BREAKING
ROCKEFELLER

BREAKING
ROCKEFELLER

The Incredible Story of the Ambitious
Rivals Who Toppled an Oil Empire

PETER B. DORAN

VIKING

VIKING

An imprint of Penguin Random House LLC
375 Hudson Street
New York, New York 10014
penguin.com

Photo Credits

Rockefeller Archive Center: page 1 (top); Library of Congress Prints and Photographs Division: pages 1 (middle), 2 (top), 3 (center), 4 (bottom), 5 (top, bottom), 6 (bottom left), 7 (top, bottom), 8 (top, bottom); Stichting Kessler–De Lange: pages 1 (bottom), 3 (bottom); Creative Commons: page 2 (bottom); Courtesy of the Drake Well Museum, Pennsylvania Historical and Museum Commission: page 3 (top); © Flagler Museum: page 4 (top); Photographic Services, Shell International Limited: page 6 (top); Imperial War Museum ©IWM A 9255: page 6 (bottom right)

ISBN 9780525427391 (hardcover)
ISBN 9780698170773 (ebook)

Printed in the United States of America
1   3   5   7   9   10   8   6   4   2

Set in Adobe Garamond Pro
Designed by Cassandra Garruzzo

For Charlotte

For a great many the oil business was more like an epic card game, in which the excitement was worth more than great stacks of chips.

William C. Mellon

Contents

Contents

Introduction

In August 2000 a group of twenty-four American and European writers, videographers, petroleum enthusiasts, and energy experts departed the oil city of Baku with a unique cargo. Secured in the sidecar of a World War II–era Ural motorcycle was a single barrel of oil. The aim of this motley caravan was to make the very first delivery of Azeri crude to the Turkish port of Ceyhan. Their route would take them along the course of a phantom pipeline.

Snaking west from the Caspian Sea, the group would climb to nine thousand feet above sea level, ride over the Caucasus Mountains, and meander across the Anatolian peninsula before reaching a spur of the ancient Silk Road at Ceyhan, on Turkey's Mediterranean coast. If it were ever to be built, this hypothetical pipeline would break Russia's monopoly on overland oil routes to Europe and unclog the crowded tanker traffic through the Bosporus, the strait at the mouth of the Black Sea. Yet despite the vast sums of political and financial capital that had already been invested in the project, this idea was still just a line on the map—a "pipeline to nowhere." For observers invested in the promise of Caspian oil, the lack of progress in constructing the Baku-Tbilisi-Ceyhan (BTC) pipeline was a source of constant frustration. By delivering that very first barrel to Ceyhan, riders in this weird convoy hoped to demonstrate the difficulties of transporting oil along ancient trade routes and past persistent conflict zones.

After almost two decades since the incredible odyssey of that single barrel of crude, the BTC pipeline is now a reality. However, the obstacles that it faced are as old as the oil industry itself. Crude is a substance that no one wants to touch, smell, or taste yet everyone wants to control. Since oil rarely occurs where it is needed most, that question of control ultimately comes down to distance, geography, risk, technology, and greed. This is certainly true in the twenty-first century, as Russia's fearsome energy monopolies defend their energy routes into Europe. It was absolutely true at the start of the last century, when a different—and equally powerful—monopoly ruthlessly did the same. Only that monopoly was American, not Russian. The company was Standard Oil, and it was led by the wealthiest human being who has ever lived: John D. Rockefeller.

BREAKING
ROCKEFELLER

CHAPTER I

The King of Broadway

For two days in late September 1889, a tropical cyclone threatened the East Coast of the United States. Approaching with little warning, the storm churned the southern shipping lanes out of New York Harbor and dumped torrents of rain along the New Jersey coast. Abruptly on the evening of Wednesday, September 25, the path of the autumn nor'easter changed. Instead of careening into New York, it turned east into the Atlantic. On Thursday morning, Manhattan awoke to a damp bank of mist and coal smoke. The fog besieged the edges of the island and shrank the limits of the visible world to just one hundred feet. It was a dangerous way to begin a Thursday.

The peculiar fog that morning created a small nightmare for the flotilla of ferryboats, freight steamers, and sailing vessels that plied the waterways around Manhattan Island. Without the benefit of sight, boat captains and slip masters conjured an eerie fugue of warning bells, ship whistles, and foghorns on the Hudson and East Rivers. With so many boats on the water and so little visibility, some kind of collision was inevitable. Surprisingly, the only calamity that morning occurred when a blind tugboat plowed into an oyster fisherman's boat at the narrow Hell Gate to Queens. There were no reported deaths.

The damage to the tug was mercifully small.[1] Aside from perils on the water, there was little else to distinguish the morning of September 26 from any other in the late 1880s. But this was no ordinary day—at least not for the richest man in America that morning: John D. Rockefeller.

Much like the island city around him, Rockefeller was a creature of repetitive rhythms, and he worked like a machine. Habitually punctual, inveterately secretive, and eternally impatient in long meetings, he explicitly exempted only Sunday from matters of money. Business consumed him on every other day. Each morning before work, he sat for a shave in the parlor of his home at 4 West 54th Street, just five blocks south of Central Park. Each evening he concluded the day's business by meticulously tallying every conceivable expense and source of income in a black notebook. More constant as a companion than any friend he had ever known, the little pocket ledger accompanied him everywhere. Finally, on the schedule of his many rituals, the commemoration of September 26 was particularly special. This was Rockefeller's Job Day, his own private holiday.

In the Rockefeller household, Job Day was rich in meaning. Typically commemorated with family and a few invited guests after work, it was the anniversary of Rockefeller's first paid position as a bookkeeper at the Cleveland-based produce brokerage of Hewitt and Tuttle. The job paid fifteen dollars a week. And a fifteen-year-old Rockefeller had secured the post based primarily on his penmanship. Over the decades, he celebrated his memory of Job Day with a mixture of solemnity and cheer. It eventually assumed such prominence that it would eclipse his own birthday as the most important commemoration of his life. Job Day was the beginning of his beginning. It was a personal dividing line that separated everything that had come before from everything that came after. "All my future seemed to hinge on that day," Rockefeller recalled. "And I often tremble when I ask myself the question: 'What if I had not got the job?'"[2]

By 1889, fully thirty-four years had elapsed since the original Job Day. Now forty-nine, Rockefeller bore little resemblance to his teenage self. The features of his broad, square face had grown angular. His wide, earnest eyes had narrowed. The boyish Cupid's bow on his upper lip had disappeared beneath a bushy mustache. Creased lines trailed down the corners of his mouth from the edges of his red whiskers. Yet even as his outward appearance had changed in the intervening years, his many inward abilities had become more pronounced. One of the most important among them was a devilish knack for ledgers.

One meaningful consequence of Job Day was that Rockefeller began his career from the perch of a bookkeeper's stool. Life among the ledgers at Hewitt and Tuttle was vastly different from the freewheeling commercial showmanship of his father, William. The elder Rockefeller made his living as a fast-talking, fly-by-night huckster, peddling miraculous elixirs to the sick across America's expanding frontier. One of William's bestsellers was a bottled cure for cancer. While his medicine did not work, his dubious sales pitch did. By contrast, John D.'s entry into the world of commerce was bereft of theatrics or the ethically dubious business practices of a snake oil salesman. Instead, his was a rigorously quantitative realm of profit, loss, credit margins, interest rates, shipping costs, and corporate expenses. For a bookkeeper, every action at Hewitt and Tuttle produced an equal and opposite reaction on his ledger. A penny earned at the company required Rockefeller to debit a cent from "cash" and to record a simultaneous credit to "income." Repeated endlessly, the rote calculations of double-entry bookkeeping represented the financial heartbeat of the firm. Recording them was mind-numbing yeoman's work. But it was a task for which Rockefeller was a ferociously quick study.

Mastering the intricacies of bookkeeping, Rockefeller began to view his ledger as more than a mere catalog of data. Instead, he saw it as an awesome cipher. By reducing every enterprise to its quantifiable essentials, the ledger could distinguish good ideas from bad, separate fortune from folly, and reduce the messy ambiguities of business relationships to rational simplicity. Prices could fluctuate, waste would go unnoticed, and unscrupulous suppliers might lie on their invoices, but the ledger invariably revealed the truth. From his earliest days in business, Rockefeller discovered that his ledgers exposed where an enterprise was succeeding, where it was failing, and what—if anything—might be done about it. Much to his astonishment, not everyone in Cleveland's business community viewed the ledger in the same awe-inspired terms. "Many of the brightest kept their books in such a way that they did not actually know when they were making money on a certain operation and when they were losing," he later recalled. It was a powerful insight. For the remainder of his life, he reserved a special reverence for the awesome power of double-entry bookkeeping.[3]

After three years at a bookkeeper's desk, Rockefeller resolved to test his own talents in business. Departing Hewitt and Tuttle, he established himself as the co-owner of a competing brokerage house along with a local Englishman named Maurice Clark. The new firm of Clark & Rockefeller bought and sold beans, pork, and other commodities from cities around America's Great Lakes. When the first shipments of petroleum began to arrive by train from western Pennsylvania in the 1860s, Clark & Rockefeller traded in oil as well. They were not alone. Around Cleveland, the firm had plenty of competition in the petroleum business. "All sorts of people went into it," Rockefeller remembered, "the butcher, the baker, and the candlestick maker began to refine oil."[4] For Cleveland's oil dilettantes like Rockefeller, the allure of petroleum was a powerful one. Startup costs were low; the method for refining crude was remarkably similar to distilling whiskey; and the profit margins on oil-based kerosene were fat—a fact that Rockefeller's ledgers doubtlessly revealed.

Established as the co-owner of his own company, Rockefeller lavished his ledgers with more attention than ever before. The previous devotion that he had shown to bookkeeping became a fixation. While he regarded this diligence as prudent stewardship of the company's finances, others around him saw only peevish zealotry. "Too exact," recalled his partner Clark. In his view, Rockefeller was "methodical to an extreme, careful as to details and exacting to a fraction. If there was a cent due us, he wanted it. If there was a cent due a customer, he wanted the customer to have it."[5] Only Rockefeller was not one to leave his zeal for pennies at the office.

During one revealing encounter on a Cleveland streetcar, a ticket attendant once charged Rockefeller for a female friend seated beside him. Rockefeller was indignant at being overcharged. "My change is five cents short," he demanded. When the attendant explained that he had only assumed a gentleman would pay for the lady in his company, Rockefeller unleashed a stinging rebuttal. "I did not tell you to take out two fares," he lectured. "Let this be a lesson to you, and never assume that a passenger is paying for two people unless he says so."[6] The tongue-lashing simultaneously betrayed its own lesson about Rockefeller: every penny mattered, even among friends.

Decades later, separated by time, distance, a marriage, five children, the growth of his company, and a new home at 4 West 54th Street, many of Rockefeller's early habits and routines from Cleveland remained essentially unchanged. In 1889 he was still in the oil business; he was still measuring his personal and professional life by the ledger; and perhaps surprisingly given his wealth, he was still taking public transportation to work. Boasting an estimated fortune of $150 million ($6 billion in today's money), he could have avoided the train altogether and commuted to the office in the privacy of his own carriage. Industrialists of lesser financial stature did just that. But Rockefeller valued efficiency, and New York's morning rush in the late 1880s was a maddening snarl of pedestrians, streetcars, horse carts, handcarts, cabs, carriages, and one omnibus line that stubbornly refused to die. As a result, the steam coaches of New York's Metropolitan Elevated Railway Company were the fastest and most comfortable way to avoid the street-level scrum. And best of all for the penny-conscious Rockefeller, a ride on the Metropolitan cost just a nickel.[7]

Traveling on ribs of wrought iron, New Yorkers had once cheered the elevated railways as a "visionary enterprise" in the 1870s.[8] Ten years later the novelty of an urban railroad had faded. By the late 1880s, all that remained was a noisy, throat-choking eyesore. The trellises of the elevated roads cast some of the city's busiest avenues into perpetual gloom and trapped the acrid smell of horse filth underneath. Overhead, the elevated trains rattled through Manhattan at fifteen-minute intervals during all hours of the day. They rained embers onto surrounding neighborhoods and coated every conceivable nearby surface in a greasy film of ashes, coal soot, and flecks of metal.[9] Uptown commuters like Rockefeller were unburdened by any of these troubles. Instead they enjoyed the comforts of cushioned seats and braided floor mats. Just like the elevated trains themselves, much of what passengers saw from their seats on the Metropolitan would soon vanish.

Departing from the 50th Street station each morning, Rockefeller's commute down Sixth Avenue blazed a path through New York's now-extinct red-light district, the Tenderloin. It was an area so famous for vice in the 1880s that, as one contemporary reported, "at least half of the buildings in the district were devoted to some sort of wickedness."[10] Below 40th Street, Rockefeller's train cut between Bryant Park and the doomed Hotel Royal, New York's home to embezzlers, confidence men, front-page suicides, and "cuisine of the highest standard." Within a year of Rockefeller's Job Day in 1889, the Royal would be devoured in a horrific fire that killed its guests by the dozen and spared only those who survived the jump to street level.[11] South of 24th Street, the train passed the fashionable department stores of the Ladies' Mile, the bygone theater district around Union Square, and the stately brick parapet of New York's Twenty-second Regiment Armory.[12] Finally, after a dogleg below Washington Square, the Sixth Avenue line reached its final stop at Battery Park. This was just a block away from the most famous business address in America: 26 Broadway, the home of Standard Oil.

At the apex of his commercial power, Rockefeller constructed an appropriately grand headquarters for the planet's largest oil company. The Standard Oil Building rose above the surrounding offices of shipping companies and foreign consulates like a slab of windowed rock. At eleven stories, it was just short of being the tallest structure in New York. Two blocks north the pointed steeple of Trinity Church clung to that fleeting honor. Nevertheless, 26 Broadway was one of the most comfortable buildings in Manhattan. It offered an array of novel amenities, including a set of elevators, offices illuminated with sunlight, and some of the highest executive suites in the city. Looking out from the top floors, the directors at Standard risked endless distraction from the slow-motion choreography of coal steamers and masted sailing ships in New York Harbor. They enjoyed an unparalleled view of Frédéric-Auguste Bartholdi's recently erected statue of *Liberty Enlightening the World*. When the coal smog dissipated, the sharpest eyes at Standard could even have discerned the outlines of the company's distant oil refineries at Constable Hook, New Jersey.

Once he arrived at the office, it was one of Rockefeller's oldest and most faithful habits to set aside formal business matters to eat an informal midday lunch with his executives. The directors of his company ate seated at a long table situated at the top of Standard's headquarters. Each one owned a minority stake in the oil giant. In return, they oversaw its day-to-day operations. Some had been with Rockefeller from his early days in Cleveland. Others had fought bitterly against his expanding dominion over the oil trade. One by one, Rockefeller had conquered them all. When resistance against Standard proved futile, these men—for there were no women among them—swapped their ownership of independent companies for a lucrative share of Rockefeller's balance sheet. "We were all in a sinking ship if existing cutthroat competition continued," Rockefeller remembered, "and we were trying to build a lifeboat to carry us all to the shore." It was a compelling story, which he used to explain the origins of Standard's supremacy—and it was a false one. As Rockefeller biographer Ron Chernow notes, Standard's founder had a "powerfully selective memory" when it came to those he had crushed in the oil business.[13] Indeed, the great irony of Standard's management team was that, at one point, many of its directors had viewed Rockefeller as the enemy. Now they ran his empire.

To a man, none of the company's directors in 1889 had begun life with any hint of the wealth or power they enjoyed atop 26 Broadway. They were the sons of carpenters, ministers, and whalers. Before trying their hand in the oil business, some had made a living as whiskey distillers or lawyers. One had once been a riverboat captain. One had been a Union general during the Civil War. Another had fought the Union as a colonel in the Confederate army. Joined together under Rockefeller, they had all reaped a windfall. However, money had not healed every wound.

One of the most obstinate directors at the daily lunch was Charles Pratt. As the former owner of the Astral Oil Works in Brooklyn, Pratt had tenaciously opposed Rockefeller's siege of the East Coast kerosene trade. He more than the others begrudged Rockefeller's victory over him. Rockefeller prized harmony and accord among his directors, but Pratt regularly denied it to him, acting as a persistent snag to consensus. Always seated beside Pratt was Henry Flagler, a man "full of vim and push," in Rockefeller's estimation, and the polar opposite of Pratt.[14] Unlike the other directors, Flagler was not one of the conquered—he had been with Rockefeller since Standard's earliest days in Cleveland. Owing to their long-standing business relationship, Flagler was more of a confidant to Rockefeller than a colleague. But by 1889 the bond between the two men was weakening. Flagler was devoting less time to the oil business and more time to his dream of constructing a new city among the orange groves and swamplands around Biscayne Bay, Florida. He almost named this settlement Flaglerville, but its residents would eventually call it by a different name: Miami.

Always sitting next to Flagler at lunch was the eerily quiet presence of Rockefeller. He was often inclined to say very little among his directors. The overwhelming size of his shareholdings in Standard said all that was needed. On his right sat John Archbold, Rockefeller's brash, handpicked successor. Boasting thick, bushy eyebrows and a thin, receding hairline, Archbold had a waistline that betrayed a lifelong fondness for the pleasures of life—especially for whiskey. While he had recently mastered his weakness for alcohol, he could never quite break his penchant for making ill-timed predictions in business. Famously, he once offered to "drink every gallon [of oil] produced west of the Mississippi," for he believed there was none. Most recently, he promoted a belief inside Standard that the public's unease with monopolies was a craze. "We do not think that much will come of the talk at Washington regarding Trusts," he famously said. "The demagogues are simply trying to out talk each other for political effect."[15] Archbold was certain that America's antitrust angst would fade with time. Just as with his prediction about oil out west, he was again going to be dead wrong.

If Archbold's biggest flaw was in talking first and thinking second, Rockefeller nevertheless respected the man's undeniable value to Standard. He was a predator, the kind of wildly aggressive entrepreneur who possessed an intuitive ability to strike an opponent's jugular vein. For Archbold, there was no such thing as good defensive strategy in business, only offense and attack. By grooming him as his replacement, Rockefeller hoped to sustain that *élan vital*, that spirit of constant attack, within 26 Broadway's corporate culture.[16] It would be a fateful decision.

In picking Archbold, Rockefeller had passed over a talented rival for the job: the "Hell Hound" always seated at Archbold's right elbow, Henry Rogers.[17] With time, Rockefeller's choice to neglect Rogers and favor Archbold would boomerang on Standard, culminating in an act of unexpected treachery. The devastating betrayal of Hell Hound Rogers would one day topple the careful wall of secrecy that Rockefeller had constructed around his empire. Once this protective barrier fell, the national outrage at Standard would embolden Rockefeller's political enemies in Washington. But in September 1889 that stunning betrayal was still far over the horizon. The veil of discretion at Standard was intact. Directors at 26 Broadway kept their secrets and ate their lunch.

Every afternoon after the conclusion of the directors' meal, Rockefeller retired to his office couch for a nap. To those familiar with the habit, Rockefeller explained that it was his way of sustaining body and mind throughout the day. "It is not good to keep all the forces at tension all the time," he would tell his son.[18] The reality of Rockefeller's retreats was more troubling. After two and a half decades of tireless struggle, the pressure of running Standard had taken a tremendous toll on Rockefeller's health. His daily sojourns to the couch were no longer a convenience—they were becoming a necessity. By the time of his Job Day in 1889, even these afternoon sojourns were failing him. Within a year, the overall decline in Rockefeller's mental state would become so great, he would require a temporary leave of absence from Standard. The oil business was slowly consuming him, and his afternoon escapes could only slow the process.

The enormous strain upon Rockefeller was certainly understandable. Starting from a single refinery along the banks of Cleveland's Cuyahoga River, he had expanded the reach of Standard's empire to fantastic proportions. His corporate domain encompassed 80 percent of the world's petroleum market, 100,000 employees, 20,000 petroleum wells, 5,000 railroad cars, and 4,000 miles of pipelines. Equally impressive was its profitability. Every year Standard generated a dividend of $380 million (in today's money). Most of this sum went directly to Rockefeller; the remainder was distributed to the minority owners of the Standard Oil Trust.[19] Yet hidden behind Standard's bottom line was a startling fact: Rockefeller had not only created the world's largest and most profitable petroleum company—he had systematically eliminated nearly all forms of competition in the oil industry.

From the "butchers and bakers" that Rockefeller had known in Cleveland to the vanquished industrial titans who now worked for him, he had bound the global petroleum business into a single, monolithic entity. By the end of the 1880s, Standard's operations were so large that the company had become an integral part of the overall American economy. It was an economy built on steel, powered by coal, and illuminated, in large part, by kerosene—Standard's kerosene. "The whole process seems a miracle," Rockefeller would say. "What a blessing the oil had been to mankind."[20] But if Rockefeller viewed petroleum in vaguely spiritual terms, the original source of this godsend was as far from a religious experience as one could possibly get. Standard had a dark side.

When oil first began to flow from the hills of Pennsylvania in the 1860s, it set off one of the greatest mineral races in human history, a competition that in many ways continues today. The revolutionary age of oil famously got under way in 1859, after a self-styled "colonel" named Edwin L. Drake drilled into a petroleum reservoir along the banks of a Pennsylvania river called Oil Creek. Raw crude flowed from Drake's well in such abundance, he scrambled to fill every container he could find, including the local supply of empty whiskey barrels.[21] That moment of hectic improvisation forged the enduring link between petroleum and the barrel.

For consumers in the mid-nineteenth century, kerosene derived from Pennsylvania crude was an instant sensation. It was far less expensive than whale oil, the most popular—and expensive—alternative in the retail lighting market. The illuminating flame from refined crude burned with a steady, yellow glow. It did not clog a room with smoke, pollute a house with a pungent smell, or smother a lamp wick with a thick carbon residue. Unlike other whale oil substitutes, such as camphene (a relative of turpentine), kerosene was less likely to explode in a customer's face when set to flame. Best of all, crude oil was available in seemingly limitless quantities across Pennsylvania. It was the perfect product.

Soon after news that "the Yankee has struck oil" rippled out from Pennsylvania, a veritable forest of man-made drilling derricks began to replace the native trees on Oil Creek.[22] The additional petroleum discoveries that followed steadily transformed the region into the global epicenter of crude, called Oildom, Petrolia, or the Great Oildorado. The boomtowns that sprouted in the oil patch boasted names like Pithole, Oleopolis, Petroleum Center, and Oil City. These settlements were a bonanza for land speculators, well borers, moonshiners, carpenters, hoteliers, bar owners, teamsters, women of easy virtue, and anyone else hoping to profit from the oil fad.[23]

If the amount of money to be made in Oildorado was astonishing, so too were the risks of earning it. One famous discovery, the Empire well, returned a jaw-dropping $15,000 in profit for every dollar invested. In addition to being the first gusher in Pennsylvania, the Empire gained the dubious honor of becoming the state's first oil well fire. Nineteen people died when the fountain of crude erupting from the well found a spark. After the ensuing inferno was extinguished three days later, the repaired well produced three thousand barrels of oil a day. And while most discoveries in Pennsylvania were far less prolific, the promise of instant wealth encouraged new prospectors to try to replicate the Empire's success. As investors lined up to find the next big gusher or flowing well, the borings around the oil region multiplied.

Across western Pennsylvania, the only reliable constants were excess, greed, and fire. In the upstream drilling camps on Oil Creek, leaking petroleum was dismissed as an unavoidable part of the extraction process. And it was everywhere. Huge quantities of crude pooled on the ground or flowed directly into Oil Creek. When it rained, the runoff of petroleum, dead mules, mud, and trash from the camps made the surrounding valley a toxic mess. "The river is dark," reported one eyewitness, "and a scum of oil glistens on its surface."[24] More than an environmental hazard, the black shimmer was a sign of great danger. With so much petroleum on the water, Oil Creek regularly caught fire, transforming the waterway into a burning river of crude. Farther downstream, the threat of inferno posed an even greater danger to the valley's plank-board boomtowns. Petroleum Center was reduced to sticks and ashes on multiple occasions. Each time the town burned, its residents diligently rebuilt. The lure of fortune in Oildorado was stronger than the fear of flame.

When they were not dousing fires, pumping their wells to exhaustion, or gambling on the future price of a barrel, the inhabitants of Pennsylvania's oil patch reveled in ostentatious displays of good fortune. Oversize diamond neck pins were a particularly popular marker of success, followed by silk top hats, lavish gambling sprees, and consumption of punishing quantities of alcohol.[25] As wealth from the petroleum mania grew, so too did Oildorado's reputation for debauchery. "The orgies of Petroleum Center sometimes eclipsed Monte Carlo and the Latin Quarter combined," wrote one bystander to the vice.[26] Unsurprisingly, this oil-soaked garden of the damned soon attracted the attention of reporters.

In 1865 *New York Times* journalist William Wright visited Oildorado on a trip into the heart of America's petroleum hysteria. He was shocked by what he found, especially the frenzied confluence of waste and excess. The mania had reached such heights, it seemed impossible to sustain. "Companies and individuals must pay the penalty of establishing conditions in which the lowest form of selfishness is the only recognized principle for action," Wright concluded. He punctuated his exposé on the oil boom by adding this prophetic warning: "Some of its people may have imagined they can snap their fingers at the natural laws," he warned, "but these will, in the end, assuredly vindicate themselves."[27] Wright's prediction would prove to be an accurate one. A reversal of fortune was coming, personified in a single individual: John D. Rockefeller.

The King of Broadway

By the time Rockefeller visited Pennsylvania in the mid-1860s, he had already carved out a modest space for himself in Cleveland's burgeoning refining business. Similar to Wright's reaction, the ostentatious displays of greed and inefficiency among the "finger snappers" also shocked Rockefeller. Rather than departing in disgust, however, Rockefeller pulled out his notepad and subjected the chaos to a careful study. How did the industry actually work? How did its pieces fit together? What were its weaknesses, and where were its strengths? To answer these questions, he traveled from one end of western Pennsylvania to the other. He visited the upstream drilling camps, the downstream boomtowns, and the multitude of refining stills that were distilling Pennsylvania's crude into the "new light" of kerosene. During his multiple forays, he asked so many questions of the oilmen that he acquired a local nickname: "Sponge."[28] It was an appropriate moniker. Rockefeller was absorbing the collected knowledge of the entire petroleum business. As the oilmen boasted of their drilling techniques, ad hoc refining methods, and schemes for getting kerosene to market, few could have guessed the significance—or the dangers—of sharing what they knew with the quiet, teetotaling "Sponge."

Based on his systematic survey of Oildorado, Rockefeller arrived at a startling conclusion. Competition, he believed, was the enemy of efficiency in the petroleum business—not its ally. In his eyes, the oilmen in the upstream camps were more akin to gamblers in a casino than industrious businessmen. Some prospered, while others went broke. The prospectors who managed to discover oil disposed of their crude as if it were plunder. As a result, well owners in Pennsylvania regularly indulged in a self-destructive flurry of overproduction. By saturating the oil market with too much crude, the upstream oilmen flung the downstream costs of Rockefeller's refining venture around like a lash. That was bad for business. It also seemed impossible to stop.

In Pennsylvania, practically anyone could be an oilman. The petroleum belowground was free for all. With little more than a drill, a steam pump, and the approval of a local landowner, would-be industrialists of all stripes bored an uncountable number of holes into the earth. Many failed to find crude, but those who succeeded were immediately thrust into a furious competition with neighboring wells. Like multiple straws all drawing from the same source, rival well owners on the surface were siphoning crude from a shared pool of petroleum belowground. This competition set off a pumping race. An oilman needed to draw off as much petroleum as possible, as fast as possible, before someone else got it first. To the victor went the spoils, or in this case, the crude.

Quantity was king in Oildorado, and it was annihilating profits. The result of the drilling bonanza upstream was a price collapse downstream at oil depots like Petroleum Center. Forcing titanic volumes of crude into the growing but still relatively small market for kerosene inevitably caused the price of a barrel to spiral downward. Supply was overpowering demand. The more oil the drillers produced, the more they pushed down prices. As prices fell, well owners had to draw off ever-larger quantities of petroleum from belowground to stay solvent. It was a devastating feedback loop.

At least in theory, the cheaper price of oil should have been self-correcting. By asking less money for a barrel of crude, the market issued a powerful signal to well owners: ease off the accelerator. But that message made little sense in the upstream prospecting camps. One oilman might dare to heed the market and slow his pumps, but there was no promise that his nearby rivals would do the same, let alone all well owners in Pennsylvania. And when the price of a barrel finally bounced back—if it bounced back at all—there was no guarantee that an underground reservoir would still have oil. Far better to pump today, when the presence of crude was guaranteed, than to have no product tomorrow, when prices might be higher.

The natural outcome of this feverish pressure to pump was a never-ending cycle of boom and bust, ecstasy and agony. During the first fifteen years of the oil industry, the price of crude plummeted from $16 a barrel (worth around $415 today) down to $0.49, then rocketed back up to nearly $8. It then fell to $2.50, rose to almost $6, and fell, once again, to around $2.[29] Up and down, rich and poor, silk hats or empty pockets, the Pennsylvania oil patch had become a muddy, noxious casino. While some gamblers lost their shirts in Oildorado, there was never a shortage of new adventurers who were willing to gamble their fortune on the next big field or frenetic boomtown.

Farther downstream in Cleveland, the whiplash on prices hit Rockefeller where it mattered most: his balance sheet. Because the cost of a barrel was hard to predict, the inherent unpredictability of the oil market wreaked havoc on the profit margins of refiners. Rockefeller considered his financial vulnerability to oil's erratic swings to be unacceptable. It stoked an intense desire on his part to impose order on the chaos. He developed his own solution to the problem. The petroleum industry needed a rule giver and gatekeeper. If anyone was going to fill that role, he reasoned, refiners like himself would have to ordain themselves. The deluge of petroleum had to be controlled.

Thanks to his early audit of the Pennsylvania boom, Rockefeller's ensuing plan for containing the flood was insightful, meticulous, and based on the worthless nature of raw petroleum. It was the basic paradox of crude. Here was a substance that no one wanted to touch, taste, or smell—but seemingly everyone wanted to control. Only after a refiner like Rockefeller transformed oil into kerosene did it offer any real value to consumers. The upstream prospectors and the downstream refiners needed each other, but it was the refiners who potentially held all the cards in the petroleum business. Rockefeller perceived that if enough refiners banded together, they could establish a chokepoint in the industry. This artificial barrier could then act as a gateway for crude. All the oil from upstream wells would have to flow through Rockefeller's refining gate. Whoever controlled that gate might even be able to establish themselves as the sovereign of crude—dictating rules, setting quotas, possibly even fixing the price of petroleum.

Emboldened by his vision of establishing a rule giver for the oil business, the little-noticed "Sponge" from Cleveland embarked upon a decades-long vendetta against upstream producers and any downstream refiner who would not join him. The undertaking was herculean, bordering on megalomaniacal. Nevertheless Rockefeller pursued his vision with unwavering persistence. Competition would be made to kneel.

As a first step, he incorporated his Cleveland refining business into the Standard Oil Company. It would serve as the corporate vehicle for his consolidation of all the refiners in the oil industry. From there, his plan was simple and unyielding. Instead of paying himself in profits, he would hoard gigantic amounts of cash on his balance sheet. The cash-rich position would be both a sword and shield for him, allowing him to endure the anarchy of the oil trade as well as to profit from it.

Whenever the price of oil collapsed, or a market panic spread fear among competing refiners, Rockefeller would deploy his cash reserve with a vengeance. If competitors were fearful, he purchased many at a steep discount. When profit margins on refined crude were low, he pummeled the companies that he could not buy with price wars. Often he manufactured his own opportunities, such as the time he engineered an artificial shortage of oil barrels to squeeze his competitors. As many of Standard's underhanded tactics were successful, plots and schemes abounded. Whether he was arranging secret kickbacks with railroad owners, undercutting the price of rival kerosene brands, offering exclusive territorial deals, or financially browbeating family shops and grocers into only selling Standard's products, Rockefeller was unyielding: the whiplash of uncertain prices had to end.

Under Rockefeller's management, the corporate culture at Standard gradually assumed a with-us-or-against-us attitude. Competing companies were divided into two categories. All those that Standard had defeated were considered "at peace" with the emerging oil giant, while all those that still resisted were deemed "at war."[30] As the list of the conquered grew longer, so did Rockefeller's original aim of establishing the refining segment as a chokepoint. Standard was becoming an empire.

By the end of the 1880s, Rockefeller's industrial behemoth was not only refining 80 percent of the world's oil, it was pumping crude from its own fields and marketing the final product directly to end consumers. Standard had ceased to be the largest refiner in America; for that matter, it was no longer the largest corporation in the oil business. Instead, Standard *was* the oil business. From upstream wellhead to retail consumer, Rockefeller's commercial dominion assumed the attributes of a fully integrated, vertical monopoly. The little refiner from Cleveland was now a fearsome anaconda that consumed the "finger snappers" of Pennsylvania, along with almost every other form of independent competition. After years of unending war and peace, the 1880s finally witnessed the establishment of the *Pax Regulae*—the Peace of Standard Oil.

Unfortunately, Rockefeller's creation embodied the idea that Rome makes a desert and calls it peace. "You have seen Pithole and Petroleum Center," said an unrepentant Rockefeller, "the places where once stood big, prosperous cities, in which men made millions of dollars out of oil. Now they are bits of wilderness, overgrown with weeds and with nothing left to tell of their greatness but a few scattered parts of old houses and the memory of a few aged men."[31] This was the obituary of competition in the early oil industry, authored by its assassin. For Rockefeller, every means, no matter how unscrupulous, justified all ends. The house always won. Standard never lost—even if Rockefeller had to deal from the bottom of the deck.

What he did not know on his Job Day in 1889 was that the *Pax Regulae* was coming to an end. A war to break his empire was approaching, one that would shatter the carefully crafted peace that Standard had established. In duration, depth, and scope, this conflict would eclipse all the previous battles that Rockefeller had fought to establish his hammerlock on the planet's oil market. Lasting for more than two decades, the battle would unfold on a global scale and shape the contours of the next century. What was perhaps most surprising about this struggle was that it began in the unlikeliest of places and was waged by the unlikeliest of men.

Far away in England, an East End London merchant named Marcus Samuel, Jr., was about to pick a fight with Rockefeller's anaconda. The world of oil would soon be turned upside down.

CHAPTER 2

The Merchant of Houndsditch

On the other side of the Atlantic, in Marcus Samuel, Jr.'s East London neighborhood of Houndsditch, visitors were wise to mind their pockets.

Bounded by London's Whitechapel district to the north and the river Thames to the south, Houndsditch was home to the same lanes and alleyways where Jack the Ripper stalked his victims in the autumn of 1888. It was a loud, bustling melee of merchants, middlemen, horse filth, and anarchists, a place where Londoners could buy a boot for a penny, a fiddle for a sovereign, and the company of a woman for a shilling.[1] When the peddlers of Houndsditch were in their stalls, "no great market or stock exchange on its busiest day ever showed more animation or made much more noise," reported one awestruck American.[2] It was in Houndsditch where the old England based on agriculture, aristocracy, and landed money was vanishing in a brine of industrial sprawl, new money, and mechanized commerce. Houndsditch was not ready yet, but it was the future of England.

In all likelihood, the name Houndsditch originally referred to a moat that once encompassed the Roman settlement of Londinium, the forerunner to the City of London. The Romans had used the pit to bury their dogs. Centuries later, when the Great Plague of 1655 ravaged the city, Londoners buried their own dead near this spot, dropping them into a mass grave forty feet long and twenty feet deep. By the late nineteenth century, the legacy of dead dogs and plague pits had slipped from living memory, and Houndsditch had become a strange intersection of arrivals and departures. It was the first place where new immigrants put down roots upon landing in London. It was simultaneously the last place to which the impoverished clung before falling off the social ladder entirely.

At this unusual crossing point between aspiring newcomers, energetic hustlers, and England's poor or forgotten, Marcus Samuel, the Jewish son of a merchant, first rented a house in the 1840s. Located at 13 Upper East Smithfield near the Thames River, Marcus and his wife, Abigail, would raise eight daughters and three sons in London's East End. Marcus Samuel, contrary to convention, named his two youngest children Marcus and Samuel. The younger Marcus, who simply added a *Jr.* to his name, was luckier than his younger brother, Samuel. Thanks to his father's eponymous flourish, he faced a lifetime of bothersome introductions as Samuel Samuel. Around the household, he was simply known as Sam.

Growing up within sight of the Tower of London, the Samuel children spent the entirety of their days on land though they were perpetually surrounded by signs of the sea. Through the rear windows of the family home, the eleven offspring of Marcus and Abigail could glimpse the armada of China clippers, Dutch galliots, and merchant schooners that lay at anchor in the Thames. These craft arrived in London from every corner of the globe. The cargo from their holds supplied Victorian England's growing demand for foreign commodities. In turn, the crews disembarking from the merchant vessels provided the tavern owners, tailors, and shopkeepers of Sailor Town, as the area around the Samuel home was known, with a constant infusion of ship's pay, mischief, and vice. Street brawls were common in the neighborhood, as was a particular species of thief who preyed upon drunken mariners.[3] All this made Sailor Town a less-than-ideal spot for raising a family, but it was the perfect place for Marcus Sr. to run a business.

A census taker who visited the Samuels in 1851 listed Marcus Sr.'s occupation as "Shell dealer and importer."[4] It was a woefully crude approximation. Nimble entrepreneur would have been more accurate but also unsuitable for a census list. During the family's years in Sailor Town, Samuel Sr. cultivated a thriving trade in the business of knickknacks. His main line of income came from supplying British holiday towns with the seashell-covered pincushions, picture frames, and keepsake boxes that English tourists habitually purchased on vacation. Victorian tourists were enthusiastic buyers of practically anything he encased in mother-of-pearl and shells. The ladies' boxes, which Marcus Sr. emblazoned with slogans like "A Gift from Brighton," were his bestsellers. To satisfy the demand for seashells, he purchased his stocks from returning merchantmen in Sailor Town; he hired young women to bedazzle everyday household items with the ocean tidbits; then he forwarded the finished goods to souvenir distributers in places like Brighton and the Isle of Wight. As the Victorians discovered the joys of tourism in the late nineteenth century, Marcus Sr.'s dockside baubles became the treasured mementos of their trips.

Bolstered by his thriving business, Marcus Sr. no longer felt compelled to keep his wife and children in Sailor Town. He now wanted his home address to reflect the family's budding prospects and prosperity. After two decades in Sailor Town, he relocated the Samuels to a middle-class London house at 21 Finsbury Square. The move was a dramatic one. The Samuels were only a fifteen-minute walk from Houndsditch, but they were a world apart from the squalor, noise, and clamor of the wharf lands.

The upward mobility of the Samuels had a formative impact on the early experiences of Marcus Jr. and Sam. Whereas the older Samuel children came of age amid the grime and smells of the waterfront, Marcus Jr., four years old at the time of the move, and Sam, a toddling baby, knew only the confidence and comforts of a middle-class merchant family on the rise. Even so, no matter where the Samuels lived or how affluent they became, the family fortune would always be tied to the Thames. The docks fueled Marcus Sr.'s reputation for charity at the New Synagogue in Great St. Helen's; they paid for the smart suits and fashionable watch chains that the Samuel men wore for formal photographs; and ultimately they provided for Marcus Jr.'s greatest asset: an education.

Around 1860, the elder Marcus dispatched his youngest sons to a Jewish boarding school in North London. Subsequently, Marcus Jr. continued his studies at a finishing school in Brussels, followed by a year with one of his sisters in Paris, where he studied at a French day school. In addition to preparation in the traditional rubric of arts and letters, Marcus Jr.'s schooling also introduced him to the cities, languages, and spaces beyond the narrow confines of London. It became an early firsthand primer on the wider world and allowed him to emulate the youthful experiences of many English aristocrats, who were also carted off to the Continent for a time. Unlike the privileged children of patricians, however, Marcus Jr.'s *tour d'horizon* would be a short one. After all, his father had a business to run.

At the age of sixteen, the younger Marcus returned from Paris to take up work at the family firm of M. Samuel & Co. During his time away in Belgium and France, the Samuels had moved, once again, to an even more spacious house at 18 Upper Bedford Place. The affairs of Marcus Sr. were thriving. The latest family residence reflected this enlarged affluence by situating the Samuels in the heart of London's smart Bloomsbury district, just a block from the British Museum. Nevertheless, Marcus Jr. returned each workday to the old family home on Upper East Smithfield Street, where Marcus Sr. continued to run the business. The teenage years for Marcus Jr. were therefore split between the intellectually fertile neighborhood of Bloomsbury and the merchants, sailors, and drunks along the Thames. This separation, occurring at the earliest point in his professional life, would endure for nearly all of Marcus Jr.'s career. Regardless of how much money he made, or how high he rose in England's social strata, his business address would almost always be located in the dodgy end of town. At the very least, it helped to keep overhead low.

Down in the wharf lands, the younger Marcus took his first major plunge into the daily operations of the family business. Much like Rockefeller's in his early career, Marcus Jr.'s initial role at M. Samuel & Co. required him to master the ledger. The family firm had expanded beyond the souvenir trade and was now a thriving import-export business. At the transition point between the 1860s and 1870s, Marcus Sr. benefited from the astonishing growth of England's maritime commerce. No longer confined to trading cash for shells with arriving seamen, M. Samuel & Co. was purchasing foreign commodities from as far away as Bangkok, Singapore, Calcutta, and the Moroccan coast. In exchange, Marcus Sr. shipped out manufactured industrial goods from England's busy factories. The souvenir business continued apace, but now it operated in tandem with ever-larger consignments of tea, silk, and imported ostrich feathers. Business was beginning to boom.

Propelling the expansion at M. Samuel & Co. was a revolution in speed. Faster generations of British steamships were shrinking travel times between ports. Simultaneously, long-distance telegraph lines, such as the new connection between London and Bombay, were cutting the interval of international messages from months to minutes.[5] All the while, Victorian consumers were becoming more prosperous and numerous. With the right financing, a reliable telegraph office, and a network of trusted commercial agents in the Orient, a merchant house like M. Samuel & Co. could run a sprawling global enterprise from the comfort of London.

When the younger Marcus was almost seventeen, the patriarch of the Samuel household died at the age of seventy-three. The firm was well established, and his passing brought a new period of commercial independence for his sons. Whether or not Marcus Sr. knew that death was approaching, he was at least prepared for it. Seven weeks before he died, he finalized his will. In the document, he calculated a net worth of £40,000 (around $5.6 million in today's money), including £10,000 worth of seashells. From among his earthly possessions, he left the family business to his oldest son, Joseph. To his two surviving sisters, he allocated £1,000 each but insisted they could be paid only upon "their respectably marrying according to the rites of the Jewish religion." Finally to his youngest sons, Marcus Jr. and Sam, he set aside £2,500 each. The brothers could claim their inheritance at the age of twenty-five or "at an earlier age if my said son Joseph Samuel shall give his consent." Finally, and most important, the elder Samuel implored that "all my said sons will be united, loving and considerate and keep the good name of Marcus Samuel from reproach."[6] These last lines enshrined the most valuable possession Marcus Sr. could give: the name of Samuel itself. It represented a carefully crafted reputation, a credit rating between merchants, and a bond of good faith. In death, Marcus Sr. was entrusting his sons with the harvest of his life's work. But what precisely did it mean to keep a "good name" free from reproach? Interpretations could vary. This last provision laid the groundwork for a lifelong source of tension between Marcus Jr. and Sam.

In the years to come, Joseph would step aside from the family business, leaving the legacy of his father in the hands of Marcus and Sam. As they matured, the younger Samuel brothers would develop wildly divergent opinions as to the best way of maintaining the "good name of Marcus Samuel." Seeing the benefit of new markets and faster growth, Marcus became the risk taker. Conversely, Sam was more cautious, placing a premium on business decisions that never endangered the family's reputation. Both aspects were essential to their father's success, but the debate could not last forever. The time would come when the brothers faced an irrevocable choice: to fight or not to fight a bare-knuckle commercial brawl with Rockefeller, the most dangerous oilman on the planet. Upon that decision would rest the Samuels' modest fortune, the "good name" of their father, and—larger still—the evolution of the global oil industry itself. And while all this was still many years in the future, its origin rested in the final words of Marcus Sr. to his sons.

Three years after his father's death, in the summer of 1873, Marcus resolved to take his first significant step toward independence. Almost five years before his inheritance was officially set to come due, Marcus was determined to leave England to reconnoiter the Far East. Ostensibly, the trip had a commercial purpose: to serve as an introduction to the overseas shipping agents with whom M. Samuel & Co. did business in the Orient. At the same time, Marcus also wished to see for himself the source of all the foreign cargo that had become the mainstay of the family's trade with Asia. Even in the age of steam travel, this would be an ambitious trip.

Departing London by steamship, he planned to call upon the island of Ceylon (now Sri Lanka), Singapore, and Siam (now Thailand). More than the distance traveled, the voyage would also mark the end of Marcus's apprenticeship at the ledger desk and open his career as a merchant trader in his own right. At roughly the same age, Rockefeller the "Sponge" plunged into the oil-crazed mania of Pennsylvania's boomtowns. Now Marcus was beginning his commercial life in the distant colonial ports of the Far East. And what a beginning it would be.

As an early milestone on the journey, he crossed the recently opened Suez Canal by steamship. He rounded the Arabian Peninsula through the Gulf of Aden and made his first port of call at Colombo, Ceylon. From there, he crossed the Indian Ocean to the Crown Colony of Singapore. Located at the southern inlet to the Malacca Strait, down the long arm of the Malay Peninsula, the colony lay at the midpoint between East and Far East. Marcus had left the West far behind.

Approaching by sea in the darkness of night, a traveler could see Singapore from fifteen miles away. The first hint of the city appeared as a lonely glow in the distance: the navigational lamp atop the giant flagstaff of Fort Canning, the garrisoned hill overlooking Singapore's harbor. Lying at anchor below the fort, an armada of red lights and lanterns bobbed and swayed in Singapore's famously calm waters. The port required every cargo vessel, paddle steamer, clipper, junk, and fishing boat, when remaining overnight in Singapore, to hoist a red light for safety.[7] The ships and lights were legion, as most east-west máritime traffic paused in Singapore to take on coal.

When the sun broke over the horizon, the colony came to life. Disembarking at Singapore in the fall of 1873, Marcus would have found as much of the Far East as he could possibly absorb. Holding fast to the harbor, the expanding British colony was crammed with 100,000 people at the time of his visit. Half of them were Chinese; the rest represented a shifting kaleidoscope of Malays, Burmese, Siamese, Abyssinians, Americans, natives of India, and British colonials. In Singapore, everyone seemed to be from someplace else, and nearly all were selling something. There was opium from India, coffee from Java, aromatic camphor, birds-of-paradise, gold-mounted tiger claws, and ever so familiar to Marcus, stunning varieties of coral and seashells.[8] Here at the crossroads of the Orient, Marcus introduced himself at the offices of A. Symes & Co., a longtime commercial agent of M. Samuel & Co. And it was during this stopover in Singapore that Marcus almost certainly acquired an exceptionally valuable bit of market intelligence. That fall the city of Calcutta in British India was on the brink of famine. But for those who were resourceful, this news presented an opportunity.

For anyone living at the time, word of a famine in Calcutta would have been difficult to comprehend. India was the rice bowl of the British Empire. To discover that Calcutta was suddenly running out of food would have been akin to hearing that the Sahara was inexplicably short of sand. In the minds and stomachs of the Victorians, India meant rice. The nutrition of the empire depended on it, particularly from the fertile lands around the northeastern city of Calcutta. In a good year, this region exported close to 700,000 tons of rice annually—roughly a third of what the entire United States exports today.[9] In late 1873, just as Marcus was making his way across the Far East, the weather around eastern India began to do strange, abnormal things. The shock waves of this disaster would soon reverberate throughout the empire.

The first sign of difficulty occurred in August. The summer's monsoon was one of the wettest on record. Damaging floods ensued. By September, many farming communities around Calcutta were still recovering from the heavy rains when the sky mysteriously cleared. Over the next two months, almost no rain fell to earth in eastern India. Drought replaced the torrents of water. Crops in the fields withered.

Rice growers around Calcutta had experienced unusually wet growing seasons before. They were likewise accustomed to dry ones. The problem was not the severity of the conditions but their combination, which sent the rice harvest careening over a cliff. If the rice bowl of the empire was empty, a failed harvest could metastasize into a full-blown humanitarian crisis. Calcutta would starve. Without food, the British colonial government feared that some political or social upheaval might occur. Traders in eastern India felt similar alarm. The price of rice began to skyrocket, signaling that a famine could be just around the corner.

This roused the colonial government of India into action. *Panic* was another word for it. In an unprecedented and highly controversial move, colonial officials set aside £3 million (roughly $500 million in today's money) from the Crown's budget to establish a famine relief fund for northeastern India. The amount of cash designated to buy food was astonishingly large. When parliamentarians back in England learned of the allotment, they were aghast at the massive outlay, but the money was already earmarked. With a stroke of the colonial pen, British officials had provided Calcutta with the cash it needed to buy emergency foodstuffs.[10] The question was, where would Calcutta get the rice?

For a young man of Marcus's talents, the news of a potential famine in Calcutta had all the hallmarks of opportunity—humanitarian and otherwise. This was a chance to save lives while turning a profit in the process. Since Calcutta was running out of food, he needed to find ample supplies somewhere else. This search promptly put him on a ship from Singapore to Bangkok, where his father's old agents at

A. Markwald & Co. told him that local merchants were flush with rice and eager to sell.[11] The freakish weather might have decimated India's crop, but the rest of Southeast Asia had escaped the threat of famine. Luck was on Marcus's side.

Using "his father's name and his brother's credit" in Bangkok, Marcus orchestrated a masterful maritime relay of food.[12] Cargo space in Bangkok was limited, so instead of moving his rice purchases directly to India, he sallied the shipments to Calcutta in stages. First, he lined up cargo vessels headed down the Malay Peninsula. Then, almost certainly with the assistance of A. Symes & Co. in Singapore, he arranged to have his cargo transferred onto separate vessels headed back up the Malacca Strait to India. When his rice finally arrived in Calcutta, it fetched a hefty 30 percent premium over his original purchase price in Bangkok.[13] Buy low, sell high, pocket the difference—it was the first principle of being a trader. In Bangkok, Marcus executed his craft with precision.

The logistical wizardry that Marcus demonstrated on his Bangkok rice run was a smashing success. The feat was even more impressive given his relative youth and inexperience. Navigating the intricacies of geography and international shipping was no easy task for an untested novice; he nevertheless came out on top. Significantly, the basic outlines of his famine run could be replicated. While the market dislocation in Calcutta was an extreme example, shortages of one commodity or another were always emerging in ports across the Far East. Marcus learned that bridging the gap between supply and demand *within* Asia could be profitable. As he would also discover, point-to-point business within the Orient was wide open, since most merchants focused on long-distance trade with England.

In the final accounting, this was a business trip for the record books. On his first solo voyage to the Orient, Marcus had discovered a specialty, acquired a taste for the deal, and helped save Calcutta from starvation.[14] He had witnessed firsthand how the distances of the world were shrinking, England's commercial reach was growing, and profits could be made. He was hooked. If ever there was a time to become a merchant in the Orient, it was the ideal moment.

As consumer goods poured into Great Britain from the Far East, Victorians quickly became enamored of new flavors, strange fashions, and the romanticism of distant places. On stage, Gilbert and Sullivan's Japanese-themed operetta *The Mikado* played to packed houses at London's Savoy Theatre. On canvas, painters such as Claude Monet depicted their wives (and sometimes their mistresses) in lavish silk kimonos. Vincent van Gogh experimented with Japanese-styled *ukiyo-e* woodcuts. James McNeill Whistler designed his famed Peacock Room around the Chinese porcelain collection of shipowner Frederick R. Leyland. On the street, ladies wrapped themselves in kimono-styled tea coats and silks copied from Chinese fans. At home, they decorated their interiors with an explosion of ebonized wood, ginkgo leaves, bird feathers, and vases from the Orient. The hallmarks of the Far East were becoming ubiquitous in England. Escaping them was almost impossible.

Along the Thames, imported goods from Asia accumulated in vast quantities. Indeed, the inventory of London's dockside warehouses during this period reads like the wedding registry of Scheherazade. There were carpets from Persia, tusks from Siberia, beads from India, ivory and tortoiseshells "massed in bins," stacks of dried parakeet and ibis pelts, and entire floors devoted exclusively to silk, cashmere, or spices.[15] If the wharves of London were any indication, Victorians did not have to leave England to experience the Orient. Firms like M. Samuel & Co. ensured that the Far East—and for that matter, the world—came to them.

The Merchant of Houndsditch

At the very center of Marcus's Victorian world was the sovereign of her own age, Her Imperial Majesty Victoria Alexandria, Queen Empress of Great Britain, Ireland, and India. Like the sprawling geographic empire around her, the ranks of England's gentry circled Victoria in ever wider rings. Situated closest to the queen was her husband, Prince Albert, and their son Edward, the Prince of Wales. Outside the tight nucleus of the royal family orbited the august aristocratic rings of dukes and marquises, followed by expanding spheres of earls, viscounts, barons, Scottish lords of parliament, baronets, and assorted knights. At the furthest edges of this system were the lesser members of the gentry, including Scottish feudal barons, clan chiefs, and swarms of gentlemen who held no title but doubtless schemed to snatch one.

Recognizing the bewildering array of pedigrees and honors in this structure, it is perhaps surprising that in the final act of Victoria's reign, England's entire aristocracy included little more than two hundred families. As a group, this clump of crossed lineages were tightly knit, curious but not overly inquisitive, habituated to comfort, conservative in outlook, and almost universally fond of their own appearance. They also had a tendency to state the obvious as profound. "To be a lord is still a popular thing," asserted the great aristocratic icon of his generation, Lord Ribblesdale.[16] And why would it not be?

From winter through fall, the calendar of the gentry was a choreographed schedule of distractions. After the seating of Parliament in January, the menagerie of London social clubs around Piccadilly offered the most immediate respite from the duties of the City season. Additionally, there was horse riding in the morning, carriage driving in the afternoon, and the opera or theater in the evening. When summer arrived, the patrician families who ruled England habitually decamped London for the ceaseless recreations of the countryside. The annual running of the Ascot Stakes inaugurated the start of the country season. In 1889 the gentry packed the Ascot to watch the Duke of Portland's thoroughbred Donovan win the derby "with great ease. . . . amidst the wild cheering of the crowd."[17] After the Ascot came the estate parties, which lasted until late September. The summer consumed entire months with the idylls of fox hunting, shooting, more racing, teas, dinners, and garden receptions. Of course, not everyone had the stamina for such a circuit. Those with less resilience could stick to drinking or cards if they wished—and many did.

It was a resplendent world, but the finale was near. By the late Victorian period, the lifestyle of the gentry had become unmanageably expensive. They had homes in London, estates in the country, second homes in Scotland or at Epsom, holiday villas in France, shooting boxes, deer forests, racing studs, and hunting packs to maintain.[18] These properties employed a veritable army of butlers, underbutlers, valets, footmen, pantry boys, hall boys, governesses, nannies, tutors, cooks, and at least nine different types of maid. Given the size of their domestic payrolls, let alone the incessant costs of real estate improvements and landscaping, some of the most prestigious families in England were staggering to support their immense overhead. For many, the inevitable financial collapse would be catastrophic.

At the end of the nineteenth century, the organizing dilemma of England's gentry was revolutionary—literally. Over the previous decades, the industrial revolution had transformed Great Britain into one of the most powerful countries on the planet. The benefits of that revolution, such as railroads, steamships, telegraph lines, and mass-produced manufactured goods, had propelled the expansion of England's vast maritime domain. The families that existed at the apex of the British class system reveled in the prestige that the empire conferred upon them. Behind the glimmer of Britannia unbowed, however, the economic drivers of the empire's power were quietly eradicating the gentry's primary source of income: rented land.

For nearly a millennium, the families who ran England had financed their existence by renting the sprawling acreage of their estates to farmers. These rents generated income for the estate owner, who conveniently endowed the English language with the word *landlord* to describe the arrangement. Over the centuries, some of these lordly possessions become so enormous, they defied any contemporary concept of personal real estate. By the time of Victoria's reign, 45 individuals owned at least 100,000 acres (156 square miles) of Great Britain each. Another 115 owned 50,000 acres (78 square miles).[19] Generation after generation, the steady, predictable flow of rental income from their estates had buttressed the gentry against the tumult of war abroad, civil war, plague, invasion, the beheading of three monarchs, and the madness of one.[20] It was a suitably impressive run, but all sprees must end.

The same revolutionary advances in technology that pried open distant markets for merchants like Marcus also allowed agricultural producers in the United States, Russia, and India to dump inexpensive foodstuffs onto English tables.[21] This was good news for everyone with a stomach, since falling commodity prices translated into cheaper meals. It was simultaneously devastating for English farmers, who felt the inevitable pinch of low-cost foreign competition. As the century bounded to its conclusion, fully 60 percent of all the calories in England were shipped in from someplace else. The financial hit on domestic agriculture careened into the upper reaches of the gentry. As tenants made less money off their land, estate owners grudgingly accepted lower rents or offered outright abatements to struggling farmers. Rather than subsequently cut their own expenses, however, many aristocratic families opted to keep on spending. These doomed lineages made the fatal decision to borrow against the promise of future rent. At that point, the end became inevitable. The stealthy pairing of new debts with declining rents became a trap from which many patricians could never escape. The less rental income the gentry collected, the more they needed to borrow. But as long as banks would lend against the hope of better days tomorrow, the glittering world of Victorian distraction could shimmer on for one more season, then another, until the interest consumed everything.

It was at this moment, when the financial fortunes of the landed gentry entered terminal decline, that successful entrepreneurs from England's industrial centers began to surge up from below. These self-made individuals represented a new kind of social creature. They had no difficulty affording the lifestyle of the aristocracy. They did, nevertheless, struggle to ingest the unwritten rules, behaviors, and rituals that patrician youths customarily acquired at public school and "the university"—Oxford or Cambridge.[22] Those who had been educated with the imprint of the gentry could identify the newly rich by its absence.

No less a figure than Joseph Chamberlain, a premier example of the self-made Victorian industrialist, suffered from the quiet demerits of his origin. Chamberlain made a tidy fortune manufacturing screws in Birmingham. By the age of thirty-eight, he retired from business to begin a new life in national politics. The drive, charm, and entrepreneurial talents that propelled Chamberlain's success in the screw trade proved to be decisive assets on the political stage. Within six years, he crafted one of the fastest-rising careers in government, opening the door to subsequent appointments in Prime Minister William Gladstone's second and third governments during the 1880s. Even accounting for these tremendous talents, Chamberlain's upbringing betrayed his otherwise perfect exterior.

The Merchant of Houndsditch

With a monocle over his right eye and signature orchid through his lapel, Chamberlain cut the ideal image of a dashing gentleman. He was certainly one of the best-dressed members of Parliament. He was also immensely popular and could regularly be seen entertaining duchesses at tea, sometimes three at a time, on the terrace of the House of Commons. All the same, for Chamberlain life among England's patricians was an imperfect fit. As Earl Arthur Balfour, that great defender of the dying patricians, once confided, "Joe, though we all love him dearly, somehow does not absolutely or completely mix, does not form a chemical combination with us."[23] The imprint of the gentry was missing.

While the "chemistry" of the aristocracy worked against the social aspirations of self-made individuals like Chamberlain, it was an especially powerful barrier to affluent members of England's Jewish community. Anti-Semitism was not only pervasive among the gentry, it was downright fashionable in some corners.[24] For men such as Marcus, overcoming the inherent prejudices of some in the British upper class was an added impediment. By the 1880s, he had achieved everything that a person could reasonably hope to gain. He had married the love of his life, Fanny, and she loved him greatly. He was a father to four spirited young Samuels. His merchant business was successful. Neither he nor anyone in his family ever wanted for food or comfort. But no matter how talented he was or what he accomplished, many Victorians dismissed him outright. In their view, he was a Jew—an impossible outsider.

In middle-class districts around Houndsditch, non-Jews openly compared their Jewish neighbors to foreign invaders and decried the transformation of East London's streets into "little Jerusalems."[25] The influential *Evening Standard* went further, asserting that Jews from Poland in particular were "a social cancer" in England.[26] Only with the battering ram of an immense fortune could an aspiring Jewish entrepreneur like Marcus hope to breach the higher echelons of the Victorian elite. Anti-Semitism might have been fashionable in Marcus's day, but being fabulously wealthy was even more stylish.[27]

The queen and the Prince of Wales helped to clear the road. Racial and class prejudice were among Victoria's "pet hates," along with smoking and women's rights.[28] Meanwhile the Prince of Wales famously enjoyed a close and public friendship with the well-heeled English Rothschilds. The fact that the Rothschild family was Jewish mattered little. At the same time, not all patricians were as friendly as the prince. Once the Duchess of Buccleuch reluctantly condescended "to entertain a Jew, whom she did not know, as a specially marked compliment to the Prince of Wales."[29] Social cues from the queen's inner circle were not to be ignored. And while attitudes toward England's Jewish community were changing in some quarters, the pace of transformation was slow.

Perpetually sensitive to the delicacies of status, Marcus despised his distinction as an outsider in Victorian England. It propelled his intense personal desire to be not only accepted but respected by those on the inside. The only sure way that he could achieve this feat was to do as the Rothschilds had done. Being well off was not enough; he needed to acquire a fortune so large it would eclipse his background from Sailor Town, his lack of a university education, the imperfections of his accent, and the fact that he had not been "born to rule."[30] Since the social barriers to affluent Jews in Victorian England were great, Marcus's wealth needed to be greater. But he was failing.

In the fall of 1889, M. Samuel & Co. was making Marcus a respectable living. The Far East trade was growing, but buying low and selling high had not generated the kind of fortune that Marcus needed. It was certainly not enough for him to reinvent himself as a member of the gentry, to purchase an appropriately grand estate, finance the lifestyle of a patrician, or at least to gain recognition worthy of a knighthood. Something had to change. Luckily for him, the petroleum business was teetering on the brink of its first truly global conflict.

Far away from London in the wilds of southern Russia, two brothers had recently picked a fight with Rockefeller's oil monopoly. The ambitious merchant from Houndsditch was about to get his battering ram.

CHAPTER 3

The Insider

In September 1885 a unique weapon of mass destruction sailed up the river Thames to London. It was a new kind of steamship, named the *Sviet*, after the Russian word for "light." And it was carrying a rare kind of cargo: situated belowdecks were two gigantic tanks, both brimming with kerosene from Russia. It was a groundbreaking moment in the history of oil, and a potentially catastrophic one for the dockside residents of London. In symbolic terms, the *Sviet* was a harbinger of the end to the monopolistic "peace" of Standard Oil. In the realm of public safety, the *Sviet* was a gigantic floating bomb.

At first glance, the cargo aboard the *Sviet* was unexceptional. After all, the British had been burning kerosene ever since a Scottish chemist named James Young first developed a substance called "coal oil" nearly four decades earlier.[1] The arrival of petroleum by sea was equally mundane. The international arm of Standard had been exporting tins of excess American kerosene to Europe for nearly fifteen years. What was novel was that the *Sviet*'s cargo originated not from America but from Russia. Its arrival in England was a brazen attack from Russia on Standard's global dominion over kerosene.[2]

The intrepid owners of the *Sviet* were two Swedish industrialists named Ludwig and Robert Nobel. Outside Russia, most people had never heard of the Nobel brothers; it was their brother Alfred who had become a household name. He was the infamous international arms dealer, inventor of dynamite, and future "merchant of death" who would eventually endow the Nobel Peace Prize that lives on today. Nevertheless, talent ran deep in the Nobel family. Inside Russia, and particularly within the oil business, Alfred's brothers were capitalists of the first order.

A decade before the *Sviet*, just as Marcus was embarking on his solo voyage to the Far East, Ludwig and Robert Nobel had made their first foray into the Russian oil business. Combining their family's commercial ties to the tsarist government with a fluent knowledge of chemistry, Ludwig and Robert were a powerful duo. Savvy Ludwig leveraged his political connections to secure low-cost oil rights around Baku, the tsar's Black City of crude. His brother Robert eagerly threw himself into the refining side of the kerosene business.[3] Like the Samuel brothers, the Nobels plied the good name of their family to expand a business, and their leap into Russian petroleum was no small-time affair. In short order, the Nobel Brothers Petroleum Production Company (known commonly around Baku as Branobel) had established itself as one of the largest oil firms in all Russia. That unchecked growth was now half the problem for Branobel.

Situated on the western shore of the landlocked Caspian Sea, Russia's oil fields were the stuff of legend. All around Baku, Russian oilmen were unleashing mammoth fountains of petroleum. The gushers were so great, reports of Baku's wells seemed far-fetched when compared to those in America. Some of Russia's wells produced a whopping 77,000 barrels of crude a day. Even today the prolific volume of Caspian oil seems as unbelievable as a magic lamp that gives wishes.[4]

As beneficiaries of the drilling craze around Baku, the Nobel brothers expanded their business along with the rising tide of Caspian oil. Unfortunately, so much petroleum was flowing from the region's oil fields that the refineries of Branobel and other producers began to oversaturate the Russian market with kerosene. Across the whole of the tsarist empire, there were simply not enough homes, estates, factories, and people to burn all the refined crude that Branobel could produce. The playground of the Romanov tsars was large, but paying customers for oil were relatively few. Worse yet, Russia's almost limitless territory was unconnected. This was the other half of the Nobels' woes.

Unlike the petroleum fields of the United States, which were close to large population centers and major transportation networks, Russia's oil was far away and hard to ship. From the shores of the Caspian Sea in the late 1880s, the Russian Empire sprawled over the map "like a giant organism moving in several directions at once." Russia's European territories alone exceeded the modern size of France, Germany, Spain, Sweden, and the United Kingdom plus Italy, Norway, and Romania combined. The tsar's Asiatic territory was larger still. Explained one awestruck American traveler, "If a geographer were preparing a general atlas of the world and should use, in drawing Siberia, the same scale that is used in Stieler's 'Hand Atlas' for England, he would have to make the Siberian page of his book nearly twenty feet in width to accommodate his map."[5]

During the previous centuries of conquest and exploration, the growth of the tsar's lands had outpaced the Russian Empire's build-out of serviceable roads, rails, and canals. That transportation gap could be ignored inside the parqueted receiving rooms of the Winter Palace in St. Petersburg, but to anyone standing in the oily muck of Baku, it was a gigantic impediment. Before a single tin of refined kerosene from Baku could reach lucrative markets in western Europe, it first had to travel more than five hundred miles up the Caspian Sea to the port of Astrakhan. But arriving at the ancient Mongol outpost was just the beginning of the daunting journey of Russian oil. From Astrakhan, petroleum shipments had to be transferred onto barges and hauled an additional twelve hundred miles over rivers, irregular highways, and rudimentary railroads to the Baltic Sea. Even then the journey was not over. From the Baltic shore, it had to be loaded back aboard a seagoing ship and sailed an additional fifteen hundred miles to the North Sea and down the western edge of Europe to waiting ports such as London.

Every mile from Baku added an incremental cost to Russian kerosene. Once these shipments from the Caspian finally reached consumers in the United Kingdom, they were no longer competitive against the high-quality, lower-cost kerosene that Rockefeller was already offering for sale. If Ludwig and Robert were going to break out of the tsarist empire, they would need to crack the old conventions of shipping; and since Branobel's fundamental impediment was the Russian land barrier, why not go over water?

Enter the *Sviet*.

On September 1, 1885, the Lindholmen Engineering Works in Gothenburg, Sweden, gave rise to one of the world's first made-to-order bulk tankers. Bow to stern, the Nobel brothers' *Sviet* was nearly as long as a football field (289 feet). When fully loaded, she could make a respectable speed of ten knots per hour and carry seventeen hundred tons of petroleum.[6] That was what made her so commercially and physically dangerous—both to Rockefeller and to anyone within the blast radius of the hull. After nitroglycerine, the *Sviet*'s highly flammable cargo was the most hazardous liquid a boat could carry. Unafraid of the risk, however, Ludwig and Robert intended to sail their combustible fireship into some of the most populated ports in Europe.

As a family, the Nobels' genius for devastation knew few limits. Alfred's dynamite could level mountainsides. The destructive potential of Branobel's tanker could incinerate a sizable portion of a city if it caught fire. Adding to the danger, the *Sviet* was woefully difficult to captain in rough seas. The petroleum belowdecks sloshed from side to side, making the ship hard to sail. More terrifying, seamen aboard the new bulk tankers noticed that rich concentrations of combustible petroleum gas tended to collect belowdecks. If a wayward spark ever found these fumes, the *Sviet* and her sister tanker ships would be transformed into floating visions of hell. Understandably, most sailors of the day valued their lives too dearly to ever go near these dangerous inventions. As one maritime expert noted at the time, "It was with the greatest difficulty that the crews to man these vessels could be procured, sailors regarding shipping on a steamship laden with oil in bulk as nothing less than suicide."[7]

Nevertheless, the Nobels' oceangoing vessels were a sea change for the petroleum industry in Baku. As long as boats like the *Sviet* did not blow up, oilmen like the Nobels could move massive quantities of product over water at low cost. All they needed was to get their kerosene from Baku to the Black Sea.

Once again geography was no friend of Russian oil. Standing between the petroleum fields of Baku and the warm waters of the Black Sea were the Caucasus Mountains, some of the most unforgiving real estate on earth. For nearly a millennium, successive waves of Mongols, Persians, Tatars, Turks, and Russians had fought to control the peaks and strategic passes of the Caucasus. Peace was often transitory, making the mountains a home for "massacres, bloodshed, treachery, and cruelty."[8] And while the topography of the Caucasus was not insurmountable, the mountain range was still enough of a barrier in the late nineteenth century to force Baku's oilmen to choose the alternative route, the long overland trek to the Baltic Sea. The final breakthrough for Caspian oil would have to wait for the arrival of the steam locomotive and two of the most unlikely railroaders in all of Russia.

In 1885, the same year Branobel christened the *Sviet*, Alphonse and Edmond Rothschild, sons of the noble and spectacularly wealthy French House of Rothschild, suddenly found themselves in possession of an obscure railway in southern Russia. It was a turn of good fortune for the Rothschild brothers. Unfortunately, it came at the expense of two ambitious dreamers named Sergei Palashkovsky and Andrei Bunge. The oil business had just claimed two new victims.

Two years earlier, in 1883, Palashkovsky and Bunge had held the world on a string. They had secured approval from the tsarist government to build a 560-mile stretch of track over the Caucasus. Once completed, their feat of audacious railroading would link the oil bonanza in Baku with the sleepy port town of Batumi on the Black Sea. The concept was simple. The potential windfall was enormous. The only hitch was the price tag.

The act of hammering a railway across one of the world's great geographic frontiers was going to cost Palashkovsky and Bunge a small fortune. In order to cover the project's expenses, the entrepreneurs secured financing from the Rothschild brothers—owners of an incredibly large fortune. With backing from the world-famous banking house, Palashkovsky and Bunge got to work building their dream. They negotiated transportation deals with Caspian crude producers, laid track through the mountains, purchased a fleet of railroad cars to transport oil, and constructed storage tanks in Batumi to hold all the petroleum that would soon arrive from Baku.[9] There were a lot of jagged pieces to their plan, but remarkably, they all fit. Within a year,

Palashkovsky and Bunge had successfully constructed an entirely new oil export channel from the Caspian to the Black Sea. Entrepreneurial zeal had triumphed over some of the planet's most imposing mountains. The floodgates of Baku were finally open to the world.

At first, the Baku-Batumi railroad seemed a resounding validation of Palashkovsky and Bunge's investment thesis: build it and they will come. Within twelve months of opening, the railroad was carrying 45 percent of all the oil pumped in Russia. Only something appeared to be terribly wrong with their idea. The firm that Palashkovsky and Bunge created to run their business, known as the Batumi Oil Production and Trading Company (BNITO, for short), was losing money hand over fist. Baku's oilmen had certainly come to the railroad; they were just not paying enough to keep the trains running.

The perpetual whiplash of the oil market snapped a hole in BNITO's business plan. Shortly after the railroad began running, the bottom fell out of the Russian petroleum market. As the price of Russian crude collapsed in 1884, transit revenues from the Baku line plummeted in lockstep. Hoping to ride out the shortage, Palashkovsky and Bunge floated a desperate corporate bond to buoy their capital. Watching this financial misadventure from a distance, the House of Rothschild purchased the additional bond offering with gusto. Alas, cash-starved BNITO was too sick to be saved by the emergency injection of cash from Alphonse and Edmond. After just two years of running oil over the Caucasus, BNITO went bust.

When Palashkovsky and Bunge failed to make a loan payment in 1885, the Rothschild brothers seized BNITO's collateral, which amounted to the company itself as well as its impressive array of storage facilities in Batumi, the railway link to Baku, and titles to upstream oil wells around the Caspian. Thanks to a single corporate default, the Rothschild brothers now possessed turnkey access to the Russian petroleum business. Granted, BNITO was low on cash, but that was not a problem for the eminently well-capitalized French bankers. They could easily recapitalize BNITO. The reason they were willing to make this additional gamble was that the railroad was not fundamentally flawed. Palashkovsky and Bunge had simply made an amateur mistake: their idea had been bigger than their balance sheet.

The merciless booms and busts of the oil trade were cruel to undercapitalized dreamers like Palashkovsky and Bunge. In the petroleum business, bold ambition was never a guarantee of success, and neither was a solid business plan, local political protection, and a natural monopoly on a transport chokepoint like the Baku-Batumi railroad. Palashkovsky and Bunge had tended to all of their bases except for one—working capital. Like founders of other ill-fated startups across the ages, these entrepreneurs had gathered enough money to open the doors of their business but were unprepared for an abrupt and unexpected change in the marketplace. The deep-pocketed Rothschilds were far better protected from the turbulence. They could survive a market slump. In their hands, BNITO was not a liability—it was a kraken waiting to be unshackled. Upon assuming control of BNITO, Alphonse and Edmond installed themselves as managers of the company, bolstered its balance sheet, and kept the oil moving. Palashkovsky and Bunge were out; Alphonse and Edmond were in; and Branobel was topping off the kerosene tanks on the *Sviet*. Russia's oil had finally carved a path to the sea.[10] The flood of Russian kerosene only had to find its way into British lamps.

Back in London, the unassuming maestro tasked with orchestrating the *Sviet*'s arrival, and thereby filling English lamps, was Fred "Shady" Lane.[11] As a middleman and shipping agent, Lane's network of business connections extended across most of the major trading and financial centers in Europe. Nonetheless, his true talent was in bringing the right people together for a deal. In fact, he was so deft at linking sellers, shippers, and buyers that most times no one knew what side of a transaction he represented—or hoped to profit from. This was the origin of Lane's "shady" reputation. He was the insider's insider—the perfect fixer, facilitator, and proxy. He knew his trade, managed it well, and always seemed to keep his own clients guessing.

With his thick neck, wide shoulders, and smart, narrow eyes, Lane looked more like a pub brawler than the best-connected businessman in London. He tempered this imposing physical presence with a quiet, modest personality. It was a disarming combination. Always keen to listen, and immensely practical when negotiating a deal, he possessed the added gift of making friends easily. In fact, the line between his personal friendships and commercial partners was often nonexistent. If a man was a friend of Shady Lane's, he was also very likely doing business with him—and vice versa.

Owing to Lane's gold-plated reputation as an effective middleman, the Nobel brothers contracted him to offload their inaugural shipment of kerosene in London. Lane was so intrigued by the financial prospects of Russian oil that after clearing the sale of the *Sviet*'s cargo, he made an exploratory visit to Batumi. It was during this trip in 1885 that he met the Rothschilds and immediately dropped his allegiance to the Nobels. Shady Lane was true to his moniker. Instead of representing Branobel, he agreed to act as the exclusive agent for BNITO's oil in London. It was an invaluable pickup for Alphonse and Edmond and a blow to Branobel. The Rothschilds' timing was also impeccable. The *Sviet* had kicked the hornets' nest at 26 Broadway. If they were going to face off against Standard, Alphonse and Edmond would need all the talents that Shady Lane had to offer.

Viewed from Rockefeller's office, it made no difference if competition in the oil business arose from glorified moonshiners in Pennsylvania, a family of dangerous chemists, or the richest bankers in the world. The deluge of crude had to be controlled. Taking a page from his conquest of the American oil market, Rockefeller began to leverage his immense economies of scale to defeat this new threat from Russia. As kerosene from the Rothschilds, the Nobels, and other Russian producers began to appear in Europe, Standard immediately responded by slashing prices in local markets. These new contenders from the East would have to match Standard or find their order books dried up. This was the basic concept behind Standard's wildly effective "cut to kill" strategy. The American oil giant had cut the price of kerosene wherever it found competition. It had been a mainstay of 26 Broadway's business practices in the United States, and it worked equally well in Europe. By slashing prices on illuminating oil, Rockefeller and his directors ensured that their competitors would always lose money when they tried to provide an alternative to Standard's product. As a result of "cut to kill," 26 Broadway could make its rivals as unprofitable as it wished, for as long as it wished.[12]

In a typical price war, Rockefeller and his rivals should have felt equal financial pain from lower sales revenue. A rock-bottom retail price for illuminating oil meant less money for anyone trying to sell it, including Rockefeller. But he was no typical seller, and neither were his tactics. Rockefeller had devised a devious twist to the time-honored practice of a price war and used it to his advantage. Thanks to his globe-spanning monopoly, he could recoup the losses from a price war in one market by raising the cost of kerosene someplace else. What was more, he could do so with impunity, since he had purged his competition from practically every other market in the world. Hapless customers in the United States were oblivious to the reason for a sudden spike in the price of kerosene. They could not have known that it cost more to light their home because Rockefeller was giving a "good sweating" to a rival far across the Atlantic in Europe.[13] Nor did consumers have any choice but to pay more. They were the hostages to his monopoly. Standard prospered. Its customers suffered.

As the Rothschilds discovered throughout the late 1880s, the buzz saw of "cut to kill" was cunning, unpitying, and effective. Branobel's innovative maritime engineering, BNITO's extreme railroading, and the deft corporate finance of the Rothschild brothers were no match for Standard. As the merciless attrition of 26 Broadway's price war took its toll, all Caspian producers felt the pain. Writing to a colleague at the time, one desperate Russian oilman lamented, "On the oil markets, as a result of the maneuvers of the Standard Oil Company, prices do not increase, although the exchange rate of the ruble is rising adversely all the time: this situation threatens to become critical in the Caucasus."[14] Of course, the plight of the Russian oilmen had to become critical. The deluge had to be controlled.

Once Rockefeller had forced his competitors sufficiently into the red, he either allowed them to go bankrupt or sued for "peace" on advantageous terms. Those he could not break, he bent. Sometimes he bought competitors outright. Other times he forced them to accept a designated slice of the overall market. This was ultimately what Standard offered to the Rothschild brothers. They could accept a place in Standard's dominion by selling kerosene up to a set quota. If the Rothschilds did not like the terms, they could return to "war" and suffer the consequences.

Faced with the prospect of an endless, money-losing fight against "cut to kill," the Rothschilds agreed to Standard's terms of peace. They would now live by the rules of the *Pax Regulae*. But BNITO's allotted slice of the European market from Standard was too small to accommodate all the oil that was piling up in Batumi. The Rothschilds needed someone who could offload their excess kerosene in large allotments. A seller needed a buyer. Alphonse and Edmond needed Shady Lane.

Desperate to offload their gargantuan surplus of oil following the peace agreement with Standard, the Rothschild brothers tapped Lane with a mission. He was to find someone who could purchase their illuminating oil dockside in Batumi and sell it someplace else—anywhere else—just as long as it was not in Europe. It all seemed simple enough. The catch was that the Rothschilds had already been burned by an earlier attempt at such an arrangement. That deal imploded after the Scottish firm of Wallace Brothers & Co. encountered "cut to kill" when trying to sell rebranded shipments of BNITO kerosene in the Far East. Awakening to the dangers of competing against Standard, Wallace Brothers pleaded with the Rothschilds to be released from their contract. Alphonse and Edmond agreed, but that meant finding a new candidate for the slaughterhouse. Whomever Lane found to replace Wallace Brothers had to be brazen—and possibly foolish—enough to scrimmage against Standard. Most important, this new partner had to be capable of making unimaginable volumes of oil disappear from Batumi. True to his reputation, Lane knew an individual who fit that description. He was the "Merchant of Houndsditch," purveyor of seashells, foodstuffs, and affordable Asian finery: Marcus Samuel, Jr.

To the uneducated eye, the offices of M. Samuel & Co. at 31 Houndsditch Street might not have inspired much confidence in Lane's abilities as a talent scout. For starters, the firm did not even have a respectable entrance. The only way to visit Marcus at work was by passing through a narrow alley off the main road. Once a visitor arrived inside M. Samuel & Co., Marcus's spartan taste in office decor was even less impressive. There was only a table, a few chairs, a book-keeper, a senior clerk and his underlings, an office boy, and a large map of the world that dominated a wall.[15] Out in back, Marcus maintained a large storage depot. Here a visitor could have misjudged the contents as belonging to either an eccentric hoarder or a well-traveled madman. From top to bottom, Marcus's storehouse was crammed with exotic seashells, both rare and common; a mélange of porcelain china, mostly inexpensive; rice from Burma, Indochina, and Japan; feathers from points unknown; tapioca from the Philippines; odd Oriental curios; furniture; silk; and enough imported sugar to rot half the teeth in England. As an added twist, part of M. Samuel & Co.'s offices doubled as a workshop. During the day, around forty female employees meticulously applied seashells to trinkets and keepsakes for the tourist trade. Marcus might have seemed like the last person in England who could resist the might of Rockefeller's *Pax Regulae*, but looks were misleading. Superficial impressions masked the reality that, amid the low-rent disorder, Marcus commanded one of the most agile trading houses in all of London. He was more than up to the fight.

During the late 1880s, Lane had frequently called on Marcus at Houndsditch. Owing to his work as a shipping broker, Lane's ad hoc commercial ties with Marcus gradually grew into a genuine friendship. It would have been odd if Lane had not counted Marcus among his innumerable friends. As a businessman, Marcus had an impeccable reputation among the close-knit network of Scottish merchant houses that dominated trade with China. Indeed, Marcus financed his transactions on their credit. Who needed bankers when one had a good name for paying debts among peers? Marcus had also established a number of minor milestones in the Asian trade: his firm was the first to export British spinning machines to Japan; it held the exclusive right to export Formosa camphor oil from all Japanese-controlled ports; and together with his brother Sam, who split his time between Yokohama and Kobe, Marcus brokered half of Japan's annual rice exports, most of its sugar, and all its foreign coal sales. The Samuel brothers were so well connected inside Japan, they would soon arrange for the very first syndicated loan for the imperial government in Tokyo.[16]

Clearly, Marcus had carved out a niche for himself in Japan. At the same time, his broader knowledge of the Far East was second to none. After years of running long-haul shipments to England and exploiting point-to-point arbitrage trades between Asian ports, there were few in the business who could navigate the complexities, customs, and quirks of the Orient as he could. His style might have been unorthodox, along with his weird distain for overhead or any semblance of organization, but Marcus was a natural at solving complex commercial puzzles. If any firm could clean up the Rothschild kerosene mess, Lane believed, it was M. Samuel & Co.

Marcus was immediately skeptical. On a small scale, he had already dabbled in the oil trade by shipping limited loads of case oil to Japan. And people talked. Through his close ties with the Scottish traders, he almost certainly knew of Wallace Brothers' disastrous gamble with the Rothschilds. It did not take a great leap of deduction to determine that Lane's offer was probably a financial pitfall.

Viewed cynically, the Rothschilds were—in actuality—asking to dump their inventory predicament onto Marcus. They would be rid of their kerosene surplus in Batumi, and Marcus would assume all the risk. More ominously, there was little reason to believe that M. Samuel & Co. would not end up in the same bind as Wallace Brothers. If Marcus tried to offload BNITO's kerosene in the Orient, "cut to kill" would likely take his legs off. Marcus demurred on the deal from Lane. Besides, he already had more on his plate than a single man could handle.

In 1890, at precisely the time when Lane was lobbying Marcus on behalf of Alphonse and Edmond, the Merchant of Houndsditch was edging closer to his own personal breakthrough. Ever so slowly, Marcus was chiseling his way through the barriers of the British class system. Now he could see a hint of daylight. On account of his success at the helm of M. Samuel & Co., he was rising in stature among the traders of London. He resolved to use this prominence as a means of becoming an alderman in the City of London. Compared to his highest ambitions in life, the alderman's post would be a modest honor. It was nevertheless within reach of a merchant's son from Sailor Town. This was no time to dabble in distractions with Lane.

Importantly, Marcus's desire to become an alderman provides a crucial clue to his character. Distinct from Rockefeller, who measured life by the dollars and cents in his black pocket ledger, Marcus valued wealth for the status it could purchase. His success at M. Samuel & Co., the good name of Samuel, and his growing affluence had all put him within striking distance of civic office. What remained was for him to apply the light artistry of some face-to-face politicking. A major nuance of politics was that it consumed time. Marcus already had too little of it. As it stood, he was working twelve-hour days, arriving at 31 Houndsditch each morning by eight o'clock and remaining at work until eight at night; he "not infrequently failed to catch the last omnibus home from the City," he recalled in later years.[17] Having maneuvered to within reach of an alderman's seat, it would be foolhardy to stretch himself any thinner.

Always persistent, Shady Lane counteroffered with a compromise.[18]

The Insider

Since Marcus was dubious about Russian oil, why not see Batumi for himself? This idea echoed Lane's own trip to the Black Sea back in 1885. Marcus would not have to go alone, either—Lane offered to accompany him as a guide to the world of Caspian crude. On the Black Sea coast, they would glimpse the magnitude of the opportunity together. The inherent dangers in the oil business were admittedly high. But the greater the risk, the larger the reward. And considering the scale of this venture, the potential payday from the Rothschild offer was incalculably large. At a minimum, it was sizable enough for Marcus to set his sights higher than a mere city alderman's post.

The allure of greater status would have resonated strongly with Marcus. As of 1890, his aspirations were as yet unrealized. He desired the kind of social rank that his current line of business could never purchase. The Rothschild deal could provide that missing piece to his ambitions. But succeeding with the Rothschilds meant stepping over the heap of dead companies that had failed before him. As Palashkovsky and Bunge had shown, the petroleum business gave no quarter—not even to talented individuals with bright ideas. Likewise, the failure of Wallace Brothers demonstrated how easily Standard could pummel small-time operators working on tight budgets and minuscule economies of scale.

Against this heap of evidence, it is a testament to Lane's persuasive powers that Marcus agreed to leave London at all. The bait proved more tempting than the dangers. Perhaps there was an unforeseen way of making the kerosene trade work where others had failed. However, if he was going to make the trip to the Black Sea with Lane, Marcus insisted that the journey had to be a short one. He did not want to be away from London for very long.

In 1890 the fastest way to reach the Black Sea from London was by way of Paris. And the shortest way to Paris started with a ticket from Victoria Station. The steamers of the London, Chatham, and Dover Railway Company could make the Channel run in seventy minutes. Trains departed daily, including Sundays.[19]

Marcus and Lane were headed east.

CHAPTER 4

Rascality of All Descriptions

In the fall of 1890, Paris was a capital of contradictions, simultaneously ambitious and insecure, Catholic and socialist, fiercely rationalist and perilously romantic. It was a city so eager to reach the future that it built the Eiffel Tower out of naked steel, yet it was so preoccupied with the past that it could not escape the memory of defeat. Nearly two decades had elapsed since Germany laid siege to Paris during the ill-fated Franco-German war. This disastrous conflict ended with Germany's victorious parade down the Champs-Élysées, Paris's humiliating surrender of Strasbourg and Alsace to Berlin, and the violent collapse of France's Second Republic. Outwardly, Paris's physical scars had healed, but inwardly they tingled and burned. Nowhere was the legacy of defeat more enduring than the Gare de l'Est train station, in the city's tenth arrondissement. Crowning the building's neoclassical facade, sculptor Henri Lemaire's female representation of Strasbourg still reigned over the capital's gateway to the East. When Lemaire carved his stoic homage to the city, it had belonged to France, not Germany. And even though France's eastern gem was now in the hands of the Kaiser, rail service from Paris ensured that Strasbourg was never more than a seven-hour train ride away. Much like the other tangled contradictions of Paris, this was both comforting and sad.

The railroads did more than tie the French capital to distant parts of Europe. They fundamentally altered the city's topography and rhythm. By the end of the nineteenth century, train lines reached out from Paris like unnatural tributaries of the river Seine. They exhaled smoke and inhaled passengers from the city's boulevards at precise intervals each day. The remarkable predictability of train travel fueled the era's obsession with timetables. Aficionados published entire catalogs on the subject. Travelers parsed these volumes and constructed elaborate routes to shave minutes or even hours from a journey. The fastest itineraries were the most prized, and it was for this reason that the Gare de l'Est could also claim one of the greatest attractions of the day. The city's gateway to the East was also the origination point for the Express d'Orient. Already famous by 1890, the Orient Express could take a passenger farther east faster than any other means in Europe.

At seven o'clock in the evening, on three nights a week, the Orient departed Paris on a marathon burn across nineteen hundred miles, eight countries, three time zones, two empires, and the length of a continent. Posting an average speed of twenty-seven miles an hour—notable for its time—the train completed the journey in less than three days. This made the Orient incomparably faster than a similar voyage by steamship, which could take as long as twenty days to reach the Bosporus. Along the way, passengers delighted in the Orient's lavish saloon cars, liveried service, and relative immunity from the incessant border stops and customs houses that plagued most overland rail trips. This exemption from border stops was what made the Orient an express.

For travelers heading east, dinner on the first night aboard the Orient was usually a memorable, swift, and smooth experience. The well-manicured rail bed in eastern France kept the train from bouncing. Along this stretch of track, the Orient's coal-burning engine could reach a top speed of thirty-seven miles per hour without spilling a drink in the dining car. Thanks to regulations requiring that all food served on the train originate from the country of transit, a typical meal on the outbound leg from Paris consisted of tapioca soup, olives and butter, bar fish with hollandaise sauce, boiled potatoes, leg of mutton à la Bretonne, Le Mans chicken with watercress, spinach with sugar, fruit tart, and cheese. Sadly, the rules on food cut both ways for travelers. In the final push to Constantinople, passengers on the Orient reported "lively recollections of Romanian fowls" and other misadventures with eastern European cuisine.[1] For now, ladies in stitched corsets and men in dress coats sat two by two on extravagantly upholstered chairs. Their meal was served on white linen and porcelain china. Kerosene chandeliers and embers escaping from the locomotive's chimney offered the only illumination.

When settling into the train's overnight *coupes* after dinner, European travelers found the Orient's sleeping cars comfortable and well appointed. To Americans they were unfathomably small, especially when compared to accommodations on the express lines running between New York and Chicago. Returning from a trip on the Orient, one particularly unimpressed American complained of sharing "one of those rooms with a French prince, an Austrian count, and a Romanian general; and all were obliged to sleep with their clothes on" since the sleeping compartments lacked enough space to store clothing at night. More difficult were conditions inside the confined "wash room, privy and *urinoir*" of the Orient. These too were judged to be "scandalously bad" by U.S. standards of the day.[2]

This was continental travel at the peak of its coal-fired glory. Express trains like the Orient were making the world smaller by the trip—and doing so in fantastic style. Yet a great deal of the modern mystique surrounding the Orient is blurred by nostalgia and recollections from the oil-powered age that followed. Later fuel-burning locomotives would possess far greater horsepower and travel at vastly superior speeds. After the eventual transition from coal to oil (and electricity) to power engines, the next-generation locomotives on the Orient would pull more weight and support heavier, more luxurious carriages. This later diesel and electric era would be the one depicted by novelist Graham Greene in his thriller *Stamboul Train*. Agatha Christie would sear it into eternal memory in her *Murder on the Orient Express*. Compared to the oil-fed beasts of the twentieth century, the coal-burning engines of 1890 were weak forebears. Within a decade, oil would begin to topple the reign of king coal and send the underpowered locomotives of the nineteenth century to the scrapyard. But in 1890 coal was still plentiful, cheap, and dominant on the world's rail lines.

Although it was still king of the rails, coal's deficiencies as a transport fuel became apparent once the Orient pressed east from Stuttgart. Passengers were likely asleep when the train slowed to a crawl at the northern end of the Jura Mountains, so they missed the first topographic test of the Orient's coal-stoked boiler, which labored to break the summit of southern Germany's hill country. Safe on the other side, the train recouped lost time by racing down the back slopes of the range and onto the plains beyond Munich's eastward reaches. The stop for water in Salzburg marked the Orient's crossing into the Austro-Hungarian Empire and the start of its determined climb through the Alps to Vienna.[3]

As the seat of the royal Hapsburg monarchy, Vienna was a city of ornate ideas and endless procrastination. It offered the greatest parks in Europe, ten world-class theaters, forty-one cafés, the finest shopping this side of Paris, and a bizarre penchant for cultivating "suicides, madness, or quarrels" among its residents. It was the place where Sigmund Freud began his revolutionary studies on hysteria in 1890; where Friedrich Nietzsche's seductive vision of the Superman was just being discovered; and where Richard Strauss's orchestra created "fantastic pictures of vanished splendor" with nothing but horns, percussion, and strings. Strauss attempted to evoke an impression of Rome's ancient ruins when he composed the first of his musical "tone poems" four years earlier.[4] He could just as easily have conjured Vienna for all that was splendid, imperial, and vanishing about the Hapsburg capital. At the trailing end of the nineteenth century, the Viennese were uncoupling from the past and rushing headlong into the future. Freud was prying open the modern mind. Nietzsche was preoccupying it. And Strauss was giving it an unforgettable score.

After passengers on the Orient bade farewell to Vienna, views of the Danube River offered them gorgeous consolation. East of the Hapsburg capital, the train coursed alongside central Europe's most important waterway as it passed through the Slovak capital of Pressburg (today Bratislava) and the conjoined Hungarian cities of Buda and Pest. The train ascended the Transylvanian Alps beyond Copsa Mica, then left the Austro-Hungarian frontier behind as it charged south to Bucharest, capital of the newly independent Kingdom of Romania.

Two sunrises and seventy hours after departing Paris, passengers on the Orient would at last reach the seaside Romanian port of Constanta. For almost a decade, Constanta had been the final stop for the Orient. Before the rail line was completed through Bulgaria in 1890, most passengers closed the remaining distance to Constantinople by steamship. For travelers who wished to venture farther east into Romanov Russia, Constanta also offered maritime passage to the Black Sea ports of Odessa and Batumi. A steamer from Constanta was therefore the most expedient way to travel from the shores of continental Europe to the oil-rich boomtowns of the Caspian. And it was in Batumi that Marcus arrived at the tail end of 1890.

When approached by water, Batumi promised to be a bustling town of squat buildings and tall ships. Amid clumps of brown and white houses that clung to the harbor, the minaret of Batumi's Aziziye Mosque was the most prominent structure in the port. Twice as high as the Russian vice-consul's office near the waterfront, the minaret only slightly exceeded the tops of the three-masted cargo steamers in the harbor. The view was so picturesque that Italian diplomat Luigi Villari waxed poetic when describing his arrival at Batumi near the turn of the century. "The magnificent bay is surrounded by an amphitheater of hills clad with rich vegetation of the most exquisite velvety green," he reported. "To the south and east are the wild Adjar mountains, purple, blue, and pink, extending to the Turkish border and beyond, while the Anatolian mountains jut out into the sea in numerous rocky headlands, hazy and indistinct."[5]

Upon landing, Batumi promptly robbed its visitors of their picturesque first impressions. It was a "filthy mushroom town" when the famous oil broker Calouste Gulbenkian visited in the late 1880s. Batumi reeked of oil, "and the inhabitants seemed to exist almost entirely by smuggling." Aside from the smell, Batumi's most striking feature was the chaotic mixture of dress, customs, and people. "Few towns present such a collection of different specimens of humanity, from the swarthy Persian to the blond Russian," added Villari once ashore. "In all seaports of the Levant the ruffianly element is conspicuous, but Batum almost takes the palm for rascality of all descriptions."[6]

This was the scene that confronted Marcus when he disembarked at Batumi. The smell of petroleum would have indicated that he had come to the right place. Upon surveying the port, two additional facts were immediately apparent. First, the Rothschilds were clearly the biggest game in town. Second, they were trading in a flood of Russian crude.[7]

In less than a decade, the Rothschilds' rail link had transformed Batumi from a quiet fishing village into one of the world's busiest harbors. The depth of Batumi's harbor made it a natural location for maritime trade. The BNITO railroad had given it a purpose. The number of ships that now called upon the port each year exceeded that of Boston or Philadelphia. Batumi had become a raging boomtown. The Rothschilds had been busy.

By 1890 the Rothschilds' oil enterprise was running at full bore. It employed fourteen hundred people—equal to 8 percent of Batumi's swelling population—and had eclipsed all local competitors in the port, including the flagging Nobels. When petroleum shipments arrived by train from Baku, the Rothschilds either diverted the crude to their secondary refineries in France and Greece or processed it on-site into illuminating oil. In Batumi, workers packed the locally refined kerosene into specially designed wood and metal tins. These tins were stacked two by two into cases and loaded by the thousands onto ships waiting in the harbor. With enough crude from Baku, the Rothschilds could produce 38,000 tins of kerosene a day. There was never a shortage for the refining stills. At the other end of the line was Baku, the tsar's Black City of crude. It was home to one of the world's largest known deposits of hydrocarbons. And the oil trains never stopped running.

It was said that the name for Baku originated from a dead Persian word meaning "City of God." For centuries, Baku had been home to the fire cult followers of the god Zoroaster. They worshiped an "Everlasting Fire" that burned miraculously of its own accord. In the fourteenth century, on his famous journey east, Marco Polo traveled through Baku, where he witnessed a wondrous "fountain from which oil springs in great abundance. This oil is not good to use with food," he stressed, "but 'tis good to burn."[8] Other adventurers followed. In 1742 the Englishman Jonas Hanway visited Baku. Upon his return to London, he became famous for introducing the English to the umbrella and for retelling stories of his adventures in Russia's wild lands. Included among these tales was the description of a curious liquid Hanway encountered on the shores of the Caspian. Locals used this substance as both an elixir of health and as a stain remover. While the liquid wonder could remove spots from wool or silk, Hanway cautioned, "the remedy is worse than the disease for it leaves an abominable odor."[9]

This was Baku. Located at the end of the world, it was an ideal destination for wandering explorers. Beyond its strange curiosities, few people gave this outpost on the Caspian a second thought. That was, of course, until the rise of oil.

Soon after the tsarist government disbanded its monopoly on oil in the 1870s, adventurous wildcatters from the United States began to arrive in large numbers. They carried with them new innovations in drilling, honed in the oil fields of America. However, the established methods for extracting oil from the rocky geology of Pennsylvania proved to be wholly inadequate for Baku's sandy substrata. Instead of boring into the ground with a rotary drill, as was common in the United States, the oilmen of Baku adapted a form of percussion drilling from China. Using this technique, drillers harnessed the power of a steam engine to repeatedly smash a weighted "pounder" into the earth. When the pounder breached subterranean oil reservoirs on the Caspian shore, it released underground pressure that had been building for 70 million years. The results were legend.

Rascality of All Descriptions

The tall tales of Baku's titanic gushers were entirely true. One of the most spectacular erupted at the Bibi-Heybat field in 1886. Oil rushed through the drilling derrick with such force that it launched a column of crude twenty stories into the air, nearly twice as tall as Rockefeller's headquarters at 26 Broadway. The roar of escaping gas and petroleum from Bibi-Heybat could be heard from two miles away. As the residents of the Black City marveled at the distant bellow, many were even more surprised when a shower of dark oil suddenly rained upon downtown buildings. The local *Baku News* dispatched a journalist to the scene who struggled to explain what he had witnessed to readers. The gusher, the correspondent reported, looked like a "colossal pillar of smoke, at the crest of which clouds of oil sand detached themselves and floated away a great distance without touching the ground." It took two weeks for derrick workers to control the Bibi-Heybat well. During this interval, the single boring produced an unthinkable 1.4 million barrels of crude oil. This was at a time when the entire state of Pennsylvania yielded 25 million barrels annually. Not all of Russia's wells were gushers—or even as productive. But collectively, these wells were the instruments that transformed Baku from the ancient City of God into the Black City of oil.

By 1890, Baku was the source of 30 percent of the world's petroleum. It was where amateurs and professionals alike boasted of their refining skills and where kerosene stills operated in nearly every blighted home. For anyone willing to hustle, toil, or steal in Baku, great fortunes were waiting to be won. It was a place where an illiterate oil millionaire, incapable of writing his own name, kept eunuchs as house servants; where an oilman could never be certain if his *kotchis* bodyguards would rob him when given the chance; and where the Everlasting Flame of the Ateshgah Temple burned long after the last priest of Zoroaster had departed the city. When the English writer

Charles Marvin visited Baku in 1888, he was stunned by the Black City's man-made forest of derricks. The oil fields of Pennsylvania had sprouted a similar sight, but in Baku the forest was larger and denser than anywhere else in the world. "At present, there must be at least five hundred wells and fountains situated close together on less than a thousand acres of ground," Marvin wrote. "The supply is simply prodigious, and every year, as the borings get deeper, the fountains become more prolific."[10]

The Black City had produced so much oil that it was physically impossible to store it all. With too much supply and too few places to keep it, local oilmen constructed immense artificial lakes of crude near their wellheads. If there were not enough buyers for the petroleum, owners simply torched the ponds to eliminate the excess. Even with the rail link to Batumi and bulk tankers like the *Sviet* to transport it, the oil supply in Russia was growing far beyond the point of market saturation. Similar to the impulsive overproduction in Pennsylvania, the manic compulsion to drill in Baku intensified with each new field and every exciting gusher. As more oil from the Black City crossed the mountains to Batumi, the Rothschilds' inventory impasse grew by the month. Locked into their restrictive quota from Standard, BNITO's stockpile of kerosene expanded to gargantuan proportions. No matter how much oil the Rothschild brothers sold, the outflow from Batumi could not keep pace with Baku's production.

Looking out across Batumi's harbor in 1890, Marcus grasped the scale of Alphonse and Edmond's predicament. Their oversupply pains were obvious. With Standard barring the door to the markets of Europe, it was logical that the Rothschilds would wish to unburden themselves onto Marcus. Redirecting kerosene to the Far East was the obvious option. Outflanking Rockefeller in the Orient would be difficult, however, and present a host of complications, representing an intriguing puzzle of distance, geography, risk, technology, and greed. If Marcus was going to succeed in the oil business, he would have to solve that enigma.

The first hurdle would be distance. Oil from the Black Sea could not reach Asia directly: it would have to traverse a daunting eighteen thousand miles of ocean before reaching large markets in the Far East. All of Asia was hungry for kerosene, consuming 3 million tins of the stuff each year. Pent-up demand was more than ten times that amount.[11] If Marcus could get it there, the Orient would burn every last drop and more of Russia's kerosene. It was the journey that would be tricky.

It was no small task to close the distance between Batumi and lucrative ports like Shanghai or Hong Kong. Russian kerosene sailing out of the Black Sea would usually have to cross the Dardanelles of Ottoman Turkey, travel west to the Strait of Gibraltar, journey down the West Coast of Africa to the Cape of Good Hope, and then double back through the Indian Ocean to the Strait of Malacca. After reaching that crucial crossroads of the Orient near Sumatra, Russian crude would still have to move north along the coast of French Indochina before finally crossing the waters of the South China Sea. Every stage of this ocean voyage would add to the cost of a shipment. The greater the distance, the higher the overhead. As Wallace Brothers had discovered earlier, the long journey to Asia would ultimately put Marcus at a distinct cost disadvantage against Standard. That was, of course, without leveraging the benefit of geography. Cutting through the desert wastes of Egypt, the Suez Canal offered Marcus a solution. By running his oil through the canal, Marcus could slice the travel distance to China. That was going to be crucial, since he needed to eliminate every extra mile from the trip if M. Samuel & Co. was going to compete against Standard's pricing power. Saving on transportation costs would also be essential in order to overcome the largest obstacle: greed.

As the Rothschilds previously discovered, Rockefeller jealously defended his monopoly in the kerosene business against all comers. By competing against Standard in the Orient, Marcus would be committing to an all-out war with 26 Broadway. That fight would be intense. Much as Standard had done to the Rothschilds in Europe, it would predictably slash prices wherever Marcus attempted to sell kerosene in the Far East. If there was going to be a price war—and there almost certainly would be—Rockefeller's monopoly would ensure that Marcus lost money. If he succeeded in finding a way to outmaneuver Standard, he stood to reap a windfall. If he failed, the gambit would likely bankrupt M. Samuel & Co. It was a classic trade-off. The Rothschilds were offering the hope of a large payday, but only if Marcus assumed a great deal of their risk in the oil trade. The promised windfall was large because the chances of defeating Standard were so slim. Stupid money chased long-shot bets. Marcus needed to change the odds. But if it was possible to stack the deck against Standard, surely someone would have already done so. No one had.

Down at Batumi's docks, Marcus watched as dockworkers loaded cases of Rothschild kerosene into the hold of a waiting cargo ship. It was a laborious, time-consuming process. The scene would have horrified Marcus, who had a disdain for unnecessary costs of all kinds. To begin with, the containers into which the Rothschilds' kerosene was packed were expensive. They had to be durable in order to survive a long journey at sea, but durability cost money. That extra cost squeezed the profit margins on exported product. Even more appalling, the cases themselves occupied wasteful physical space inside a ship. Every inch of packaging was one less inch that could have been devoted to additional kerosene. If the Rothschilds were in the oil business, why did they devote so much space to something other than oil—in this case, packaging material? The answer was obvious. The product should be shipped in bulk—not in prepackaged, expensive containers. That meant moving the kerosene in tankers.

For Marcus, the idea of shipping petroleum in bulk was the loose end of a knot. As many had tried before, he pulled on the slack and tightened the rope. The moment he solved one riddle (cost), he reintroduced another (geography). He could not take bulk kerosene through the Suez. The potential for a tanker explosion inside the canal, bringing the world's oceangoing traffic to a standstill, was such an enormous risk that the International Suez Commission, the operator of the waterway, steadfastly refused to let oil tankers pass through the Suez. Marcus could transport petroleum in bulk if he wished, but his shipments would be taking the scenic route to the Orient. It was a frustrating snarl. It all seemed to hinge on the canal. This was clearly the center of the issue. If he could find a way to exploit the geographic shortcut through the Suez, he could move the world.

Standing on the docks of the Black Sea, Marcus studied the cargo steamers in Batumi's harbor. What if there was an oil tanker that did not explode? It was a straightforward question. A safe tanker would solve the puzzle. From this starting point, he began to shape the contours of a strategy to beat Rockefeller at his own game. If a new ship design or technology could eliminate the risk of an explosion, then the Suez Commission might be convinced to allow a bulk tanker, or even a fleet of bulk tankers, to pass through the canal. It was a sizable *if*, but a great many things followed from that single leap of imagination.

With the Suez open, Marcus could reduce the distance to the Far East. That would save money. Transporting oil in bulk tankers would make each load more profitable, since he would be able to move more oil without wasting space on packaging like other shippers. Finally, there was the size of Marcus's potential market. It was immense. In China alone there were 380 million people—all potential paying customers for his kerosene. Just to satiate demand in that one part of Asia, let alone the whole of the Orient, Marcus would need every barrel the Rothschilds could give him. He would then sail that kerosene through the Suez, arbitrage the rock-bottom price of oil in Baku against the oversize demand in Asia, and clobber Rockefeller's economies of scale with even greater scale of his own.

Here was a business strategy on a truly grand scale. If it was going to work, Marcus would need some help—and not just from the Rothschilds. What he was envisioning was nothing less than the largest undertaking that M. Samuel & Co. had ever attempted. He would have to muster every agent, middleman, and merchant house with whom the Samuels had done business in the previous decades. Most important of all, he would need to convince his inscrutable brother Sam that it was a good idea. This was not a commitment that Marcus could make on his own. It was a decision Marcus and Sam had to make together.

Risk-averse Sam was not going to like Marcus's idea.

CHAPTER 5

It Can't Be Done

When spring arrived, the cherry blossoms at the Moon Temple atop Japan's Mount Maya were worth the journey. In truth, there was no such thing as a Moon Temple on Mount Maya. Only the foreigners living at the base of the mountain in Kobe called it that. Its true name was the Maya-san (Tenjō-ji) Temple. Dedicated to the mother of the Buddha, the site had no connection to the moon at all. The reason anyone called it the Moon Temple likely originated from a nighttime procession of pilgrims who trekked the mountain during Japan's summer O-bon festival. During the O-bon, the faithful visited the temple to honor their ancestors. When foreigners ventured to the temple grounds at all other times of the year, they typically came in sunlight and as tourists.[1] If the temple held no interest for them, the mountain's visitors could gaze upon the nearby Nunobiki waterfall, or marvel at the spectacular views of the distant harbor. Spread out below Mount Maya was the awakening port town of Kobe. It was new, bustling, and filled with foreigners.

For more than two and a half centuries, the harbor of Kobe had slept under the willful isolation of the old Tokugawa shoguns. Seeing no need for the outside world, the shoguns had shunned it, ruling

Japan as a closed, militaristic state based on rice and feudal allegiances. After reformers forced the reopening of Japan in 1868, Kobe roared back to life. This process, known as the Meiji restoration, was cracking Japan's old barriers to the world. As part of the transformation, Japanese officials designated Kobe's harbor to be one of the country's official entry points for all foreign trade. The walls against commerce fell. Foreigners came in fleets. Kobe grew at an exponential rate.

The most visible signs of Kobe's awakening could be seen in the Foreign Concession along the waterfront. Here the paved streets, gaslight lamps, and mixed assortment of European architecture clashed with the surrounding shrine and temple structures of old, sleepy Kobe. In the eyes of one visiting American, Kobe's newly built Concession had a "very English look." But that was only if a visitor looked beyond the obvious rickshaw traffic, the adolescents in dark *uwagis*, and the clumps of local laborers who milled around the gates of Kobe's foreign consulates.[2] The Concession was decidedly not London, nor even Liverpool. It was a special bubble world created for one purpose: trade.

The merchants who populated Kobe's Foreign Concession enjoyed all the amenities of gracious living. There was a daily English-language newspaper, a post and telegraph office to connect Kobe with the outside world, and even the illumination of an electric lighting company. Most important of all, the foreigners of Kobe had the Hyogo Hotel, the epicenter of the town's expatriate social life, its billiard games, and its local pricing scheme for rickshaw runners. In fact, the Hyogo was so central to the foreigners of Kobe that when one of them wished to go anywhere around town, the cost of a rickshaw ride would be quoted in terms of the distance to or from the hotel.[3] It was little wonder then that Sam Samuel chose a location only a few blocks from the Hyogo in which to open the new offices of S. Samuel & Co. of Yokohama and, now, Kobe, Japan.

It Can't Be Done

Becuse the youngest Samuel son spent a good deal of his adulthood in Japan, the rules and rhythms of the Orient had come to define his professional life. Sam first arrived in Japan after the initial shock wave of the Meiji restoration in the early 1880s. It had been his task to expand the family's commercial foothold on this new frontier of the Far East. Operating under the trade name of S. Samuel & Co., the build-out of S. Samuel's first foreign office, in Yokohama, had proved to be one of Sam's major successes in Japan. The opening of the second office, in Kobe, gave him a nice bookend to that accomplishment. In between Yokohama and Kobe, Sam had established a thriving business importing British spinning machines and exporting Japan's camphor oil, rice, sugar, and coal to ports around the globe.

As the head of the family's operations in Japan, Sam enjoyed a wide degree of freedom from Marcus back in England. One way this autonomy manifested was in Sam's total disregard for regular business hours. Unlike Marcus, who arrived at work in Houndsditch promptly by eight o'clock, Sam's appearance in the office was more lackadaisical and harder to predict. On Saturdays, the final day of the business week, Sam typically breached the office doors at the leisurely stroke of eleven o'clock, whereupon he promptly ordered lunch and a double whiskey soda, and then proceeded to dig through the firm's weekly finances. Officially, Sam's employees were supposed to work only a half day on Saturday, but this was rarely the case. Instead, his ritual inspection of the books became a harrowing daylong affair. No one could leave as Sam methodically inspected, disputed, and calculated every expenditure and invoice that had steadily accumulated on his desk during the previous week. Being on time for work could be dispensed with, but neglecting the family's ledger was unacceptable. Rockefeller would have approved—at least about the ledger.

During his time in Japan, Sam had collected a colorful cast of characters who floated through the offices of S. Samuel & Co. There was "Smiling" Zensuke Tanaka, Sam's expert on the silk trade; Tatsuji Ando, the virtuoso of all imports; and Walter Finch Page, the seasoned British expatriate, full-time railroad expert, and part-time transportation adviser to the Japanese government.[4] Finally, in 1886, a highly capable Scottish trader named William "Foot" Mitchell joined the merry band of Sam's office staff. The arrival of Foot Mitchell was a turning point for Sam: older brother Marcus felt it was time for Sam to come home, and Foot Mitchell would take over in Japan. After Sam had spent his early adulthood in the Orient, his world of misnamed temples, shaved foreheads, rickshaw rides, and carefully calculated wagers in the local rice market was about to disappear. For Sam, returning home meant losing his relative independence from Marcus. The readjustment for both brothers would not be a tranquil one.

Reunited in London before Marcus's trip to Batumi, the contrast between the Samuel brothers was stark. In physical appearance, the tall, lean Marcus loomed above the shorter Sam, who was beginning to bulge at the waist. In personality, Marcus played the introvert to Sam's extrovert. In love, Marcus had eyes only for his wife, Fanny, while Sam was a committed bachelor. However, the brothers' most decisive difference lay in the realm of business. By now, the older Marcus had emerged as the risk taker, while young Sam approached business decisions with much more caution. Naturally, their management styles and temperaments in the office also differed, especially as the last will and testament of Marcus Samuel, Sr., still hung over both of them. The Samuel brothers had not forgotten their father's final request.

Nearly two decades had passed since Marcus Sr. instructed his sons to "keep the good name of Marcus Samuel from reproach." While these words remained sacrosanct, friction persisted between the brothers over day-to-day decisions. Once they began to work side by side in Houndsditch, Marcus and Sam locked pincers like scorpions in a bottle. Arguments between them were frequent, loud, and hostile. It was usually Marcus who tried to steamroll his younger brother's objections. Sam invariably refused to yield ground. Epithets sailed. Savage curses followed. Cutting words escalated into outbursts. Just when the flare-ups seemed to reach a climax, there would be an abrupt silence. "The two brothers would always go to the window," remembered one eyewitness, "their backs to the room, huddled together close, their arms round each other's shoulders, heads bent, talking in low voices, until suddenly they would burst apart in yet another dispute." In this way, business was conducted at M. Samuel & Co. "Mr. Sam with loud furious cries, Mr. Marcus speaking softly, but both calling each other fool, idiot, imbecile, until suddenly, for no apparent reason, they were in agreement again."[5]

It was into this high-tension environment that Marcus returned from the Black Sea in 1890 with his plan to flood the Far East with kerosene. Seen through Sam's naturally cautious outlook, the intrigue that Marcus had cooked up in Russia represented nothing less than commercial suicide. There could be no doubt that Standard would try to eliminate any competition from the Samuels. Wherever they tried to offload illuminating oil in Asia, 26 Broadway was sure to slash the market price for kerosene. Worse, Marcus's bright idea about cutting through the Suez was a nonstarter. The canal was closed to oil tankers because "safe" tankers did not exist. The risk that one of them might blow up inside the Suez was too great to endanger the flow of global commerce. Even if the Samuels could somehow build a fleet of these vessels, the up-front costs of the gamble were astronomically expensive. The brothers did not have enough liquid assets to cover the capital costs. How would they ever finance the idea?

Much like the strategy itself, Marcus's solutions to these practical impediments were equally bold. Taking a page from his original Bangkok rice run in the 1870s, he intended to draw credit from the Far East merchant houses with whom the brothers did business and with whom they enjoyed a trust cultivated over the course of decades. This would eliminate the need for bank loans, which the brothers steadfastly avoided in business. If they agreed to pursue the venture, Marcus could lower their overhead even further by piggybacking on the merchant houses' ready-made distribution channels into the hinterlands of the Far East. That would translate into greater sales volume and higher revenue. But lowering costs would help only if the plan could be executed—which was far from guaranteed.

The most important elements of Marcus's plan would be scale and speed. By opening the spigots of Russia and moving product in bulk, he could surprise Rockefeller with a preemptive price war across every major kerosene market east of the Suez. That would turn the tables on 26 Broadway. Instead of getting a "good sweating" from the American oil giant, he would force Standard to lose money instead. He needed to turn all of Asia into his battlefield in order to short-circuit the threat of "cut to kill." Economies of scale had always been on Rockefeller's side. Marcus would turn that advantage against Standard by making the scale of his commercial attack larger than anything Rockefeller had yet experienced.

In the past, when Standard used the devious strategy of "cut to kill" against competitors, the contested market or country had always been a limited one. If 26 Broadway wished to deploy its old weapon against Marcus, it would have to do so in every major port, market stall, and distribution channel in the Orient. The financial pain from such a price war would be immense and would require Standard to compensate by imposing across-the-board price hikes in America. When that occurred, savvy Russian oilmen would pounce on Rockefeller. Why fight for scraps in Europe, when premium prices in America would invite every oil baron with a tanker to offload their product in New York or Philadelphia?

In the rough-and-tumble world of oil, Marcus was preparing to open his attack on Standard with shock and awe. Nothing of this magnitude had been attempted in the petroleum business before. The catch was that it required an all-or-nothing bet from Marcus. If his gambit failed, then he endangered his own personal fortune. More alarming, he would very likely bring all of M. Samuel & Co. down with him. The "good name" of Marcus Samuel, Sr., would end in disaster, bankruptcy, and liquidation. On the other hand, if Marcus succeeded, the financial upside was potentially boundless. The wealth that would flow from his venture could propel Marcus, as well as the entire Samuel family, into an entirely new echelon of class and social status. That was, of course, only if Sam agreed. Marcus could take no action without Sam's support. The Samuel brothers might fight all they liked, but in the end, forming a consensus was the unbreakable family rule of their business.

The precise manner in which the Samuel brothers finally came to an agreement on the oil gamble remained between them. What mattered was that both brothers were of one mind. Marcus had prevailed. Sam consented. The youngest sons of Marcus Samuel, Sr., would wager his good name on an all-or-nothing bet in the kerosene business. It was a point from which there could be no return. Marcus and Sam were going to be oilmen. If they failed, they would be bankrupt oilmen. From this point forward, they raced to assemble the pieces of their strategy before Standard got wind of it.

Starting in early 1891, the Samuel brothers hit the seas. Sam departed London for the Black Sea: like Marcus and Lane before him, he would see the Russian oil business with his own eyes. Next Marcus set sail for Asia, to confer with the family's Far East agents. It was imperative that he line up both financing and distribution arrangements for the new venture. Secrecy and the personal touch remained essential to success. Marcus needed to conduct these conversations face-to-face and with considerable discretion.

In many respects, this new journey to the Orient echoed Marcus's original sortie to Asia in 1873. He called on familiar ports like Singapore and Bangkok and reconnected with the merchants at A. Symes & Co. and A. Markwald & Co. At the same time, this voyage highlighted just how much Marcus had accomplished in the two decades since his first visit. When he was twenty, the good name and credit of the Samuel family had been sufficient to pay for his rice relay into Calcutta. Now that he was thirty-eight, the family name was enough of a marker to borrow the vast supply of capital needed for a run against Rockefeller, the most powerful oilman in the world.

As he journeyed through now-familiar ports in the Orient, Marcus at last reached his farthest destination in Kobe, Japan. There he met with Foot Mitchell and briefed him on the plan. Marcus intended to execute the strategy on a frighteningly short timetable. In July 1891, M. Samuel & Co. would begin the process of acquiring land, designing holding tanks, ordering equipment, building onshore facilities, and arranging for overland transportation to inland depots across the Far East. His initial targets were the kerosene markets of Bangkok, Calcutta, Madras, and Singapore. The second wave would be centered on Burma, the Straits Settlements, Java, Siam, China, and of course Japan.[6] Aside from Foot Mitchell, execution of the plan would be strictly a family affair. Since his own children were too young to bring to the Orient, Marcus intended to deputize three nephews—the oldest sons of his sister Julia Abrahams—to act on his behalf. In Japan, he told Mitchell to expect the arrival of nephew Harvey. While Harvey was under Mitchell's wing, Marcus hoped that he might also learn the silk trade. After all, constructing a nationwide oil distribution chain without the slightest measure of experience was sure to leave Harvey with plenty of spare time to learn an entirely unrelated line of business, or so Marcus thought.

The final element of the effort was the most essential—and still unresolved. Marcus did not yet have a "safe" tanker that could pass through the Suez. Lacking that one asset, his entire strategy fell to pieces. As long as the canal remained shut, M. Samuel & Co. was dead in the water. Only with a new kind of vessel could the Merchant of Houndsditch achieve the impossible and breach the Suez.

CHAPTER 6

The Carnivorous Snail

In 1891 the highway of the world began at the breakwaters of Port Said. Running in an almost direct line through 105 miles of the Egyptian desert, the Grand Maritime Canal of Suez was a marvel of hand and shovel engineering. For its French creator, Ferdinand de Lesseps, it was also a dream made real. The Aztecs erected the Pyramid of the Sun, the Chinese constructed the Great Wall, and the Romans built the Aqueduct of Segovia. De Lesseps designed a trench in the desert. When water flooded his glorified ditch, it made a canal—*the* canal.

The cost of transforming de Lesseps's dream into reality was as monumental as its construction. The Suez had devoured more than £16 million ($2 billion today) and nearly twenty thousand lives by the time of its completion in November 1869. The return on such a colossal investment in human lives and fortunes was a smaller world. De Lesseps's narrow slit through the Suez Isthmus cut the overseas distance from Europe to Calcutta by a third. The length of an ocean voyage to Shanghai shrank by a quarter. Merchants paid less to transport their goods. Travelers arrived at their destinations earlier.

Even more important than its convenience was the canal's strategic value to the British Empire. As the nineteenth century drew to a close, the Suez had become essential to the Royal Navy. Famed British maritime strategist John "Jacky" Fisher calculated it to be one of the five "keys to the world."[1] Each of these keys represented a critical geographic chokepoint for commerce, navies, and the ambitions of Great Powers. Whoever controlled these keys commanded the oceans. When de Lesseps began digging his ditch in 1854, there were only four keys to the world: the Strait of Dover, the Strait of Gibraltar, the Strait of Malacca, and the Cape of Good Hope. When de Lesseps finished the Suez, there were five.

The fact that the planet's most preeminent sea power, Great Britain, did not originally control the canal was more than a mild embarrassment; it was a frightening vulnerability. From Britain's perspective, it was bad enough that the Suez passage was owned by a French company, operating under French law, and headquartered in Paris. The deeper threat was that Victoria's seagoing empire had come to rely on the canal for its sustenance and survival.[2] The Suez was now the main artery through which the United Kingdom shuttled goods, navies, and armies to its colonial possessions in the East. In the event of a military crisis, a foreign power could exploit that dependence by closing the canal to British shipping. That could never be allowed to happen. Britain had to have more control over this powerful new key to the world.

In 1875 British prime minister Benjamin Disraeli determined that England could not afford to live without the Suez, despite the fact that it could not afford to purchase it. This tension came to a head in 1875, when Egypt indicated it might sell a controlling stake in the canal to London for a mere £4 million (in the neighborhood of $500 million today). The catch was that Disraeli's government had no money to spare. The onerously expensive Crimean War in the previous decade had cleaned out the British Treasury. Disraeli's finances were so upside down that each year his government set aside an astonishing 40 percent of its expenditures just to pay the country's creditors. With no way of assembling £4 million on his own, Disraeli famously turned to the "world's bankers," the House of Rothschild.

On twenty-four hours' notice, Disraeli brazenly requested a £4 million line of credit with the English Rothschild family. As a branch of the extended Rothschild family in Europe, the English Rothschilds were relatives of the French Rothschilds, Alphonse and Edmond, with whom Marcus would later partner in Batumi. Although the creditworthiness of Disraeli's treasury was questionable, the English Rothschilds were staunch patriots and inclined to consider the appeal on behalf of the country's broader interests. Also in Disraeli's favor was the knowledge that England always paid her debts. No government in the country's long history had ever broken the sacred trust of a loan. Disraeli's credit was good with the Rothschilds at 5 percent interest, plus a 2.5 percent commission for their trouble.

It was one of the greatest purchases ever made: Disraeli snatched a controlling stake in the canal and cabled the news to Queen Victoria: "You have it, Madam."[3] The fifth key to the world dropped safely into the royal pocket. By financing Disraeli's canal maneuver, the House of Rothschild inscribed its first mark on the fabled history of the Suez. Marcus Samuel was twenty-two years old when that drama unfolded. He could not have known it at the time, but this monumental event would one day alter the course of his life.

Sixteen years after Disraeli's canal deal went through, Marcus faced his own quandary linking the Rothschilds and the Suez. The strategy that he had devised to outflank Rockefeller required obtaining kerosene from the French Rothschilds in Batumi and opening the canal to bulk petroleum tankers. Marcus held the first element well in hand.

His contract with Alphonse and Edmond would be finalized by July 1891. But it was the locked canal that mattered most. Britain's powerful fifth key to the world was inconveniently beyond his reach.

From the outset, when oilmen like the Nobels began to pour petroleum into tank steamers, the Universal Suez Ship Canal Company unilaterally refused to allow them passage through the shortcut to Asia. The company would not risk an oil tanker running aground, springing a leak, or spontaneously exploding inside its narrow waterway. That could potentially bring global commerce through the canal to a sudden, costly standstill. Not even Rockefeller could break the ironclad rule against bulk steamers. As recently as 1890, the Canal Company had denied Standard's request to slip its own bulk tankers through the Suez.[4] As long as the moratorium remained in place, the strategy to break Rockefeller's monopoly in the Far East would fail. Marcus's new bulk steamer had to be so different, and so unimpeachably safe, that the managers of the canal would have no choice but to change their policy. Unfortunately, Marcus was not a naval engineer. Among his many talents, designing steam tankers was not one. Still, a businessman did not need to know everything. He just needed to know Shady Lane.

Thanks to an introduction from Lane, Marcus had struck up a friendship with James Fortescue Flannery. The match was ideal for both men. Flannery was fast becoming a rising star in the English shipbuilding industry. His specialty was in the design of cargo steamers. It was to Flannery that Marcus turned for a solution to his Suez riddle, offering him the commission of a lifetime.[5]

The concept behind Marcus's plan for a petroleum tanker seemed simple. The vessel had to be small enough to fit through the Suez yet large enough to carry vast quantities of kerosene. The crucial snag was that it also had to be safe enough to lift the ban on bulk oil shipments. It would be up to Flannery to define *safe*. However he defined it, the design had to be compelling. Otherwise, the canal's managers would deny Marcus passage just as they had done to Standard. Should that occur, the financial consequences for M. Samuel & Co. would be catastrophic.

For Flannery, the design challenge was a chance to push the envelope of maritime construction. The kind of tanker that Marcus requested needed to be significantly different from every other that had previously been put to sea. Envisioning the contours of such a steamer, Flannery saw a huge craft. She was to be wide, long, and very safe. Throughout 1891 he drafted the plans for this new class of petroleum steamer. Bow to stern, she would stretch 349 feet—fully 60 feet longer than the *Sviet*. Across the beam (width) of his tanker, he saw the vessel filling out at 43 feet. When her topmost portions were finished, she would stand just over two and a half stories tall in a dry dock. That would be large for her day, but even greater ships were already sailing the world's oceans. Size alone would not make his vessel special. It was what Flannery planned for her insides that would make her unique.

Above the tanker's keel, the very spine of his vessel, Flannery placed not one bottom but two. This double bottom would serve as an extra watertight layer of steel and run the length of his ship. It was an innovative safety measure. Never before had an oil tanker possessed such a thing. Flannery then transformed this *safety* feature into a *stability* feature by dividing the ship's double bottom into three separate segments. A segmented double bottom would allow the ship's captain to adjust the water level in each individual compartment, giving her more or less ballast where needed. That additional ballast would make Flannery's tanker more nimble at sea. If an unforeseen accident ever occurred and his ship ran aground, the extra ballast in the double bottom could be flushed to increase the vessel's buoyancy. Added buoyancy in an emergency might lift her up from the canal floor and prevent a potential closure of the Suez.

In addition to being buoyant and stable, Flannery also wanted his craft to be exceptionally strong. Inside her hull, he partitioned the vessel with nine transverse bulkheads. These upright partitions divided the vessel into individual compartments. Each one granted the ship added strength, and importantly in the case of an oil tanker, they could prevent the spread of leaks or fire. Flannery placed two particularly durable bulkheads near her bow and stern. He ran the bulkheads from the bottom of the ship's keel all the way to the top of her main deck. If a part of the vessel's hull were ever damaged at sea, these watertight slabs of steel might just be enough to keep her afloat. In between the partitions, Flannery placed the ship's reason for existence: ten gigantic oil tanks.

The petroleum tanks were the business end of Flannery's ship. Collectively, they gave her the ability to ship four thousand tons of oil, a 135 percent increase over the Nobels' old floating bomb, the *Sviet*. Since the cargo in the tanks was dangerous, Flannery took extra precautions to protect them. Leaking petroleum was the first hazard he wished to guard against. As such, he diligently separated the watertight tanks with an extra airtight cofferdam—an impermeable void nestled in between each tank. When his steamer put to sea, Flannery envisioned that the cofferdams could be kept empty for even more buoyancy or be filled with water for added ballast. There would be no more sloshing around in rough waves for his ship. As an additional precaution against leaks, he installed special expansion trunks inside each tank. Liquid petroleum contracts and expands at different temperatures. These new expansion trunks would help accommodate any natural changes in volume while keeping the petroleum tanks sealed in transit.

Flannery knew that his creation would be a globetrotter, traveling great distances to reach the Far East. Once she arrived at her unknown destinations, there was no telling what kind of rudimentary conditions awaited her dockside. She would therefore need to carry her own unloading equipment wherever she sailed. For this reason, her creator endowed the vessel with his own new design for drawing oil in and out of her tanks.[6] To power his innovation, Flannery placed two massive pumps amidships, the workhorses of his tanker. Wherever she might travel, and whatever scant infrastructure she might encounter, Flannery's ship would be capable of offloading all four thousand tons of her petroleum in just twelve hours.

Delivering liquid cargo to the opposite end of the world covered only half of the vessel's journey. After she offloaded oil in the Orient, she would have to return to Batumi. Flannery considered the economics: an empty tanker would be a burdensome cost for Marcus. So why not make her convertible into a regular cargo steamer for the back end of her eastbound voyages? To achieve this goal, Flannery designed specially fitted steam pipes inside his vessel's petroleum tanks. By giving her a good steam cleaning, her crew could purge all traces of oil and fill her with dry cargo for the return trip from the Orient. It was a brilliant and profitable flourish, the signature of a master designer. In fact, Flannery's steam-cleaning innovation is still in use today on modern supertankers.[7] But when it came to adding design touches, Flannery was just getting started.

As well as making her stable, strong, and stacked with special features, Flannery had above all to protect his ship against any chance of fire. From rudder to forecastle, he considered all possible sources of onboard combustion. The most insidious danger, and the most difficult to counteract, existed in the air itself. By the time he sat down to design his ship, the accumulation of flammable petroleum vapors aboard oil tankers had become a well-known peril. Deadly experience had shown that gases from petroleum were heavier than air and tended to concentrate at the bottom of a ship. In response, Flannery installed intake vents to increase the circulation of fresh air inside his tanker. But he anticipated that this would not be sufficient: the air was going to need some extra help to prevent explosions. Since he could not halt the chemical release of hydrocarbon vapors from the vessel's tanks, he would instead prevent those gases from concentrating. He developed a specially designed fan system for the ship. Capable of sucking 7,500 cubic feet of air from the tanker every minute, the ventilation system would act like a massive vacuum cleaner. With its fan system running, the entire ship would have fresh air once every twenty minutes. As with many of Flannery's innovations, this added protection against explosion would become standard for tankers that followed.

When it came to fire, Flannery was meticulous. He considered all possible points of ignition, scouring the rest of his ship design for any source of flame. He could address the obvious risks, such as the vessel's coal-fired boilers and its galley stove. These he placed close to the rudder—as far from the forward oil tanks as possible. Next, he imagined the human element and the mischievous habits of a crew at sea. Here his talent for social engineering shone brightest. While smoking was to be absolutely forbidden, he asked himself what would happen during a cold night. Would sailors be tempted to burn coal in their quarters? Any temptation to light an unsanctioned flame was one risk too many when mariners were sitting atop four thousand tons of flammable liquid.

Foreseeing a need for heat, Flannery ran steam pipes through the crew quarters. Likewise, he eliminated any need to light candles or lamps by stringing electric bulbs into the main cabin, the engine and boiler rooms, the galley, the chart room and wheelhouse, and around the binnacle, the home of the ship's compass. These were the obvious places where sailors would need illumination. He next considered the obscure places aboard the vessel where greater dangers lurked. He determined to outfit his steamer with a set of portable electric lamps. If crew members ever needed to move through the unlit inner bowels of his ship, they would not be taking any open flames with them. And as an added bonus, the onboard electrical system allowed for the installation of a ship's telegraph for communication, as well as a twenty-inch searchlight. Should his tanker ever pass through the narrow Suez at night, Flannery wanted her to be properly equipped.

Once Flannery finalized the plans for his creation by late summer in 1891, Marcus quietly initiated his gambit with the managers of the Suez. Using a back-channel intermediary by the name of Henri Goudchaux, from the French banking house of Worms & Cie, Marcus asked the Canal Company to consider a mind-blowing question: What if it were possible to build a safe petroleum tanker?[8] The managers of the Suez had never considered what might constitute a safe tanker. They had no precedent on which to judge such a thing and absolutely no idea what the exact requirements would entail.

Conveniently for the Canal Company, Marcus knew the precise dimensions and features of a safe steam tanker—his impresario ship architect Flannery was designing one. Under Flannery's supervision, the esteemed shipbuilder William Gray & Co. would soon begin to construct such a vessel at England's famed West Hartlepool shipyards. If the Canal Company still felt at a loss to define the specifications of a safe tanker, why not defer that question to the experts at Lloyd's of London, the world-famous underwriter? Lloyd's was the most respected risk manager on earth. It would know whether something was safe—it had built its reputation on it. In fact, each year on July 1 it published a registry of new vessels, rating them on the basis of safety—

a global benchmark. When Lloyd's spoke, the shipping industry listened.

At a fundamental level, Marcus was employing a very different approach with the Canal Company than Standard had attempted. When 26 Broadway previously asked to sail its steamers through the Suez, the American oil giant had offered the Canal Company nothing new. It had simply wanted an exemption to the rules. Its tankers were going to be of the floating bomb variety—the great menace of the Suez. Understandably, the Canal Company had refused to exempt Rockefeller's ships. By contrast, Marcus was offering something unusual. The Canal Company needed only to accept that a safe tanker was possible and then place its trust in the esteemed judgment of Lloyd's of London.[9] It was a bold move, and the managers of the Suez took notice. Audacious as it was, the bet that Marcus was placing was also insane. All his chips were riding on the assumption that Flannery's tanker would be included on the Lloyd's registry. But what if his ship did not make the cut? The canal would remain closed. Marcus's gamble would collapse along with the good name of his family.

Given the huge stakes of his gamble, Marcus's negotiations with the Canal Company invited a carnival of speculation by his contemporaries and later historians. The most damning accusation was that Marcus rigged the outcome, employing "much *baksheesh*" (meaning bribery in this case) in his dealings over the Suez.[10] But there is another possibility hidden in plain sight, a far more likely scenario and one that has managed to escape notice for over a century. Perhaps Marcus did not need to bribe anyone. Perhaps all he had to do was game the system.

The clue to his brilliant ploy can be found by scrutinizing the firm that he and Flannery commissioned to construct the new tanker: William Gray & Co. of West Hartlepool, England. This company was one of the best known in the business. Its eponymous owner, William Gray, was a very busy man—possibly too busy. In addition to being the founder and senior partner of his shipbuilding company, he was also the mayor of West Hartlepool and—significantly for Marcus—the regional representative for West Hartlepool on the executive management committee of Lloyd's of London.[11] Was it remotely possible, let alone probable, that a senior representative at Lloyd's would certify one of his own construction projects as unsafe? Viewed from Marcus's perspective, the odds of that were infinitesimally low.

Marcus needed a clean bill of health from Lloyd's. Gray's double role—as the head of the firm that built the tanker and the representative of Lloyd's for the West Hartlepool shipyard—all but guaranteed that outcome. The larger mystery is, who would have been in a position to hatch the scheme? Did Marcus's sleight of hand with the Canal Committee reflect the subtle handiwork of Shady Lane, or was it Flannery's? As no one was kind enough to leave a surviving paper trail, this question is difficult to answer. What is certain is that the arrangement brought precisely the right individuals together for a larger purpose: to advance the financial interest of the Rothschilds, Lane's paying client. In order to succeed, the gambit required a fluent knowledge of personal résumés and overlapping business interests in the realms of the Far East trade (Marcus), marine architecture (Flannery), ship construction (Gray), and the Lloyd's safety certification (Gray again). Not for nothing did Shady Lane possess a universal reputation for working multiple unseen angles on a deal. It was a skill that created the conditions for Marcus's success.

By granting William Gray the contract for his new tanker, Marcus tilted the odds decisively in his favor, but he also acted prudently. Gray had earned one of the best reputations in English shipbuilding by also being in the business of distinguishing a safe vessel from an unsafe one. Moreover, Flannery personally oversaw the construction of his design in West Hartlepool. Marcus did not cut any corners. He intended for his tanker to meet the highest level of safety achievable in his day. In the process of toppling Standard in Asia, he built a vessel that set a new standard for the safe passage of oil over water. Its legacy still resonates today.

Unfortunately, the secrecy of Marcus's plan was one thing he could not completely control. By the middle of 1891, whispers about a new tanker were swirling inside the oil business. Despite Marcus's best efforts, a good secret was hard to keep. When Standard finally learned of the effort, it calculated that this new tanker had one purpose: to breach the Suez.[12] Such a breakthrough would put 26 Broadway at a tremendous disadvantage in the Far East. The tanker gambit had to be stopped.

The British law firm Russell & Arnholz spearheaded the struggle against Samuel's Suez gambit. Its early actions in the fall of 1891 revealed that only partial bits of information had emerged. Nevertheless, it was minimally apparent to outsiders that Standard's familiar nemesis the Rothschilds were somehow involved, even if the extent of their connection was still unclear. In any event, it was up to Russell & Arnholz to kill this new threat of competition in the dry dock. Standard never lost.

Ominously, anti-Semitic stories began to appear in British newspapers. They were infused with prejudicial buzzwords decrying "Hebrew inspiration" behind a plot to endanger the Suez with oil tankers. Next, Russell & Arnholz began to inundate British prime minister Robert Salisbury and his government with letters. The first of these missives arrived in late October 1891.[13] Feigning grave concern, the barristers inquired as to who exactly was behind this risky idea to sail tankers through the Suez. The barrage from Russell & Arnholz initially caught

Salisbury's government off guard. The Foreign Office forwarded the inquiries to the Canal Company and shot notes back to the lobbyists: Who wanted to know? Of course, the company that dearly needed to know was Standard.[14] Naturally, Russell & Arnholz ignored the question about their client's identity and doubled down on their line of questioning: Who would assume the enormous financial liability for a tanker mishap in the canal? Was it Salisbury himself, British taxpayers, or some private company? If the last, pray tell, who might that be? Salisbury was on guard and dodged their questions. Russell & Arnholz opted to escalate.

Across London, the mailboxes of foreign embassies soon filled with friendly, unsolicited warnings from Russell & Arnholz, asking if diplomats were aware that Britain might soon violate the 1888 Convention of Constantinople, which guaranteed the neutrality of the canal. Allowing only British tankers through the Suez would hurt non-British interests, and that was banned under international agreement. If foreign governments had any concerns about Britain's potentially egregious violation of an international treaty, they should direct their questions to Lord Salisbury. It was an inflammatory mutilation of the facts, and it backfired in spectacular fashion.

Inside the Salisbury government, the letters prompted spasms of apoplexy. Russell & Arnholz were becoming more than a nuisance—they were threatening to destabilize the diplomatic balance of the Great Powers over the Suez. Suspecting that Russell & Arnholz were acting on behalf of Standard, Salisbury demanded to know which British interest they represented.[15] Their response was to camouflage any American interests by hastily assembling a motley, artificial coalition of domestic companies. This faux constituency included anyone remotely involved in the petroleum business, from case oil merchants to makers of kerosene tins. In a joint reply to Salisbury's government, these firms bemoaned the harm that bulk oil shipments would inflict on their businesses. It was a smart tactic in principle, but the ruse was too obvious. Russell & Arnholz's coalition was too broad, and its list of potential grievances was too expansive to be taken seriously. Rather than creating a chorus, the lobbyists had produced a cacophony. Noted Salisbury, "It would be difficult to understand how so large a body of intelligent and practical men of business could have signed such a document."[16]

Despite the deficiencies in their tactics, the barrage from Russell & Arnholz could not go unanswered. It was time for the House of Rothschild to enter the fray. Unleashing their own lobbyists upon Salisbury's government, the extended Rothschild banking family made their case on behalf of Marcus. In doing so, they had a card that trumped any in Russell & Arnholz's hand; they held the loan that financed Disraeli's original canal purchase. Certainly, Salisbury's government had not forgotten the Rothschilds' powerful assistance, or why Great Britain had struck the Suez deal in the first place. The whole point of securing the canal had been to ensure that the Crown's interests in the Suez were protected. And here was M. Samuel & Co., a *British* firm, hoping to advance *British* commerce by carrying oil to *British* colonies on *British*-flagged steamers. The government's course was clear. The Suez should be opened to the Samuels if the vessels were safe. Ever the empire builder, Salisbury was inclined to agree.

Back in Paris, the Canal Company issued its historic decision in January 1892. Starting on July 1 of that year, bulk petroleum tankers would be allowed to transit the Suez—if they met a very specific set of conditions. First, the tanker must receive Lloyd's of London's highest safety designation: 1A.100. Additionally, the Canal Company issued a string of extra safety and design specifications for acceptable tankers. These were so close to Flannery's design that they read like a technical description of his ship, right down to the rivets. In fact, Flannery's tanker, still in dry dock at West Hartlepool, was the only vessel on the planet that actually complied with the specifications.[17] Marcus could not have asked for a better outcome. Only tankers built precisely to his specific ship design were to be allowed through the Suez. It was a coup of the first order. Now all he had to do was christen the vessel.

On Friday, May 27, 1892, Samuel's wife, Fanny, and his daughter, Nellie, were in West Hartlepool for the auspicious naming of the family's big coup. By giving it a name, the Samuel ladies brought the ship to life. She would be the *Murex*, the world's first modern oil tanker. Named after the shell of a carnivorous sea snail that bristles with spikes, the *Murex* would soon have many sisters. All based on Flannery's design, they would each bear the name of a shell, such as the *Conch*, the *Clam*, the *Elax*, the *Bullmouth*, and the *Volute*.[18] The shell, that physical embodiment of Marcus Sr.'s legacy, would be the Samuel family's banner in their coming war against Rockefeller.

At long last, the pivotal day, July 1, 1892, arrived with no surprises. Designated as vessel number M.834, the bulk petroleum steamer *Murex* found its place on Lloyd's official shipping registry for that year. As expected, Lloyd's granted the *Murex* its coveted 1A.100 rating. Every chip Marcus possessed for the Suez gamble was spread out upon the table. Now it was time to begin the blitz.

Under the command of Captain John R. Coundon, the *Murex* called at the docks of Batumi later that August.[19] She took aboard four thousand tons of bulk Russian kerosene from the Rothschilds and departed for Port Said, at the opening of the Suez Canal. Always the savvy businessman, Marcus ensured that his long-term contract with the Rothschilds would not straitjacket him. If the price of oil fell in the future, or if Marcus found a better deal dockside at Batumi, the Rothschilds' contract gave him the freedom to buy kerosene from whomever he liked. In exchange for this concession, the Rothschilds preserved the right to act as Marcus's agent for any outside purchases. Naturally, Shady Lane, the consummate middleman, would broker all transactions.

More than a century later, on any given day, 7 billion people consume 70 million barrels of crude; $223 trillion in debt accumulates on the world's spreadsheets; and an average of ten bulk petroleum tankers casually slip through the Suez Canal.[20] But on August 23, 1892, only one tanker crossed from the waters of Europe to Asia. She was the *Murex*. By the time she safely reached the opening to the Red Sea, Samuel had flipped the oil world on its head.

By sending the *Murex* across the canal, Marcus became the first to solve the complex puzzle that prevented bulk Russian oil from competing against Rockefeller in Asia. He had shrunk vast distances, navigated difficult geography, managed gut-churning levels of risk, harnessed technological innovations, and subverted a powerful lobby. His winning solution, a fleet of safe oil tankers, would become the template that others—including Standard—would follow years later. As a result of Marcus's Suez coup, Asian consumers would tip the scales of the global energy business for the first, but not the last, time.

As the *Murex* exited the Red Sea, it ventured eastward into the Indian Ocean. The carnivorous snail from the dry dock of West Hartlepool charted a course toward the Strait of Malacca. Her first port of call would be the Crown Colony of Singapore.

As the strait narrowed on the approach to Singapore, the tropical shores of Sumatra lay far to the west off the *Murex*'s starboard rails. It would have been impossible to see from the deck, but in the distance, a light flickered on the Sumatran coast. It issued from a fire that burned without ceasing, and unknown to many, it signaled a secondary threat to the might of Standard in the Far East. Even before the

Murex completed her first record-setting voyage to the Orient, a potent rival had sprung up to flatten the triumph of Marcus's coup. The company called itself Royal Dutch. It was a dangerous rival to M. Samuel & Co. and sought its own victory in the new global struggle to topple Rockefeller's oil empire.

CHAPTER 7

The Royal Crown

It began in a tobacco shed.

In the fall of 1880, forty-year-old Aeilko Jans Zijlker was aimlessly wasting the last portion of his life working as a manager of the East Sumatra Tobacco Company. The tobacco fields of Sumatra were as far from his native Holland as Zijlker, the son of a Dutch farmer, could possibly get. When he was still a young man, he had fled to the Indies to escape a broken heart. He subsequently failed at farming for himself.[1] By middle age, he was growing tobacco for someone else on the tropical perimeter of the Dutch colonial world. That was before the sudden rains.

Zijlker was out surveying a tobacco field for his employer when a fast-moving squall approached. It was one of the island's famed *sumatras*, ferocious storms that appeared with little warning.[2] The sheets of rain fell so heavily during a *sumatra* that it was nearly impossible to see and hazardous to walk very far. The rain drove Zijlker into the shelter of an abandoned tobacco shed. There, blockaded by the elements, he settled down for an uncomfortable siege.

In the darkness, a brilliant flame illuminated the interior of the shed. Zijlker's accidental companion for the evening, a native overseer

for the tobacco company, had sparked a torch. The peculiar light cap-
tivated Zijlker, and he peppered the overseer with questions about the
flame. What kind of resin was in the wood? Where did it come from?
The overseer answered that there was nothing special about the resin
or the wood—it was merely a common torch. The difference, he explained, lay in how the fire burned. A special kind of local mineral
wax fueled it. The substance especially lent itself to making torches
and was also particularly handy when caulking boats.

Zijlker insisted on seeing the source of this wonder. Luckily for
him, it was plentiful in the area. When the rain cleared, the overseer
promised to show him the pools of water from which locals skimmed
the wax with banana leaves.[3] The unusual ingredient was, of course,
petroleum. At forty years of age, living 2,600 miles from his birth-
place, the Dutch tobacco farmer was now infected with the oil bug.

Over the next ten years, Zijlker would be a man obsessed, driven
by the single goal of hacking out a kerosene company in rugged
northern Sumatra. He would let nothing stand in his way: not his
lack of capital; not the colonial bureaucrats, who reluctantly lent him
engineers; not even the Emir of Langkat, whom Zijlker finally per-
suaded to grant him an oil concession. "What won't bend must
break," Zijlker wrote. "Whoever is not with me is against me, and I
shall treat him accordingly."[4] Ally or enemy, advantage or impediment, Zijlker thus parsed out his world.

Returning to the Netherlands to scare up capital, Zijlker acquired a
host of useful advocates and patrons for his oil venture. One of the
most important was a colonial banker named Dr. Norbertus Petrus
van den Berg. In a lucky break, Zijlker had booked passage back to
Amsterdam on the same steamship as Van den Berg in September
1889. Van den Berg was returning home to become the governor of
the prestigious Netherlands Bank.[5] Aboard ship, Zijlker had a captive

audience with Van den Berg, as well as one hell of a pitch. Zijlker carried with him an encouraging report about his oil concession from an engineer in the colonial mining department, as well as cost estimates, revenue projections, designs for a refinery, plans for a port, and a scheme to build a railroad to the sea.

After the two men reached Amsterdam, Zijlker had made a believer out of Van den Berg. Not only did the banker agree to become the chairman of Zijlker's company, he translated the tobacco farmer's collection of documents into a respectable business plan and prospectus.[6] More crucially, Van den Berg used his influence to secure a coveted seal of approval from the Dutch king, William III, the last male heir to the House of Orange-Nassau. The award of a royal warrant from the king was a breakthrough for Zijlker. Typically reserved for the most prestigious of Dutch companies, it gave Zijlker the right to use the word *royal* in the name of his firm. This transformed the small-time "East Sumatran Petroleum Co." into the impressive-sounding "Royal Dutch Oil Co."[7] Thanks to the king, the banker, and the unstoppable tobacco farmer, Royal Dutch was ready to take the Amsterdam stock exchange by storm.

When Zijlker was promoting his idea around Amsterdam, his pitch made sense on multiple levels. For the Dutch government, the creation of a petroleum industry in the East Indies would help cover the costs of running its colony on Sumatra. This money-losing territory could become a moneymaker for government coffers. For private investors, the prospect of oil in Sumatra had all the hallmarks of fortune. Situated on the adjacent Strait of Malacca, the ocean highway of the Far East, Zijlker's oil concession was close to the largest cities in Asia. Unlike petroleum from Russia or America, petroleum shipments from Zijlker's wells did not have to make a long-haul trip to the Orient. It was already there. Kerosene from Sumatra would not have to absorb the cost of long-distance shipping. This would gave Zijlker an edge over Standard's oil monopoly. How could he lose?

When shares of Zijlker's enterprise hit the Amsterdam stock exchange in the late summer of 1890, the initial public offering (IPO) of Royal Dutch fed a frenzy of greedy purchasing. Buyers outnumbered the available shares by a ratio of four to one. Zijlker was triumphant. His decade-long struggle was at last turning into an actual company. Royal Dutch had the financial capital and political backing to launch into the kerosene business.

What Zijlker did not have was time. On December 27, 1890, he was making a return trip to Sumatra when he suddenly fell over dead in Singapore. His abrupt passing, so closely following the firm's IPO, threw Royal Dutch onto its heels. Back in Amsterdam, the newly established directors of Zijlker's company scrambled to find a replacement for the deceased founder. Their eventual choice was Jean Baptiste August Kessler, the middle-aged son-in-law of the managing director at Royal Dutch. In another situation, the accusation of nepotism might have tainted this hiring decision, but that was not the case with Kessler. Royal Dutch had found the ideal candidate to continue Zijlker's mission.

Recently retired from a mediocre run as a merchant in the Far East, Kessler was thirty-eight years old and eager to make a comeback in business. Although still full of energy, he looked like a man twenty years his senior. The allure of youth had entirely departed Kessler's face, leaving behind a map of stress and concentration. His hooded eyes gave the impression of someone who had not slept in months, and the crooked bridge of his nose hinted at a brawler's past. However, the veil of premature age was deceptive. Kessler possessed a deep well of personal leadership, unflagging stamina, and most of all, the makings of an oilman. He was precisely the kind of manager who could contend with the mosquitoes of Sumatra, cross the language divide with Chinese laborers, ride herd over a rowdy bunch of imported American oilmen, and still keep a steady hand on the firm's finances. If ever there was a right person for the world's toughest job, it was Kessler.

While the wary eye of Standard Oil trained on Marcus Samuel's Suez gambit, Kessler quietly set out for the Far East in September 1891. His official mandate from Royal Dutch's directors at The Hague was straightforward: kick-start kerosene production as fast as possible. In the time since Zijlker's death, Royal Dutch had been burning through cash at a startling rate. Kessler needed to bring large volumes of refined illuminating oil to market in a very short time span. Luckily for Royal Dutch, Kessler was impatient for the task, determined to make his second chance in business a success.

As the new leader of Royal Dutch, Kessler brimmed with confidence. Upon making landfall in Sumatra at the end of October, he promptly issued a note to the company's directors: his work on the island could be wrapped up by February 1892. The projected timeline was cutting it close, since that was at the same point that Royal Dutch's Sumatra operation was scheduled to run out of money.[8] What Kessler did not know was that his assessment of the situation was outrageously optimistic. The reality of Royal Dutch's predicament was daunting in the extreme. The jungle would see him humbled.

When Kessler reached Royal Dutch's jungle concession at Telaga Said, he discovered a chaotic mess. The company's petroleum was six miles upriver from the coastal settlement of Pangkalan Brandan, the nearest outpost of civilization. That could be solved, but conditions around the wellhead were confused and cluttered. Goods and materials were strewn in every direction. Critical parts for some equipment had gone missing. Other parts were either damaged or incompatible, since half had been purchased from Europe and the other half from the United States. When it came to financial management, there was none. The closest approximation of accounting that anyone could muster was a lowly cashbook. Appalled by what he found, a lesser manager might have penned a resignation letter. Instead, Kessler fired the country manager on the spot and got to work.

In principle, the overall task in Sumatra was manageable. Kessler needed to move his crude across only six miles of bush to Pangkalan Brandan on the Strait of Malacca.[9] It was a relatively short distance to cross, but in the swampy forests of Sumatra, the work was anything but simple. Every week produced new mishaps or misfortunes. The jungle rotted everything. If Kessler was not dealing with floods, his crew was running short of food. Even when his men had enough to eat, the rain and constant humidity turned metal into rust. Floodwater from the nearby Lepan River was an additional headache. When the river overflowed its banks, Kessler's partially completed tramline to Pangkalan Brandan became an underwater tramline. The flooding showed that Kessler's plan for a rail link to the coast was going to be unfeasible. Weeks of hard labor to construct the rails were lost. All the while, fever cut through his workforce like a scythe. Among those who escaped infection, many simply disappeared into the jungle—never to return.

At The Hague, Royal Dutch's insatiable appetite for news added further stress to Kessler's ordeal. Company directors were waiting to hear positive reports from Sumatra, but Kessler had none to give. When he was not suffering from jungle-borne illnesses, contending with broken equipment, or corralling his stubborn American oilmen, he penned explanations as to why Sumatra created endless, costly delays. The scale of his task began to wear him down. "I do not feel very cheerful about the business," he confided to his wife. He was in a "godforsaken, out-of-the-way-place" where bad news came in torrents.[10]

After scrapping plans for a tramline, Kessler opted instead to move his oil through a pipe. This resulted in a painfully slow construction process, as his crew manually screwed each individual segment together across the six miles of heavy vegetation. The pipeline was among the least of his worries, though. Far more urgently, he discovered that Royal Dutch was going to need more oil down at the refinery. His tribulations in the jungle truly knew no end.

The need for more crude was clear. Based on the rate of petroleum that flowed from Royal Dutch's upstream oil play, Kessler was going to be perpetually short of raw crude once his refinery began operating on the coast.[11] Come hell, fever, or floodwater, his operation had to produce a thousand tins of kerosene a day for the company to meet its revenue projections.[12] Failing to meet that goal would mean lower profits, disgruntled shareholders, and less money to recoup Royal Dutch's investment in the jungle. All of Kessler's herculean trials in Sumatra would mean little if Royal Dutch could not produce enough kerosene to cover its sunk costs. Somehow he had to find more oil.

Unaware of what he was asking, Kessler dutifully ordered his crew to drill another well upstream. If the fortunes of his company rested on finding a new source of petroleum, then that was what he would do. Never mind that he gave this order without any knowledge of subterranean geology or actual experience in oil exploration. As he would later come to discover, finding crude in Sumatra was not nearly as simple as picking a clearing, drilling into the earth, and pumping the hydrocarbons that flowed from below.

Perhaps predictably, nature did its utmost to impede Kessler's progress. For days on end, his American rig builders and drillers cobbled together a new derrick amid constant, heavy rains. Compared to the hills of Pennsylvania or even the mild pleasures of Amsterdam, the forested hills of Sumatra were a bewildering, alien, and hostile environment. Kessler's ill fortune seemed as constant and pervasive as the humidity. But his share of bad luck was coming to an end. At the company's emergency well in the jungle, later known as Telaga Baru, he finally caught a break. His countless setbacks washed away when drillers ripped open Sumatra's first petroleum gusher. The bounty of crude could upend the worst of luck.

The placement of the Telaga Baru well was a rare stroke of providence for Kessler. His imported American oilmen had almost blindly hit their mark: their drill had plunged directly into a small reservoir of high-pressure petroleum. Once released, the underground oil sprayed into the air, reaching a height of ninety feet, higher than most of the trees around it, and splattered the surrounding hillside in a slick coating of greenish-brown Sumatran crude. For the first time since Kessler's arrival at Pangkalan Brandan, Royal Dutch was edging closer to becoming a fully operational oil company. All it needed now was a working pipeline.

On February 28, 1892, at five minutes before eleven o'clock in the morning, Kessler waited downstream at Pangkalan Brandan in front of his newly completed refinery and a pipe. During a moment fraught with expectation, he stood next to an empty oversize petroleum tank holding a stopwatch.[13] Standing around him was a group of nearly four hundred people. They were Americans, Europeans, laborers from China and Indonesia, and Sikhs. It was a Sunday. Everyone was working. Everyone was waiting.

Six miles away, oil from Royal Dutch's concession flowed from an open-air pond of crude into Kessler's pipeline. Gravity did the rest, pulling the raw petroleum down a natural slope of the earth to the coast. Kessler and his crew stood at the other end of that pipe, waiting for the fruits of their labor to emerge. For every infuriating obstacle, he had improvised a solution over, around, and sometimes through the hassle. As a final monument to his brawl with nature, the last section of his pipeline sat wedged into the hacked remains of a tree that had previously blocked the path. But no stump, no matter how stubborn, was going to impede Kessler now.

If the calculations that he had in hand were correct, 10:55 a.m. should have been the precise minute when the oil reached Pangkalan Brandan. The assembled crew around Kessler watched and listened. The arrival time approached—and then slipped away. There was nothing. The pipe remained silent. Empty.

Once again it looked as if something had gone wrong. Something always went wrong for Kessler. Visibly dejected, the beleaguered manager turned his back on the entire scene. *Godverdomme.* If there was ever a good time for an oath, this was it. Mercifully, the defeat was only momentary. An audible sound soon began to emanate from deep within the pipe. The noise intensified, coming closer, until it culminated in "a roar as a mighty storm."[14] A rush of acrid air preceded an outburst of dark crude into Royal Dutch's holding tank. Kessler's link had worked. The company's oil was finally flowing. Telaga Said was offering up its petroleum.

As for the delay, that had been the result of a calculation error. When Kessler's team initially determined the velocity at which their oil would travel through the pipe, they had neglected to account for friction. The small oversight had caused nothing more than momentary churn of the stomach on opening day. As unrefined crude surged from the pipeline, the men of Royal Dutch cheered. Someone unfurled the tricolor Dutch flag. Everyone toasted the company's success. Kessler's enduring nightmare in the jungle was ending. His refinery could begin its work.

Nestled around a bend in the shallow Babalan River, Kessler's refinery at Pangkalan Brandan was hardly a paragon of innovation.[15] Instead, it was an exact replica of the refining stills used in the oil fields of North America. When Royal Dutch recruited American oilmen to work its oil field in Sumatra, the company intended to pay for their labor and know-how. Yet these men knew how to construct only one kind of refinery to make kerosene. They "clung with fanatic conservatism to their American experience."[16] How high were the stills in Pennsylvania filled with crude? That was precisely how high the one in Sumatra was to be. It did not matter that the petroleum in Sumatra was chemically different from Pennsylvania crude. Neither was it important that Standard had already begun to employ more sophisticated methods for refining raw petroleum into its composite "fractions," as they were known, such as lubricating and illuminating oils. Royal Dutch had asked for a refinery, and its American workmen built just that—a prototypical American refining still.

Using imported methods from Pennsylvania, Royal Dutch's first refinery at Pangkalan Brandan was essentially a very large moonshining distillery. Crude from Royal Dutch's holding tank was heated until it vaporized. The vapor was then cooled until it gradually condensed back into a liquid. This was the transformative process that separated petroleum into different fractions. At least initially, Royal Dutch's rudimentary stills could transform only 35 percent of Sumatran crude into kerosene. An additional third condensed into a dreadful, useless waste product known as gasoline. On warm days, so much of it resulted from the refining process at Pangkalan Brandan that the still was cloaked in a dense fog of vaporized gasoline. The vile substance irritated the eyes, skin, and nose. Anyone who spent too much time near "that wretched stuff," as Kessler called it, could develop splitting headaches, blurred vision, slurred speech, and convulsions.[17] Kessler needed kerosene to keep his company afloat. As for his enormous stockpile of gasoline, he had no time for it.

As a large volume of waste gasoline accumulated at Pangkalan Brandan, Kessler's men were at a loss as to how to dispose of it. At first, they attempted to burn the vile liquid a short distance from the stills, but the inferno grew so large that it threatened to incinerate Kessler's entire operation. By now, he knew better than to risk a return of his bad luck, so the company's workmen subsequently hauled their evil liquid to a nearby gravel quarry on the coast. There they unceremoniously dumped it onto the rocks and set it alight. This fire burned for years. In fact, Royal Dutch's gasoline fire blazed so brightly and so constantly that sailors of the day adopted it as an aid to navigation.[18] The light of Sumatran crude, which had once dispelled the darkness of Zijlker's tobacco shed, was now illuminating the Strait of Malacca, crossroads of the Far East. Such a light was bound to attract the attention of Standard.

By the winter of 1893, Standard was aware that it faced a two-pronged danger in Asia. On one flank, Samuel's inexpensive kerosene from Batumi was steaming through the Suez and locking down the low-end segment of the market. On its other flank, Kessler's higher-quality "Royal Crown" illuminating oil was gaining ground. Because the chemical composition of oil from Sumatra made for better kerosene than did blends from Russia, Royal Dutch's product commanded a slightly higher price than Samuel's shipments. This gave the Royal Crown kerosene greater appeal to buyers at the top end of the market. Together, Standard's new competitors were grabbing its consumers across the board. Adding to the alarm, breathless reports about Royal Dutch were reaching 26 Broadway from its commercial spies in Sumatra. They raved about Kessler's accomplishment. "In the whole history of the oil business," wrote one agent, "there has never been anything more phenomenal than the success and rapid growth of the R. D. Co. (Royal Dutch)."[19]

Viewed from Standard's perspective, Royal Dutch and the Samuel tankers represented a twofold dilemma—one of supply and one of price. Both difficulties were linked. On the supply side, the oil fields of America were old and entering into decline, with U.S. wells pumping less crude each year. Twenty years earlier the oil market had been different. Back in the 1870s, American oil fields were pumping more crude than domestic customers needed, and Standard began to export American kerosene to gigantic foreign markets like China.[20] Any surplus that Rockefeller could not sell to his U.S. consumers, he packed and shipped overseas. So much oil was flowing to foreign countries that it accounted for 70 percent of America's total production. As a welcome bonus, Standard discovered that Asian consumers would pay a higher price for kerosene than U.S. consumers would. It had been the perfect system for Standard. Americans got all the oil they could burn; Standard got rid of the excess; and Rockefeller padded his balance sheet with fat profit margins on exports. But as is always the case with oil, the good times could not last. By 1890, just before Royal Dutch and M. Samuel & Co. began to contest Rockefeller's grip on the Asian market, the share of U.S. oil exports had fallen to just 34 percent. Standard no longer possessed the arsenal of petroleum it would need to deploy the old, reliable "cut to kill" strategy against new competitors in the Orient.

The flip side of Standard's supply dilemma was price. By selling massive amounts of kerosene from Russia and Sumatra to Asia, Royal Dutch and M. Samuel & Co. pushed prices lower across the Orient. The abundance of new supplies sent the price of crude tumbling in places like Baku. This put Standard in an exceptionally perilous position. The price of oil was suddenly higher in America than everywhere else in the world. By continuing to keep the cost of oil high, Standard was laying out a banquet before the starving. It was only a matter of time before some enterprising competitor sailed bulk Russian kerosene to the East Coast in the hope of cashing in on that high price. Standard had to cauterize that threat or face the unthinkable: a flood of foreign petroleum in the United States.

Bowing to tremendous commercial forces on its shoulders, Standard caved. In a historic move on January 23, 1895, its agents in Oil City, Pennsylvania, posted a stunning notice. Going forward, the American oil giant would purchase American crude at a price only "as high as the market of the world will justify."[21] This was more than a mundane piece of news. It was the birth of a global price for oil. Standard was losing its power to dictate the cost of a barrel everywhere in the world. The battlefields of the petroleum business were becoming too numerous and too far-flung. Rivals like Royal Dutch and Samuel were too nimble. The wells of Baku and Sumatra were too abundant. The technology of bulk maritime transportation was becoming too common. Rockefeller had tried to hold back the deluge of crude, but now it was spilling over the top of his monopoly.

By accepting a global price for a barrel of crude, Standard was protecting itself against the immediate threat that foreign imports would reach the United States in large quantities. After the switch, the cost of kerosene in the United States sank to levels on par with international markets. Russian sellers no longer had a temptation to dump their oil onto consumers in Boston or New York. Standard's home front was safe—for now. The next move for 26 Broadway was to reestablish dominance over the "ruinous competition" that was annihilating its market share in the Far East. At the top of its list of enemies were Royal Dutch and M. Samuel & Co.

Viewed from the perspective of 26 Broadway, Samuel's tanker syndicate looked meddlesome but manageable. The contract that Samuel had signed with the Rothschilds made him little more than a cash-and-carry middleman. What he bought in Batumi from the Rothschilds, he sold east of the Suez. Samuel had likewise secured for himself a small oil concession on the island of Borneo, but Standard's spy in the East Indies reported that production from this field was paltry. More amusingly, Samuel's refinery in Borneo was so poorly constructed that it was wildly inefficient and unlikely to offer a serious challenge to Standard. Unless he could find more oil and refine it in greater quantities, Samuel was not a real threat.

The greater danger to Standard was Royal Dutch. In Sumatra, Kessler had created everything that Standard desired in the Far East. The Dutch insurgent possessed a proven source of high-quality crude, a small but growing commercial network to market its product, and was close to massive markets like China. More impressively, the output of Royal Dutch was rising fast. Over the span of one year, from 1896 to 1897, Kessler had raised his exports from 5 to 15 million gallons of kerosene. Revenue was rising so quickly that shares of Royal Dutch began to trade at 900 percent above their face value. Anyone holding a share of the company's stock enjoyed a gratifying 52 percent dividend.[22]

Rather than exterminate Royal Dutch, 26 Broadway wanted to buy it. Standard made an offer, but it seemed too low—this was the official reason that Kessler and his directors gave for rejecting Standard's advance. In truth, there was almost no price at which Standard could buy its Dutch rival. National pride was tied too closely to the company. Kessler, his board members, and most of his stockholders had no desire to become part of Rockefeller's sprawling oil empire.[23] There were too many benefits to Sumatra, and too many sacrifices had been made in the jungle.

The Royal Crown

Unable to get through the front door with Royal Dutch, Standard's next best option was to try a back one. The nature of Royal Dutch's ownership structure offered the opening. Unlike Samuel's privately run business, which the Samuel brothers owned exclusively, Royal Dutch was a publicly traded company. The shareholders were the owners. Should anyone wish to own a piece of Royal Dutch, all they had to do was purchase shares on the Amsterdam stock exchange. By controlling enough stock, a single buyer could control the board of Royal Dutch and therefore the company. Standard did not have to "cut to kill" Kessler; it merely had to buy him on the open market.

The danger of a hostile takeover ceased to be hypothetical when Royal Dutch's stock price took a suspicious tumble immediately after it rejected Standard's buyout. Was the short selling of Royal Dutch part of a natural market correction, or was something more devious afoot? Standard was well known for spreading rumors about its rivals to lower their share price; the Royal Dutch management team suspected 26 Broadway was to blame in this case. Whatever the cause, rumors that Royal Dutch's wells in Sumatra were running dry wafted through the Amsterdam bourse like smoke. Shareholders invariably clamored for the exits. As panicked investors offloaded shares, the selling became a rout. The value of the company's stock fell from 900 to 400 percent of face value by June. By October, it would be down to 250 percent.[24] In all, shares of Royal Dutch would fall by a devastating 600 percent in less than a year, and the ride was not over.

Every leg down on the share price increased Royal Dutch's vulnerability to a hostile takeover. The immediate task for Kessler was to fortify the company against a surprise attack from Standard. Since the perceived danger to Royal Dutch was new, the company opted to build an equally unprecedented layer of protection around its boardroom. For the first time in Dutch commercial history, Royal Dutch issued a special class of preferred shares that had the unique power to appoint members of the board. As a foreign entity, Standard would be excluded from owning these shares, thereby protecting Royal Dutch from any mischievous attempt to seize control of the company in the open market. In 1890s Amsterdam, this was cutting-edge corporate governance. Coupled with a loan from the House of Rothschild to shore up Kessler's operating capital, Royal Dutch had—once more—found its footing.[25] Unfortunately, the larger peril for the company was more insidious and harder to fix. The rumors about falling production were true. Kessler was actually running out of oil.

As early as March 1897, a weird phenomenon began to appear in the wells on the Telaga Said concession. Salt water was inexplicably mingling with the petroleum that flowed from belowground. Inside Royal Dutch, there seemed to be no explanation for the source of the salt water, nor any indication as to what it meant. Standard knew. The appearance of salt water signaled the impending death of Telaga Said and—potentially—Royal Dutch.[26]

For the better part of a year, 26 Broadway's commercial spy in Sumatra sent updated reports to John Archbold, Rockefeller's hand-picked successor in New York, concerning the appearance of salt water at Royal Dutch's oil play. Archbold was a veteran of the Pennsylvania boom, where the phenomenon of saltwater incursion was a well-documented menace. Salt water came on gradually at first. It was as easy to ignore as the first symptoms of an illness. Over time, however, the symptoms grew more acute. The longer an oilman pumped his well, the more salt water he would produce. Eventually all the oil would be gone, leaving behind a stream of undrinkable, brackish water. This was what was occurring now at Telaga Said. The field was dying. Making matters worse, Royal Dutch was ignorant of its own peril.

Thanks to detailed updates from Standard's commercial spies, Archbold often had a better picture than Kessler about conditions at Telaga Said. As the run on Royal Dutch stock unfolded during the summer of 1898, one spy cabled exciting news to New York. "Have picked up information that production of Royal Dutch is falling at Langkat (Telaga Said)," he wrote. "Shall I use this information discreetly for public opinion?"[27] Kessler did not need rumors to tell him that something was wrong in Sumatra. After reaching a peak of 848,000 cases of kerosene in May 1898, the output of Telaga Said fell by half the next month, then to 300,000 cases that August. Whatever was wrong in Sumatra, it was accelerating. By mid-September, Standard received another intelligence report: "I learned that a little more salt water was manifesting itself in the R.D. & Co. wells, but no one there . . . had guessed what it meant."[28]

Royal Dutch was losing precious time to ignorance. Only at the very end of September did the hazard of salt water become absolutely clear. Kessler's bad luck had returned. His company faced an entirely new crisis of survival. With his wells running dry and his investors fearful, he needed to find more crude. Unlike his previous foray in Sumatra, however, the task was easier said than done. Royal Dutch would have to unlearn everything it knew—or thought it knew—about oil exploration. By doing so, it would make history.

CHAPTER 8

The Hidden Map

The man in the trench was no ordinary ditch digger. He was an Italian time traveler—at least of a sort. His name was Dr. Cesare Porro. And in 1898 he was scooping his way into the past on the northern edge of Sumatra.

Layer below layer, the soil of Sumatra was an autobiography of dirt. Equipped with simple tools—just a hammer, a compass, a miner's level, a triangle, and a protractor—Porro was attempting to decipher that autobiography of more than 66 million years. His enemy was the climate. In Sumatra, one of the wettest places on earth, equatorial rain and constant humidity created the ideal conditions for the erosion of rocks. Porro was on the hunt for specific stones that had survived the water. And since there were so few outcroppings of readable rock on the surface, he was digging pits into the earth to find them. He was hoping to discover a revealing detail about Sumatra's history. Finding it meant getting dirty.

Far to the west of Porro's pits, the volcanic Barisan Mountains stretched for more than a thousand miles along the western edge of Sumatra. Some of its tallest peaks were more than ten thousand feet above sea level. They were so high, in fact, that atop the Barisans there existed one of the world's strangest living realms: a tropical pine forest. Lower down the slopes, a thick canvas of jungle gorged on the island's rain. Every year sixteen feet of precipitation fell on Sumatra. A few regions received more than twice that amount. Season after season the rainfall washed over the Barisans. It dissolved the volcanic peaks into the rich soil, which fed the island's mangrove forests, its banana trees, and its insatiable tobacco plants. As the eroded dirt and water washed down from the mountains, it also created a clue.

Much like the palimpsest writing on ancient manuscripts, where successive generations of scribes penned their words over the scrawling words of others, Sumatra's layers of rock told the whole story of the island at once. Some portions of that narrative were linear and cogent. Elsewhere, the tale was warped and damaged. Words on top of words, centuries of soil were written on top of others. The weight of that record gradually compressed itself into vast timescales of stone. Ages became epochs. Glaciers expanded and receded. Oceans rose and fell.

Far underground the deep time of Sumatra's stone decoupled from the rhythms of organic life. Heat from the earth's mantle and pressure from the surrounding strata cooked the bodies of long-dead plankton into buried lakes of oil. The earth wobbled on its axis. Epochs became long geologic periods. Sumatra gradually assumed its modern shape.

Compared to the lifespan of the rocks, the obsessions of the humans who walked on the surface were as meaningful as dust. The stone had no regard for the rebels of Atjeh (today Aceh) who toiled in their endless war of rebellion against the Dutch colonials; nor for Sumatra's native soldiers, who drilled on the esplanade of Meden wearing magnificent European uniforms but no shoes.[1] Equally as insignificant were the oilmen who blindly drilled into the soil of Sumatra. Lacking any useful knowledge of the earth's hidden strata, they were handing great fortunes to chance and receiving nothing in return. The holes that the oilmen drilled were barren of oil. Blindness had a price.

Standing waist high in his pit, Porro was not blind; nor was he ignorant of the stones around him. In fact, the bespectacled geologist was in Sumatra precisely because the wisdom of the oilmen had failed. He did not need to guess at the location of the island's oil. He would read it in the rocks themselves. It was an entirely new technique on the frontier of science. Porro was among its pioneers.

As far back as the early days of Oildorado, one basic principle had defined the exploration for crude: go where the oil was. Following this rationale, wildcat drillers placed their wells close to obvious signs of petroleum on the surface. In Pennsylvania, Baku, and elsewhere, the ironclad logic of this approach proved to be outrageously successful. Indeed, it was this method that Zijlker had used when sinking his very first well in Sumatra. Kessler did the same when he ordered an additional well to be constructed at Telaga Said. What was unknown at the time was that the logic of the oilmen was deceptively wrong.

Signs of a flaw in the conventional wisdom of oil exploration were legion. Even when drillers did what was logical and placed a well directly on top of a petroleum seepage, these holes were frequently dry. For every flowing well around the prolific field of Oil Creek, Pennsylvania, for example, early drillers created dozens of empty borings into the earth. When production at a successful oil play eventually collapsed—and it always collapsed—drillers simply extended their borings deeper into the earth. Sometimes the technique found more crude; other times it just made a bigger hole. The randomness of petroleum exploration hinted at the organizing conundrum for oilmen. After more than three decades of existence, the entire industry was still largely in the dark when it came to understanding the exact nature of petroleum reservoirs. In the case of Royal Dutch, that knowledge gap now endangered the company's survival.

Acting according to convention, Royal Dutch did everything right once Telaga Said began to fail. The company embarked on a drilling frenzy, boring more than one hundred new wells around the area. But none of them struck oil. Proceeding on the assumption that more oil might be found deeper underground, Royal Dutch pushed the borings of its existing wells to great depths. One of these efforts reached twelve hundred feet before drillers gave up on the effort. Running low on options at Telaga Said, Royal Dutch finally widened its search. These frantic exploratory borings yielded even more dry, expensive holes. The reason for these failures was simple: the conventional wisdom of the oil field was wrong. Royal Dutch was drilling in the wrong places, but it did not know any better.

As far back as 1866, an American geologist named E. B. Andrews had suspected there was something special about the location of underground crude. He correctly identified that finding it was not entirely random: petroleum seemed to collect in the cracks of folded or broken rock.[2] Around the same time, a fellow American, Thomas S. Hunt, determined that petroleum in western Ontario was appearing between impermeable layers of clay. Acting as a barrier, these formations seemed to trap oil in place.[3] As scientists examined other geologic formations around the globe, their observations slowly pointed to an odd theory, one that a geologist named Israel C. White advanced in the 1880s: underground petroleum was actually *moving*. Rising through layers of buried rock, it was only when oil reached the top of an underground arch—known as an anticline—that its buried journey came to a halt. If drillers wanted to find oil, White proposed that they look for anticlines.

In different parts of the world, a suspiciously large amount of data supported the anticline theory. The same kinds of buried rock arches could be found at petroleum discoveries in the United States, Romania, and the Caucasus. The evidence was so compelling, the anticline theory made zealous disciples out of the geologists who studied petroleum. Unfortunately, they attracted few adherents among actual oilmen. It was a strange divergence.

Seen from inside the oil industry, the problem with geology lay in its application to the brass tacks of the business. By the 1890s, the anticline theory could go a long way toward explaining why crude accumulated in specific spots, but it had not yet been able to predict where someone could find the next gusher.[4] Adding to the incredulity of the oilmen was the apparent folly of the scientists. Because the hidden folds of the earth could be slanted in different directions and angles, the anticline theory suggested that sometimes the best place to drill for oil might be a great distance away from any previously known source of crude. This was directly contrary to the received wisdom of the oilmen, who clung to the belief that the best place to find petroleum was either where it occurred on the surface or in the vicinity of a producing well.

The geologists saw things differently. All things being equal, the presence of surface crude usually indicated that a small amount of oil had escaped from a larger, hidden reservoir. Drilling on a seepage was a fool's errand. An oilman might get lucky, but only for a time. Why waste money to find a puddle of petroleum when a huge lake might be hidden elsewhere?

It was to be in Sumatra where sweat, science, and financial desperation gave geology the chance to prove its usefulness. Using every conventional method in the oil industry, Kessler's drillers had failed to bring in any sustainable, flowing wells. Royal Dutch was out of ideas. Since the traditional techniques had failed, why not try something unconventional? It was this thinking that brought Porro and a fellow geologist, Dr. C. Schmidt, to the attention of the company's managers. Both scientists had garnered a small bit of renown for mapping the anticlines of petroleum-bearing rocks in Romania and the Caucasus. Royal Dutch opted to bring Porro and Schmidt aboard as hired guns. The company gave them an urgent mandate: pinpoint where it could find new oil—and fast. The jungle would be their laboratory. The survival of the company would depend on what they found.

Thrown into the wilds of Sumatra in 1898, Porro and Schmidt grappled with a four-part riddle. Before they could point to a likely source of new oil, their first task would be to determine the precise sequence in which the rocks of northern Sumatra had been laid down. Second, they needed to identify where—and how—the earth had warped and twisted underground. If there was an anticline underfoot, and they believed there was, the geologists wanted to map it. Third, they had to calculate the precise depth at which oil had likely accumulated. This would pave the way for the fourth and final task: to recommend where Royal Dutch should drill a new well.

Working separately to cover the most ground, Porro and Schmidt set out across the rugged country of Sumatra on foot. They traveled light, wading up streams and trekking through heavily forested swamps. As they systematically addressed each aspect of their riddle, the geologists kept a lookout for virgin outcroppings of rock, places where fresh stone had not yet been weathered away on the surface. Unfortunately for them, the frantic pace of tropical erosion in Sumatra made virgin outcroppings a rare prize. It was for this reason that Porro and Schmidt took to digging pits. Typically stretching 10 to 20 feet long and 1 to 3 feet wide, these exploratory holes allowed the geologists to record the direction and dip of the island's rocks—crucial clues to deciphering the hidden map of the island's strata. The more pits the geologists excavated, the more accurately they could determine how Sumatra's stones had been broken, bent, and deformed over the ages. Knowing these facts would be crucial for revealing where the island's oil was buried.

It was hot, solitary work—and there were predators. Safe in towns or fortified on their plantations, Sumatra's Dutch colonists claimed that the island's indigenous population of tigers posed no threat to humans. One common belief held that the predatory cats ate too many wild pigs to hunger for people. Such boastful confidence was cold comfort when the eyes of a three-hundred-pound meat eater peered out from the underbrush.[5] And even if Porro and Schmidt avoided becoming a meal for large animals, they were a potential feast for the island's mosquitoes.

Back at Telaga Said, time was running out for Royal Dutch. As Porro and Schmidt surveyed their strata, Kessler's wells experienced a catastrophic decline in production. Between 1898 and 1899, the output of crude from company wells in Sumatra fell by 70 percent. It was a sickening descent. Downstream at Royal Dutch's Pangkalan Brandan refinery, workmen nervously examined the facility's oversize holding tank. Each morning only a few feet of crude was typically visible—barely enough to supply a full day's work at the refinery.[6] Should the tank ever run completely empty, Royal Dutch would be an oil company without any crude.

As he appraised the supply crisis from the Netherlands, the latest petroleum crunch weighed heavily on Kessler. "Everyone is talking about it, even old women and school children," he confided in a letter to his protégé, Henri Deterding. "Truly, I am bowed down by cares."[7] In an act of supreme humility, he sheepishly lined up an emergency purchasing agreement from independent oil sellers in Russia. As with

Samuel, this deal allowed Royal Dutch to buy its product in bulk, but Kessler could arrange to ship his oil only in outdated tankers. The Suez was closed to such vessels, meaning that Royal Dutch would have to go the long way around the Horn of Africa. It was an unattractive deal, but Kessler had no meaningful alternative. If his wells ran completely dry in Sumatra, it would be his responsibility to keep the doors of the firm open for as long as possible. He prepared for the worst.

Back in Sumatra, Porro and Schmidt were ready to deliver their official findings to Royal Dutch on April 30, 1899. Their dauntless walkabout on the island had produced a remarkable document. Not only had they created an extraordinarily accurate picture of the island's underlying geology, they had identified a region of northern Sumatra where Royal Dutch was likely to find oil. This was both good news and bad for the company. According to the geologists, there was not one but three anticline folds beneath this part of Sumatra. The largest formed a dome underneath Zijlker's original well. If Royal Dutch wished to find new oil, Porro and Schmidt recommended that it drill into a different fold, one that was far to the north of Telaga Said. That was the bad news.

The area that Porro and Schmidt recommended was situated in the region of Atjeh, several miles up the Perlak River (today Peureulak). For twenty years, this region of Sumatra had burned in a never-ending war between native rebels and the Dutch colonial government. Upriver on the Perlak, the Dutch ruled in name, but a tribal network of Islamic warlords ruled in fact. By 1899 the struggle to pacify the region had become a fight that the Dutch government could afford neither to win nor to sustain.[8] Should colonial authorities march into the region with a show of force to protect Royal Dutch, they would almost certainly inflame a new round of violence, sabotage, or revolt.

Royal Dutch was free to venture up the Perlak, but if it tried, it would be unprotected. Not that Royal Dutch had much of a choice. Its only alternative was to endure a slow, painful decline into bankruptcy.

The historic oil expedition to save Royal Dutch departed from Pangkalan Brandan on September 7, 1899. Leading the mission into the unknown was an eminently skilled colonial manager named Hugo Loudon. As the son of a former governor-general in Sumatra, Loudon possessed the demeanor of an aristocrat, the mind-set of an engineer, and the gentle tact of a diplomat. Loudon would need all three traits once he arrived upriver. Also joining the adventure was Porro. It was only natural that the Italian geologist should accompany the expedition as a technical adviser, since it was on account of his recommendation that Royal Dutch was launching itself into this risky, war-torn part of the island.[9]

For those traveling up the coast from Pangkalan Brandan to Perlak, the shoreline of Sumatra was a primal place. The only signs of human settlement were scattered fishing villages that clung to the outlets of mediocre streams. The rest was unpacified swamp forest. The Perlak River itself was unimpressive. In fact, its mouth ran so shallow at the opening to the Strait of Malacca that it was practically dry land at low tide. A prudent vessel waited until high tide before proceeding inland. As an old river, the Perlak snaked its way to the sea through a series of wiggly oxbows and switchbacks. Its lower banks were flanked by marshes. Only on the distant higher ground could a visitor catch sight of pepper gardens and plantations.[10] Ten miles in from the coast sat an unassuming village. It too was named Perlak, and it was the closest approximation of civilization on the river. This was where Royal Dutch would make its stand as an oil company.

Upon reaching Perlak, the first order of business for Loudon was to gauge the attitude of the local raja, Teungku Tji. Much to the team's relief, his welcome was surprisingly hospitable. In a letter back to Amsterdam, Loudon happily reported, "The Rajah has made himself personally responsible for the expedition."[11] Next came the question of the underground geology. As the expedition soon learned, Perlak was situated close to a notable seepage of crude. But it was unlike the typically deceptive puddles of surface oil, which lured lesser oilmen into a false sense of fortune. Instead, Porro believed, the Perlak seepage likely coincided with a large reservoir and nearby anticline. Additional surveys of the area bolstered this expectation. In fact, the more the expedition explored, the brighter the outlook for petroleum became. Upon returning to Pangkalan Brandan, Loudon could barely contain his enthusiasm. "I have never seen a structure more likely to contain a rich oilfield than now in Perlak," he wrote Amsterdam.[12] It was time to strike.

Operating on the time-honored principle that it was better to beg forgiveness than ask permission, Loudon issued the order to drill. In doing so, he was operating outside the limits of his authority. He had not waited for formal approval from Amsterdam; nor did he have the Dutch government's final sign-off to claim the concession.[13] Royal Dutch was racing against the clock, and urgency defined Loudon's actions. On December 4 he accompanied a second, larger expedition from Pangkalan Brandan. This time the group included two drillers, 125 native bearers, and "a few dozen heavily armed Achinese."[14] Colonial Dutch soldiers were out of the question in Perlak, but Royal Dutch still needed muscle.

During Loudon's absence upriver, the Sultanate of Atjeh learned of Royal Dutch's recent foray up the coast and feared the worst. Intending to check the advance of Dutch interests into this portion of the island, the sultan dispatched a deputy, Nja Daud, with orders to repel Royal Dutch by force if necessary. This was the point where Loudon's talent as a diplomat would be truly valuable. Rather than triggering a fight, he opted for a summit.

Meeting at Perlak, Loudon first rained a deft mixture of guilt and greed on the local raja, Teungku Tji. He reminded the wavering leader that it was on his personal promise of protection that Royal Dutch had invested great sums of money. The raja could reverse course—but why should he? The village of Perlak was about to get rich on oil royalties. Loudon was equally adept at reading the sultan's well-armed deputy, Nja Daud. In his case, the promise of wealth was only half of Loudon's selling point. More important, he pledged that Royal Dutch's activities in Perlak would not invite an accompanying force of colonial soldiers. Royal Dutch had no tiff with Atjeh. As long as Loudon's drilling operations were unimpeded, the sultanate's revolt against the Dutch government could continue. It was an extraordinary performance. The hostility toward Royal Dutch quickly abated. And although Nja Daud technically violated his instructions from Atjeh, he conceded to the company's presence in Perlak without firing a shot.

On December 9 the second expedition to Perlak got to work. The team unloaded its gear, erected shelters, and began constructing a steam engine for the drilling derrick. Thirteen days later, at noon on December 22, the company broke ground on its first well at Perlak. Given Royal Dutch's past woes in Sumatra, the drilling process was surprisingly free of drama. At 70 feet, workmen saw their first indications of crude. At 250 feet, they found more. Shortly afterward natural gas began to escape from the borehole. As the drill edged deeper underground, the flow of gas increased. Finally, on December 28, the well came to life. With little warning, a rush of drilling fluid sprayed out of the boring, followed immediately by a slippery gusher of Sumatran crude. Royal Dutch was back in business.

The Hidden Map

After drilling more than one hundred dry wells to the south, Kessler's company had finally brought in a successful new field at Perlak. Loudon's men had found the anticline reservoir predicted by Porro and Schmidt—and it was a monster. The future of Royal Dutch would no longer depend on the dying field of Telaga Said. Within four years, the company would be producing 4.5 million tins of kerosene a year—mostly from Perlak. The geologists had prevailed.

Thanks to the work of Porro and Schmidt, the anticline theory was no longer a niche concept. Geology ceased to be a "paper science."[15] After Perlak it would be a real-world asset for oilmen. From this point onward, the science of geology and the business of oil exploration would be permanently intertwined. As more advanced theories, better equipment, and many more geologists populated the petroleum business, the methods and language of science would become second nature to the oil industry. Every new frontier needs its pathfinders. In Sumatra, Porro and Schmidt led the way.

The pendulum of fortune now swung violently in Royal Dutch's favor. All anxiety over the company's future immediately vaporized into a new cloud of greed. When news of the Perlak discovery hit the Amsterdam stock exchange, shares of Royal Dutch spiked 100 percent in a single day's trading. For the second time in ten years, Royal Dutch had escaped death. Standard missed its opportunity to snatch up the company at an embarrassing discount. The crisis of the late 1890s was abating.

By November 1900, Kessler was back in Sumatra on business but preparing to leave. Surveying his accomplishments, he could have been proud of what he created in the Indies. Through enormous effort, Royal Dutch was now on solid financial ground. The potentially hostile indigenous population around the Perlak River had acquiesced to the company's drilling operations. Beginning in January, a new

125

pipeline would start transferring crude from the Perlak field to Royal Dutch's coastal refinery at Pangkalan Brandan. Output at the field was approaching the old production levels at Telaga Said. And more than half of the fresh crude from Perlak produced kerosene. The remaining fractions either settled out as heavier oils or resulted in more useless gasoline. Kessler had saved his company—again—but this latest victory was purchased at tremendous personal cost.

Kessler now looked very old. The thin wrinkles on his face were becoming deep grooves. The hoods around his eyes drooped lower. His body was spent, and his health was failing. Just before he set sail for Holland, he fired off a haunting cable to company headquarters in The Hague. In the dispatch, he confessed to being "in a very nervous condition."[16] The long journey home did little to improve his health; if anything, it grew worse. On December 14, Kessler was in Naples when his heart finally stopped beating. Had he lived just one more day, he would have seen his forty-seventh birthday, but it was not to be. The surrogate father of Royal Dutch had ended his time on earth.

Once again Royal Dutch required a new leader. Having suddenly lost Kessler, the company was not only bereft of his talents, it now needed to find someone to fill his very large shoes. This was a tenuous moment for the company. Any transition to new leadership had to be swift. The company likewise had to demonstrate clear continuity with Kessler's management. In order to pull off this delicate feat, the company's directors turned to Kessler's determined protégé, Henri Deterding. It was to be a monumental decision.

On December 15, 1900, only one day after Kessler's death, the leadership of Royal Dutch passed to Deterding. Owing to the circumstances of his succession, Deterding opted to assume the humble title of "interim manager," in a nod to Kessler's colossal contribution to Royal Dutch and the suddenness of the transition. However, the "interim" part of Deterding's title was deceptive.[17] He was about to scale the heights of the global petroleum industry, fundamentally transform the company he inherited, and redirect the flow of oil through new, unimagined channels. For the next thirty-five years, he would accomplish these wonders under the modest cover of a simple manager. It was a hint of his charm.

With seemingly boundless energy and a hearty laugh, Deterding was methodical and ambitious in the extreme. As a former banker, he possessed "a lynx-eye for balance sheets and figures" and a keen instinct for a deal.[18] This made him a natural peacemaker in business, since he was perpetually on the lookout for a beneficial contract or arrangement that might align divergent commercial interests with his own. Unsurprisingly, many of his commercial rivals viewed him as anything but a pacifist. The Nobel brothers reserved a special disdain for him. To them, he was a "terrible sort of being whose mission was to slaughter everybody and pick up the carcass."[19] Peacemaker or one-man slaughterhouse, in Deterding the two concepts were interchangeable.

As a first order of business, Deterding intended to extend Royal Dutch's commercial reach across Asia. It was a reasonable ambition given his background. Prior to replacing Kessler, he had served as the company's marketing manager. But his expansion plans would require him to wrestle customers away from Samuel. It was a divergence from Kessler's old strategy, which had assumed a live-and-let-live approach to Samuel. As challengers to Standard, the two businessmen had even experimented with an arrangement to market their kerosene jointly in the Orient. Now Deterding was preparing for a different path. He was going to launch an internecine war against Samuel. It was not personal. He simply needed the leverage.

In the time since the *Murex* first blitzed the Suez, Samuel had consolidated his loosely affiliated network of bulk distributers into the Shell Transportation and Trading Co.[20] Through this move, Samuel increased his control over the tanker syndicate by formalizing the role of M. Samuel & Co. as "Managers of the Shell." Buoyed by his corporate reorganization, Samuel had re-upped his export contract with the Rothschilds and solidified his production in Borneo—albeit at a low level of output. Even so, Samuel had become too strong for Deterding's liking. He needed to weaken Shell in order to make room for Royal Dutch's planned growth.

The opening of Deterding's expansion strategy started a savage price war in the Far East. Just as Samuel had done to Rockefeller in 1892, Deterding attacked nearly every major market in the Orient at once. By undercutting Samuel's price in the Far East, he hoped to steal Shell's customers while simultaneously punching a hole in its balance sheet. There were advantages to dividing the Asian market between Royal Dutch and Shell instead of fighting for it. But before Deterding could make peace, he needed to inflict the maximum amount of financial pain upon the Merchant of Houndsditch.

It was the beginning of a long rivalry between Deterding and Samuel. Fraught with twists, half-bluffs, partial truths, and blatant displays of bravado, the clash of these two gigantic egos would shape the future of the global oil business.

CHAPTER 9

The Knight in the Mote

Beautifully positioned on the overlook of an artificial English lake, the Mote was a grand country estate with a fine pedigree. The lands around the estate near the southeastern town of Maidstone, Kent, traced their lineage back to the time of Henry III in the thirteenth century. Over the years, several knights, two beheaded earls, and the consort of King Edward IV had called this place home. During most of the nineteenth century, an old noble family had owned the Mote. When they put it up for sale in the early 1890s, Marcus Samuel eagerly snatched it up.

The Mote was a worthy escape for any gentleman and the perfect place to make a home in the country. The square Georgian mansion at the center of the estate was hewn from the same kind of limestone that adorned St. Paul's Cathedral and Buckingham Palace. Surrounding it was a place of "great beauty and delight," said one visitor. It was a tranquil five-hundred-acre paradise of gardens, gentle paths, grand oaks, chestnut trees, and stately elms with seats beneath them, "very tempting on a hot day."[1] It was also about as far as Samuel could get from his family's first home in Sailor Town.

Parallel to his mercurial rise in the oil business, Samuel's ascent into the lower ranks of the gentry had begun in earnest back in 1891, the same year he launched his great oil venture in the Far East. That year he won his first elected post as an alderman in the City of London. Racing into office, Alderman Samuel looked upon this victory as an initial step into public life—not as a final one. He swiftly followed the election win by becoming a sheriff of London three years later. Situated on this lofty perch in London's city politics, he stood just second in line to the office of Lord Mayor itself. Yet all civic offices are temporary. The pride of a political position today can vanish tomorrow. Samuel desired something more permanent. A knighthood would have certainly granted him the status that he craved, but those were hard to come by. Samuel's ambition to rise ever higher into the ranks of the gentry kept him, as it always did, on the lookout for an opportunity. His breakthrough chance would come in the form of an unexpected calamity in Egypt.

The misfortune occurred in Suez. On Valentine's Day in 1898, the battleship HMS *Victorious* unexpectedly ran aground at the mouth of the canal. Thankfully for Samuel, none of his tankers were to blame for the misfortune. Even more of a relief was the fact that initial reports of the event, though often repeated, were incorrect. The warship had not actually struck bottom in the canal. Instead, it had run into a submerged sandbank roughly a mile east of Port Said. This was far enough away to allow other ships safe passage to and from Asia, but close enough for the crew of every passing vessel to catch sight of the stranded warship. The fact that the *Victorious* had become trapped in the sandy mud on a foolhardy attempt to squeeze through the canal made the Royal Navy's embarrassment all the more mortifying.

Due to her large size, the *Victorious* had had no business trying to force a transit through the Suez. In this case, the needs of geopolitical expediency had trumped good sense. Far away in China, British officials urgently required warships from the Admiralty for a show of gunboat diplomacy. Since there was no time to send the *Victorious* on the long journey around the Cape of Good Hope, the Royal Navy had stretched its problem-solving skills beyond the limits of safety. Under normal circumstances, the bottom of the *Victorious* would have sat too low in the water to pass through the Suez. If she lost a little weight, however, she might just have been able to squeeze through—at least on paper. She subsequently called at Port Said for an emergency weight-loss program. Coal and ammunition were the easiest items to toss overboard. With less cargo in her fuel bunkers and ammunition stores, the battleship rode a few precious inches higher in the water. In principle, the added buoyancy offered enough leeway to scrape through the hundred-mile journey to the Red Sea. Alas, the *Victorious* would never even get a chance to try.

As the *Victorious* neared the entry to the canal, unexpectedly high winds and heavy seas forced her into shallow water. As her plow-shaped bow burrowed into a submerged mud bank, the combined forces of gravity and suction locked the hulking ship into place. There she sat, trapped in the mud, stubbornly refusing to budge. The would-be rescuer of the Far East now stood in need of rescue herself. So much for the shortcut to China.

Samuel was in London when he first learned of the fiasco. Few ships at sea possessed the strength and power to free a vessel as large as the *Victorious*. The clear exception was in the private flotilla of Samuel's oil tankers. Included among his roster of bulk steamers was the mighty *Pectan*.[2] Named after the iconic scallop shell that symbolized Samuel's company, the *Pectan* was one of the last and most powerful additions to the fleet of oil tank steamers belonging to Shell. As it happened, the *Pectan* was on a return voyage to fill up her tanks in Batumi when a message reached her from Samuel: her new orders were to free the *Victorious*. If any ship could accomplish this feat, the five-thousand-ton sister ship of Flannery's original *Murex* would be the one to do it.

For nearly three days, the *Pectan* sat abreast of the *Victorious* in preparation for the great pull. When both crews were ready, the Shell tanker churned out to sea. As a high-tension towline stretched between the two massive vessels, it put the design of Flannery's vessel to a remarkable, and unexpected, stress test. Years earlier Flannery had purposely made his tankers strong in order to increase their safety. Now, at the mouth of the canal, his added design features would prove fortunate.

For twenty-one hours, the *Pectan* fruitlessly fought the suction of the sandy mud, sixteen thousand tons of dead weight from the *Victorious*, and the sea itself. Her large propeller clawed at the water, trying to exert enough forward momentum to pry the *Victorious* free. In the process, the natural shearing forces of the waves and the trapped body of the battleship strained the interlocking steel plates of the *Pectan*, the plates that Flannery had overengineered to prevent leaks. The foresight of that design choice was a crucial element to the operation. A less robust vessel, or one that had been thrown together in a slapdash fashion, might not have been up to the task.

It was only after twenty-two hours that the formidable struggle ended. The mud could no longer resist the *Pectan*. The underwater shoal surrendered its captive. As the *Victorious* edged forward, its heavy armored hull finally broke free. The design of Flannery's tanker was triumphant over the elements. The Royal Navy gained back its warship.

There was a sweet irony in the Suez rescue. Years earlier anti-Semitic British newspapermen had denounced Samuel's "Hebrew" plot to endanger the canal with bulk oil tankers, but now in 1898 one of those very tankers had come to the aid of the stranded *Victorious*. Instead of endangering British interests, as the insidious allegations had implied, one of Samuel's oil tankers had saved them. By salvaging the Admiralty's stranded battleship, Samuel was acting out of a deep sense of patriotism. If the Royal Navy needed help, he would offer it. Yet the salvage operation also allowed him to play for something bigger, and Samuel intended to grab fate by the towline.

Under the maritime rules of the day, the captain, crew, and owner of the *Pectan* were all entitled to compensation for salvaging the *Victorious*. As such, the Admiralty dutifully informed the Treasury that Her Majesty's government was now on the hook for £5,000 ($726,000 in today's money) to Samuel, £500 to the captain of the *Pectan*, and £500 to the crew. This mundane exchange of imperial paperwork would have proceeded smoothly had the Merchant of Houndsditch not thrown a spanner into the bureaucratic works. After receiving notice of the salvage offer, he replied with a carefully crafted letter to the Treasury feigning confusion. Why should he receive compensation for the salvage? He had only "done for one of Her Majesty's ships no more than he would expect one of Her Majesty's ships to do for him." Moreover, the queen could rest assured that "the Pectan, and indeed the whole Shell fleet, were naturally, at all times, at Her Majesty's entire disposal."[3] Now it was the Treasury's turn to be confused.

There was no template for someone refusing to take honest money for an honest salvage. By gallantly forgoing a payout, Samuel gambled that such an obvious act of chivalry would produce an equally gallant offer of a knighthood. Those three little letters—*S-I-R*—and the status they conveyed were worth much more to Samuel than any amount of money. There remained, of course, the outstanding issue of the captain and crew of the *Pectan*. Of course, they would need to be paid out from the Treasury's coffers. For in refusing money for himself, Samuel had no intention of refusing their rightful share of the salvage.

Just as he had done so many times before, Samuel the gambler came out on top. On August 6, 1898, less than six months after rescuing the *Victorious* from the sandy mud of Port Said, Samuel's lifelong ambition came to fruition. In a private investiture ceremony on the Isle of Wight, Marcus Samuel, the son of Sailor Town, at last received his coveted knighthood. As he approached the queen to be knighted, Victoria was in the evening of her life. At seventy-nine years of age, she had survived thirty-three prime ministers, one Great Power war, seven assassination attempts, the loss of one husband and two children, and she had—unknowingly—endowed the gene for hemophilia to many of the royal houses of Europe. On the balance sheet of Queen Victoria's life, the portly former sheriff of London, with his fleshy cheeks, walrus mustache, and slightly thinning, close-cropped hair, was an easily forgettable footnote. But for Samuel, kneeling before the aging queen was a pinnacle of life. Hereafter he would be Sir Marcus Samuel, alderman of London, gentleman of the Mote, "Japan merchant," and the brash president of the Shell Transportation and Trading Co. The good name of Samuel had attained heights that his father might never have imagined for it.

Enjoying the life of a newly minted member of the gentry, Sir Marcus lived in strict accordance with the rules of a country gentlemen. He fished for perch and pike in the lake beyond the Mote's front doors; he grew prizewinning grapes and peaches in the gardens and greenhouses behind his kitchen; and he watched the sportsmen of Maidstone smash bat and ball on his private cricket pitch, which he made available to the village team. On workdays in the City of London, Sir Marcus remained an early riser, but he no longer headed straight to work from his blocklong home, now located at 20 Portland

Place. Instead, by eight o'clock each morning, he could be seen out riding his beloved horse Duke in Hyde Park. Not that Sir Marcus ever fully mastered the art of horsemanship. Whenever he was on horseback, disaster always seemed imminent for the newly minted knight.

Back at Shell's new offices at 16 Leadenhall Street, just two blocks from Houndsditch, Sir Marcus ran his oil company much as he rode his horses: invariably, he managed to pull through somehow.[4] When Deterding unleashed his abrupt price war in the Orient, it struck at the core of Shell's kerosene business. In any other setting, the future of Shell might have looked dim. But Sir Marcus was surprisingly well positioned to endure the siege. The reason was encompassed by a single word: gasoline.

CHAPTER 10

The Deal of the Century

In the early hours of an August morning back in 1888, Bertha Benz, the wife of engineering virtuoso Karl Benz, awoke before her husband. Moving under the cloak of predawn, she and her teenage sons, Eugen and Richard, had appointed themselves to carry out a mission: to save Karl from himself.

Inside his workshop, Bertha's husband had constructed a remarkable invention. Known as the *Patent Motorwagen*, the motorized vehicle was revolutionary. Bertha knew it. The whole family knew it. Unfortunately, Karl suffered from immobilizing self-doubt about the commercial viability of his design. It was one reason why few people around the city of Mannheim, let alone in the rest of Germany, were even aware of his creation. Those few who did know about it did not know what to make of the unusual contraption.

If Karl had been as talented at showmanship as he was at invention, the motored tricycle in his workshop might have been called the *Wunderwagen*—for that was its true character. Harnessing "that wretched stuff," gasoline, for power, the vehicle was a monumental step forward in human engineering. It granted its driver all the mobility and freedom of a carriage but liberated them from the smell and responsibility of a horse. The device itself was amazingly simple—just three wheels, two large and one small, a sturdy bench on which to sit, a tiller for steering, and a one cylinder gasoline combustion engine mounted in the rear. Gasoline motors were not especially cutting edge in the 1880s, but most were monstrous in size, powering factories, not tricycles. That was the beautiful part about Benz's breakthrough: he had miniaturized gasoline combustion and made it portable.[1] Now Bertha would demonstrate his accomplishment to the world, or at least to southern Germany. Since her overly cautious husband would never have approved of her marketing plan, she kept the intrigue a secret right up to its execution on this late-summer early morning.

As Karl slept, his wife and sons quietly pushed the *Motorwagen* out of the Benz workshop. They guided it away from the house, so as not to wake Karl when turning over his engine. This was no easy task in the early morning. Karl's miniature gasoline motor was revolutionary, but it was also finicky. Half of the excitement with the Benz *Motorwagen* was getting the thing to start. Although the car had an electric ignition system, it required a manual spin of the flywheel to initiate combustion. At first, this effort usually produced a huff and sigh from the gasoline motor. More spins produced more puffs and little else. Only the persistent prevailed. When they did, Benz's engine whirled to life with a satisfying click. The gasoline fired, then fired again. In a matter of seconds, a rapid succession of micro-explosions inside the engine's single cylinder merged the clicks into a steady, rattling cadence. This meant that the engine was ready to roll. Once Bertha got her *Motorwagen* started, the gasoline did all the work.

Sitting behind the tiller, Bertha set out for the very first automotive road trip in history. Her famous sixty-five-mile drive to the German town of Pforzheim was not without its mishaps, however. Along the way, she had to unclog a carburetor pipe with her hatpin; insulate the car's ignition cable with her garter; invent the automotive brake lining out of necessity; and replenish the car's fuel tank with refined petroleum spirits purchased from a pharmacy.[2] Despite these woes, Bertha's guerrilla marketing strategy paid off handsomely. Word about her wild adventure in a motorized tricycle spread quickly. Within the year, interested purchasers were seeking out Karl to buy their own *Motorwagen*. By 1894 he was ready for mass production. Thanks to Bertha and her sons, Benz & Co. of Mannheim, Germany, known today as Mercedes-Benz, was racing into business.

Fuel lay at the core of Benz's design concept, and it powered the success of the motorcar. Pound for pound, the gasoline combustion engines on Benz's vehicles unleashed more energy than any previous attempts to create a horseless carriage. Similar fuel sources like coal or natural gas could not compete with gasoline's punch, or they were simply too difficult to commercialize.[3] By miniaturizing the gasoline engine, inventors like Benz and a fellow German named Gottlieb Daimler were able to harness the power of gasoline. Even so, the gasoline cars were not alone on the roads of the late nineteenth century. Internal combustion had a formidable competitor: steam.

In the modern era, the steam car stands as an extinct curiosity of a bygone age. Nevertheless, for a glimmering instant before the turn of the century, the steam car enjoyed a brief stint as king of the road.[4] Unlike the *internal* combustion engines used in Benz's design, automotive steam engines harnessed *external* combustion for power. Early steam cars burned crude oil, coal, and sometimes kerosene to boil water under the hood; the resulting steam compressed a piston and drove the vehicle. The basic concept was similar to that of a locomotive engine.[5] And since steam cars benefited from a century of miniaturization and innovation on the world's rail lines, external combustion cars were less complex and more refined than the gasoline-powered upstarts.

The Deal of the Century

Convenience aside, steam cars were far safer to operate than their early gasoline-powered competitors. An automotive enthusiast with a steam car did not have to risk breaking an arm by turning a fussy starting crank incorrectly. The driver of an external combustion car simply dropped a match onto a wick and then waited twenty minutes for steam pressure to build inside the engine. The design concept behind the steam car traded time for safety. The cars were safer to start but were useless when it came to instant, on-demand power. Gasoline cars, by contrast, were ready to drive after a few exhausting and potentially hazardous whirls of the starting crank.

Any time lost in the twenty-minute startup of a steam car could be recaptured out on the road. In the early age of the automobile, steam cars were faster than their internal combustion rivals—at least initially. Indeed, the principal drawback to the steam car lay in the fact that it required two types of fuel to operate: a burning fuel for heat and water for steam. By contrast, the internal combustion engine used only gasoline. This fundamental difference between gas and steam would eventually consign one to the history books and grant dominion of the road to the other. The gasoline engine might have been a relative newcomer in the late nineteenth century, but it was just getting revved up.

In 1894 one of the first head-to-head contests between steam and gasoline cars unfolded on the highway between Paris and the cathedral town of Rouen, near the English Channel. The French newspaper *Le Petit Journal* originally envisioned the event as a publicity stunt to increase readership. Since cars were interesting, why not drive a lot of cars to Rouen? The paper would build up the excitement, cover the proceedings, and report on the results. The scheme was a reasonable one. But *Le Petit Journal* was playing with forces beyond its control. What the paper actually created was a dusty traveling circus that doubled as an engineering stress test and advertising bonanza for early car-makers. Over seventy-eight miles of crude, unpaved road, the Rouen Trial accidentally pitted steam against gasoline in a direct face-off. Among the 108 cars that started the event, gasoline engines were in the overwhelming majority. Nevertheless, a steam-powered car, driven by the Marquis Jules-Albert de Dion, finished first and posted the best time. Rounding out the remaining top finishers were the gasoline cars of famed French car builders Émile Peugeot and Émile Levassor.

At the finish line, overzealous race organizers used the ad hoc rule-book to create trouble. They refused to grant de Dion first prize be-cause a second person had ridden on board with him to stoke the boiler of his steam engine. When the organizers published the official results, gasoline came in as the winner. But it proved a hollow victory. In actual performance, de Dion's steam car had bested all comers. If early carmakers like Peugeot and Levassor were going to demonstrate the merits of gasoline over steam, they would need to do more than exploit the rulebook.[6] Within a year, both sides were ready for a re-match.

What had begun as an isolated effort to boost newspaper reader-ship in Paris now ballooned into an event of international interest. As far away as California, newspapers billed the follow-on Paris-Bordeaux-Paris Trial of 1885 as an epoch-defining "competition of carriages without horses."[7] No simple race this; the contest would be a grueling marathon. Covering nearly 745 miles over forty-eight hours, the drive from Paris to Bordeaux and back was to be the longest trial ever attempted. Speed mattered, but endurance would be the virtue that decided this competition's winner.

As in the previous sprint to Rouen, de Dion's steam car initially set the pace. Levassor stalked him like prey from behind. The limitations of steam also became apparent. When de Dion made an unexpected stop to replenish his car's water supply on the long road to Bordeaux, Levassor motored past with his four-horsepower Daimler engine and seized the lead. The single fuel requirement of the gasoline engine provided an edge.

Levassor arrived back in Paris first; he had not slept for over forty-eight hours. His sleepless drive had been worth the sacrifice, however, since the exhausted carmaker reaped all the free advertising that came with his accomplishment. But once again the rulebook intervened to deny victory to the fastest car. The race organizers arbitrarily insisted on awarding prizes only to four-seat vehicles. Levassor had performed his feat in a two-seater. Consequently, the official four-seat winner of the Paris-Bordeaux-Paris race finished the course eleven hours behind him. This perverse result caused French car fanatics to pine for a straight-up contest whereby the fastest car would be the winner. That concept worked in horse racing—why not in motor sport? The next summer drivers finally got their chance.

The tipping point for both racing and the gasoline engine occurred at the Paris-Marseilles-Paris Rally of 1896. More ambitious than any previous automotive contest, it stands today as the first automotive Grand Prix in history. There were no arbitrary bans on two seats or four, and no nitpicky distinctions between one passenger or two. This time the fastest car to the finish line would take the laurels. But surviving to the finish would not be an easy feat. The rally course was to cover 1,063 miles of road—the longest ever attempted.[8] Out of thirty-two drivers willing to attempt the race, only four were brave enough to enter steam cars. All the other participants opted for gasoline-powered engines. The speed-hungry de Dion factored among the racers to Marseilles, but he too abandoned steam in favor of gasoline. Just two years had elapsed since he bested the internal combustion cars at Rouen, but already the performance gap between gasoline and steam was insurmountable. De Dion, no fanatical purist, wanted to win. That meant he would use gasoline.

Speed ruled the onslaught to Marseilles. Launching out from Paris, one of the gasoline cars reached the white-knuckle speed of nineteen miles per hour.[9] As the drivers departed for the second stage of the race at the town of Auxerre, the steam cars were no longer competitive. The gasoline engines dominated the front of the race, and among them death found attractive company. During the outbound run to Marseilles, Levassor established a tragic automotive milestone after being thrown from his vehicle on the outskirts of Avignon. Through grim determination, he managed to complete the course. He even lived long enough to see an eight-horsepower Panhard et Levassor car of his own design win the rally. However, his injuries—and lack of timely medical attention following the smash-up—were fatal. Instead of gaining distinction as the winner of the race, he became the very first person in recorded history to die from injuries sustained in an automobile accident. The French inventor was the first, but millions would join him. The dominion of gasoline was beginning. It was going to be a very deadly reign.

For its part, the automotive steam engine did not go entirely extinct after the Paris-Marseilles-Paris Rally. Steam cars persisted among weekend enthusiasts and a few masochistic diehards who insisted on entering them into long-distance races. Nevertheless, gasoline cars now ruled the competitive scene. Their engines possessed the speed and the reliable endurance that won races. In the frantic Darwinian competition of automotive evolution, only gasoline survived.

A delicate irony of gasoline's triumph revealed itself as the internal combustion engine proliferated on the world's roads in the mid-1890s. Even though gasoline proved to be the superior automobile fuel, few members of the general public had the vaguest clue that it even existed. This gap in public knowledge endlessly annoyed the accomplished English racer Charles Jarrott. During the early lifespan of the motorcar, he received the same line of questioning "about five-hundred times a day":

"Where is the electricity stored?" confused onlookers would inquire about Jarrott's motorcar.

"This is not an electric machine, but one driven by petrol," he informed them.

"What do you mean petrol?"

"Petrol is a spirit."

"Goodness gracious! Doesn't it always blow up?"[10]

Indeed—that was precisely the point. The rapid explosion of gasoline inside the internal combustion engine unleashes enormous amounts of energy. Since more gasoline, firing inside ever more pistons, potentially allowed for greater speeds, car engines grew larger with each successive race. Some of these automotive monsters attained colossal proportions, measuring as large as eighteen liters at one point.[11] As more gasoline cars hit the road, global demand for the motor fuel began to spike. This put Sir Marcus in a surprisingly profitable position. The same crude from his Borneo concession that was bad for making kerosene proved exceptional at making gasoline and heavier fuel oil. No longer considered a waste product, gasoline in England and Europe was fast becoming a key source of Shell's annual revenue. The problem was that the world would soon have too many cars and not enough fuel. Shell's concession in Borneo could not meet the expected demand, and neither could Royal Dutch's wells in Sumatra. The chemical composition of Baku's crude made it a poor source of gasoline, and America's oil fields were on the decline. Without more gasoline, the planet's growing fleets of automobiles would never leave the garage.

It was for this reason that, seemingly overnight, the compass of the petroleum business pegged on the small town of Beaumont, Texas. Outside the state, few people had ever heard of the place. It was so obscure that no one at Shell could find the town on any atlas in the offices at 16 Leadenhall.[12] That would change soon enough. Someone down in Beaumont had just ripped open a gigantic new petroleum field. So much crude now flowed out of Beaumont that the settlement was fast becoming a new epicenter of global oil production. As Sir Marcus saw it, Texas held a fresh chance for Shell to break free of its dangerous overdependence on Russia.

The unlikely catalyst for the Beaumont boom was a one-armed, infatuated dreamer by the name of Pattillo Higgins. Around Beaumont, he was simply known as Bud. Back in 1880, Higgins had lost his arm following an exchange of gunshots with a sheriff's deputy. The details of his run-in with the law are difficult to sort out and almost certainly obscured by multiple retellings. What is certain is that a Texas sheriff's deputy was killed; a jury acquitted Higgins on grounds of self-defense; and the infected bullet wound that was gradually eating his arm was amputated along with the limb.[13] Welcome to Texas.

Left with only one arm, Higgins tried his remaining hand in the logging industry, the real estate business, and finally the brick business. As a brick maker in Beaumont, one of his constant dilemmas was the price he paid to power a manufacturing kiln. There had to be a less expensive way to heat his bricks, or so he thought. Setting out to find a solution to his high fuel costs, he eventually went to Pennsylvania. In the shadow of the long-vanished petroleum boom, he absorbed the sights and bygone tales about oil, while studying the uses of low-cost fuel oil to fire kilns. The stories of past crude discoveries in the Pennsylvania oil patch reminded him of a swampy stretch of land back in Beaumont. Just south of the town, there was a weird twelve-foot bulge in the ground. Some called this curious bump on the horizon "Spindletop." Others simply called it the "Big Hill." Whatever its name, in Higgins's estimation, something special lay beneath it.

If a visitor happened to walk around Spindletop in the late 1890s, they would have immediately noticed the obvious smell of brimstone. Sulfur molecules floated in the air around the hill. Nearby, a naturally occurring vent of natural gas pumped vaporized hydrocarbons into the atmosphere. The noise from the spring was so loud that locals thought the sound resembled a "bunch of ducks feeding in the woods."[14] There were no ducks below Spindletop, but Higgins steadily convinced himself there was crude.

As Higgins fixated on his dream of oil at Spindletop, he cast his imagination far into the future. Around Beaumont, he envisioned a vast industrial city. The foundations of its progress would rest on all the petroleum that would rush from Spindletop. He planned to name this new metropolitan center Gladys City, after a student he fancied in his Bible class. At the center of this mirage there would be the Gladys City Oil Glass and Manufacturing Company—her namesake and his company. It was an impossible fantasy, of course, but Bud Higgins believed every bit of it.

Despite his far-flung plans for Gladys and her city, Higgins had practical reasons to be confident that petroleum existed near Beaumont. In 1888 crude had already come in around the town of Nacogdoches, 120 miles north of Spindletop. The field of Oil Springs, as it was called, initially produced three hundred barrels a day, but this rate soon declined to a trickle. Similar wells near the town of Corsicana drew a measly two to twenty-five barrels a day. While these small finds were not sufficient to excite a bonanza, they were more than enough to fuel Higgins's outsized visions of grandeur.[15] He was going to make Gladys City a reality.

In 1892 Higgins convinced a parishioner from his Baptist church to cosign a loan for half the land around Spindletop.[16] Operating as the fancifully named Gladys City Oil Co., he and a handful of partners began to drill exploratory wells into the bulging hill south of Beaumont. All they managed to produce were dry, sandy holes. Part of the trouble was their stab-and-jab strategy for picking a drill site. The other was the soil itself. Similar to Royal Dutch's experience prior to the arrival of the geologists Porro and Schmidt, Gladys City Oil Co. was blindly boring wells without any thought to the underground strata. Based on other successful wells up north, Higgins suspected by pure guesswork that his borings would have to reach a depth of one thousand feet before striking oil. The hassle was an infuriating layer of sand that existed far below the surface at Spindletop. None of Higgins's borings could reach through the barrier. His exploration efforts were not going according to plan.

Anyone who has ever tried to build a sand castle out of dry sand might sympathize with the tribulations of Spindletop. Every time drillers reached the depth of three hundred feet, they encountered the same sandy obstacle. It was "like drilling in a pile of wheat," said one contemporary of Higgins.[17] As well after well collapsed, Gladys City Oil left a trail of dead holes and dashed hopes around Spindletop. Worse yet, none of Higgins's hired drillers could find a way through the barrier. As each team departed in failure, Higgins sold off portions of his land to pay his mounting bills. The more holes he bored at Spindletop, the more money he burned. This was beginning to make the financial backers of Gladys City Oil nervous.

Aiming to calm his investors, Higgins decided that an expert's endorsement would buy him some needed time. He found a possible candidate in a scientist at the Texas State Geological Survey. Higgins proceeded to talk his ear off. After surveying the ground around Spin-

John D. Rockefeller at the height of his power, ca. 1889. Rockefeller had not only created the world's largest and most profitable petroleum company, he had systematically eliminated nearly all forms of competition in the oil industry.

Marcus Samuel, the founder of the Shell Transportation and Trading Co., in 1921. Rising from modest origins, this former "Japan merchant" from Houndsditch would eventually outrank all but a handful of the British nobility.

A young Henri Deterding with his mentor, Jean Baptiste August Kessler (left), the surrogate father of Royal Dutch. After Kessler's sudden death in 1900, Deterding would transform Royal Dutch and redirect the flow of oil through new, unimagined channels.

26 Broadway (second building from the right) in the late 1880s. It was an appropriately grand headquarters for the planet's largest oil company.

Houndsditch in 1872. Visitors were wise to mind their pockets. At the crossing point between aspiring newcomers, energetic hustlers, and England's poor, Houndsditch was the home of M. Samuel & Co.— Standard Oil's unlikely challenger.

Titusville, Pennsylvania, at the height of the oil boom in the 1860s. Soon after news that "the Yankee has struck oil" rippled out from Oil Creek, a veritable forest of man-made drilling derricks began to replace the native trees in the region.

The famous Lucas well at Spindletop, ca. 1901. The discovery of crude at Spindletop revitalized the flagging U.S. petroleum industry and spawned the ill-fated "deal of the century" between Shell and Guffey Petroleum.

A Royal Dutch gusher in the East Indies, ca. 1900. The race to pump oil in the East was a herculean struggle against jungle-borne illnesses, rusting equipment, and endless, costly delays.

Henry Flagler, the man of "vim and push" at Standard. Flagler was an architect of the original Standard Oil Trust and the closest approximation of a friend that Rockefeller had ever known.

John Archbold in 1908, prior to the final breakup of Standard Oil. As Rockefeller's handpicked successor, Archbold sustained Standard's war against competition until the very end.

"Hell Hound" Henry Rogers (left) and Mark Twain (right), ca. 1904. It was Twain who brokered Rogers's fateful introduction to investigative journalist Ida Tarbell.

Theodore Roosevelt in 1910. His reputation as a trust buster would be won thanks to his attack on Standard. By adding Rockefeller to his collection of vanquished monopolists, Roosevelt hoped to score a political victory and demonstrate that all Americans could still expect a "square deal" in the United States.

The *Murex* was the world's first modern oil tanker. By sending the *Murex* through the Suez Canal, the main artery between the United Kingdom and its colonial possessions in the East, Marcus Samuel became the first to solve the complex puzzle that prevented Russian oil from competing against Rockefeller in Asia on a large scale.

Admiral John "Jacky" Fisher, the man whom Samuel dubbed the "God-father of oil." His career epitomized the confluence of speed and firepower that prompted the Royal Navy's "fateful plunge" into oil.

The HMS *Queen Elizabeth*, the first super dreadnought to run on liquid fuel. She marked a significant crossing point between the old age of coal and the new reign of crude.

Aviation pioneer Glenn Curtiss over the Hudson River on his 150-mile flight from Albany to New York on May 29, 1910. The conquest of such a great distance by air was the springboard for future long-distance airmail and passenger services.

Daytona Beach became the "Mecca of motorists" during Rockefeller's retirement in Florida. As new generations of motorcars roared across Daytona Beach, they possessed an unquenchable thirst for "that wretched stuff," gasoline.

Trailblazing journalist Ida Tarbell. Beginning in 1902, her nineteen-part investigative series in *McClure's* exposed Standard's illegal business practices to the American public.

John D. Rockefeller (center) leaving court in 1908. Up until the very moment when the Supreme Court ordered an end to Rockefeller's monopoly in 1911, Standard attempted to expand its dominion.

dletop and imbibing the nonsensical, amateurish yammering of Higgins, the state geologist sounded the alarm about the one-armed oilman and warned the residents of Beaumont not to waste their money on the "idle dreams or insane notions of irresponsible parties" looking to find oil at Spindletop.[18] So much for the validation of science.

Bereft of ideas and running short on cash, Higgins's last hope was to advertise. After buying space in a trade journal, he carefully described the area around Spindletop. The advertisement stressed the telltale presence of sulfur around his unproven oil play and pleaded for outside help. It was that peculiar mention of sulfur that did the trick. Far to the east of Spindletop, across the Texas state line in neighboring Louisiana, one Anthony F. Lucas read the anxious plea. A former naval officer from the Austro-Hungarian Empire, Lucas had long ago abandoned his life on the water in order to try his luck as a gold prospector in Colorado. It was an ill-fated career change, at least at first, as Lucas eventually went bust as a gold miner. By the time he saw the ad from Higgins, he was making a living drilling Louisiana salt wells. The word *sulfur* grabbed his attention. As he saw it, the Texas venture was at least worth a try. Even if Higgins was wrong about oil, his land might be a good place to mine for sulfur.

Unfortunately for Higgins, the financial clock had expired. When Lucas finally arrived in Beaumont, Gladys City Oil was nearly broke. Higgins had no money left to pay Lucas for his efforts. Undaunted, Lucas offered to cut Higgins in for 10 percent of any discovery. Higgins agreed, and Spindletop immediately began to suck Lucas dry. This hunt for crude was turning into a money pit.

In all likelihood, the Lucas venture would have failed had it not been for the timely intervention of two Pennsylvania oilmen named John H. Gailey and James M. Guffey. Experienced wildcatters in their own right, they were accustomed to long-shot gambles. Their small success at finding oil near Corsicana buoyed their confidence that Spindletop might also harbor crude. They lined up $300,000 ($8 million today) in financing from the Mellon banking family in Pittsburgh and offered Lucas a 13 percent stake in a revamped search at Spindletop. Unfortunately for Higgins, the big-talking dreamer had nothing left to offer. Gailey and Guffey squeezed him out of the deal entirely.

After taking over at Spindletop, the J. M. Guffey Petroleum Co. hired a team of brothers from Corsicana to punch yet another hole into the ground outside of Beaumont. The Hamill brothers, as they were known, were experienced drillers. More important, they had tussled with the frustrating sand barrier before. Lucas would run the show at Spindletop, but it was Gailey who would choose the spot for the new well. In the oil fields of his day, there was a rumor that Gailey could physically "smell" underground crude. Even so, the merits of this claim were dubious. As he walked the ground at Spindletop, Gailey determined that the next well should sit directly atop a naturally occurring gas seepage. It was a solid, educated guess. If he could smell anything at all at Spindletop, it was the molecules of natural gas emanating from the nearby vent, a whiff of sulfur, and perhaps the rich organic odor of the nearby stock tank (known outside of Texas as a water pond). There was certainly no oil to be sniffed, at least not yet.

The Hamills got to work. Although the brothers might have been expert drillers, they still faced the imposing sand. Once again it was proving difficult to keep the well open. As the Hamills burned a veritable forest of lumber to power a steam engine and chewed through drill bits, one of the brothers, Kurt Hamill, hit upon an innovative solution to the problem with collapsing holes. Over in Corsicana, drillers commonly flushed their sandy bores with a runny mixture of mud and water. This "drilling mud" was just as efficient as water for clearing out rock cuttings and related debris from the bottom of a well, yet it had the added benefit of holding back caving sand. Kurt wanted to use a thicker kind of mud to keep his latest well at Spindletop open, but where was he going to find it?

The solution was pure Texas. Kurt and his brothers, Alan and Jim, convinced a local farmer to drive his herd of cattle into the nearby stock tank. As the cows splashed and stomped through the sloppy water, the beasts manufactured all the natural mud that the Hamill brothers would ever need. When this mud plunged down the boring at Spindletop, it did wonders for holding back the encroaching sand. Thanks to their cow mud, the Hamills swiftly powered through the barrier that had defied all previous attempts. After the Hamills' drill cleared the formidable sand, it hit a layer of black dirt. Below that, it cracked into a layer of shale—shale was a good sign. Pushing deeper, bubbles began to form in the drilling fluid at the surface—bubbles were an even better sign.

Shortly after midmorning on January 10, 1901, the Hamill brothers reached a depth of 1,020 feet. Following an equipment swap, they lowered their drill back down into the borehole. As the tip chewed through several additional feet, more bubbles appeared in the drilling mud. Then the Hamills witnessed something that had never before been seen in Texas. With the force of an enormous cannon shot, six tons of drilling equipment, rocks, and cow mud exploded from the boring. The debris heaved upward into the Hamills' derrick and then crashed back to earth. Next came a rush of natural gas. It hissed from the borehole and announced the arrival of frothy, dark green, Texas crude. At first the petroleum from below simply gurgled at the opening of the boring. Then after an eerie pause, the liquid did something astonishing.

Abruptly, a rush of crude thundered into the air, cascading upward from the boring. The ensuing column of oil reached twenty stories above the mangled derrick. All around the Hamills, the ground was covered in mud and slimy petroleum. They marveled at the sight. This was more crude than any of them had ever seen. The brothers had just unshackled a titan that rivaled some of the colossal oil giants in Baku. The great age of Texas petroleum was born.

When Lucas first set out to drill in Texas, he had hoped to squeeze five barrels a day from his well. Instead, his blowout at Spindletop produced between 75,000 and 100,000 barrels of crude every twenty-four hours, at least initially. This unimaginable flow rate was more than half the daily output of every other well in the United States *combined*.[19] If only John Archbold, Rockefeller's hard-charging director at Standard, had been there to witness the sight. It was Archbold who, years earlier, had once pledged to drink every barrel of oil west of the Mississippi. Gazing upon the black and green majesty of Spindletop, the boastful Archbold might have turned green himself.

Thanks to Higgins, Lucas, and the Hamill brothers, Guffey Petroleum had uncovered the single largest new discovery of oil in America. Up until Spindletop, the U.S. oil industry had been spiraling into a phase of terminal decline. The oil fields in America were old and overpumped. Each year they were producing less crude to meet the country's rising demand for gasoline and other refined petroleum products. The domestic oil industry would have been in a tight corner were it not for the new find in Texas. This made the gusher at Spindletop more than a geologic curiosity. It heralded the opening of one of the greatest petroleum bonanzas ever seen. The deluge of oil had returned. The Lone Star State would never be the same.

Even Higgins was transformed. Although the one-armed, big-talking eccentric had no financial stake in the initial gusher at Spindletop, he controlled the rights to property leases around the well site. These immediately shot up in value. By slicing his parcels into tiny segments, Higgins sold them off for $5,000 apiece ($140,000 today). With all the money he generated from trading land at Spindletop, he was able attract a new round of investors and start over in the oil business. His second attempt was christened the Higgins Oil and Fuel Co. Whether she was relieved or disappointed, Gladys from Bible class never did get her city. All the same, the prophet of Spindletop did get to play the part of an oilman.

After the Lucas well, Higgins jostled with six hundred newly created petroleum companies around Beaumont. The pile-on effect was overwhelming. It was made worse by the spades of illegitimate, fly-by-night hucksters and purveyors of easy profits who had no intention of buying or selling oil. These con artists were more interested in fleecing unsuspecting investors. As in the early days of the Pennsylvania boom, the onrush of petroleum lured opportunists of all varieties. It was a universal constant in the oil business. Whenever people seemed to be getting rich from crude, hustlers were always ready to glean money from the rubes. The hive of fast talkers and swindlers eventually grew so thick around Spindletop that many local residents took to calling the place ".Swindletop."[20] The chance for profit always came at a price.

It was into the high-risk investment climate around Beaumont that Shell fearlessly trod. In Guffey Petroleum, the owner of the first well at Spindletop, Shell found an ideal partner. Even though Guffey was flush with oil, it faced two significant obstacles. Most immediately, it needed someone who could take enormous quantities of oil off its hands. As a close second, it dearly wanted to prevent Rockefeller or his secret proxies from extending Standard's monopoly over Texas. Decades earlier Standard had choked off competition in Pennsylvania, and the oilmen of Texas were sensitive to any hint of the same in their state. This made Shell a natural ally. The British oil company wanted to buy large quantities of oil, and it had nothing to do with Standard. Sir Marcus had his own aspirations for Texas. Shell needed to lock down upstream supplies in Texas as a means of diversifying away from Russia and Borneo. It was a great advantage that Shell was no friend to Standard, and its tankers could carry as much oil as Guffey could offer. This had the makings of a deal, and not just any deal—one that would be as large as the Texas oil rush itself.

Six months after the Lucas well came in at Spindletop, Shell and Guffey signed the "deal of the century."[21] Under the terms of the twenty-one-year contract, Sir Marcus agreed to buy at least 15 million barrels of petroleum at the guaranteed price of 25 cents a barrel ($7 today). It was the biggest oil agreement in the world and an immediately profitable one for Guffey. As more wells came online at Spindletop, the ensuing flood of crude drove the market price of Texas crude down to 10 cents, and then 5 cents a barrel. This was perfect for Guffey, since Shell was on the hook to pay 25 cents for every barrel its tankers picked up off the coast. Since oil was suddenly cheap, the Guffey contract essentially meant that Shell was paying a premium for its supply diversification. Thanks to the new shipments from Texas, Sir Marcus had access to oil from three different parts of the world. Everyone seemed to win from the deal, but there was a hidden danger. In signing the "deal of the century," both Guffey and Shell were making a blind bet. Each side assumed that the prolific oil field around Spindletop would never run dry. In time, this minor detail would grow into a major crisis. But for now everyone was too optimistic to cautiously consider the future.

Down in boomtown Beaumont, fear of a pending oil collapse was hard to find. Seemingly overnight, the tiny settlement had too much oil and far too many people hoping to make money from it. One symptom of the town's instant population spike could be seen in the long lines of people, which snaked in every direction at once. There were two-hour lines to get a meal, equally long lines to use a bathroom, and the line to make a phone call literally took days. Down at the Crosby House, the finest hotel in Beaumont, the throngs of new arrivals, land speculators, and stock boosters grew so large, the proprietors sectioned off the building's front porch, its back garden, and even individual chairs in the lobby for traders. When this real estate ran short, the spillover of speculators and land traders from the Crosby House soon filled the corners of adjacent saloons. Yet no matter where people congregated, the only topic that anyone wanted to discuss in Beaumont was crude. "Oil insanity was strictly monomania," reported one witness. "Food, drink and raiment were forgotten. The oil crazed man or woman lived on oil. They never thought of sleep as long as they could keep their eyes open. They heard nothing but oil and talked nothing but oil."[22]

One result of the oil hysteria could be seen at Spindletop itself. The original Lucas well was soon indistinguishable from the surrounding forest of tightly packed derricks. As speculators jockeyed for parcels of new drilling land from inside the Crosby House, the size of individual lots around Spindletop shrank to just 50 feet. If they grew any smaller, the legs of one derrick would physically touch those of a neighbor. Not that the proliferation of wells seemed to matter. Almost every new hole struck oil.

Fortified by his "deal of the century" with Guffey and the unstoppable production at Spindletop, Sir Marcus was riding high during the summer of 1901. His upstream supplies of petroleum were safely diversified. Linking the distance and geography between wellhead and consumer, Shell's tanker fleet was transporting 70 percent of all the world's ocean-bound oil shipments. Even more gratifying, Shell was still the only company that could get bulk petroleum through the Suez. It was from this coveted position of strength that Sir Marcus could finally put Deterding in his place.

If ever there was a time for Shell to leverage its success from Texas, this was it. What Sir Marcus did not know was that the time available to corner his rival was terrifyingly short. When it ended, Shell would be on the ropes.

CHAPTER 11

The Rivals

S hady Lane had never been shadier. It is a testament to his incalculable talents as an interlocutor that, during the late summer and fall of 1901, Sir Marcus and Deterding both believed that Lane was conspiring to aid them individually in negotiations with the other. Lane's intervention in the rivalry between Royal Dutch and Shell occurred at a decisive moment in the world's transition from coal to oil. At the time, Deterding and Sir Marcus were battling each other as much as they were fighting Standard. Lane endeavored to bring an end to the internecine conflict between Standard's challengers and, eventually, forge a lasting union between them. In the process, he would do more than make business history—he would help to alter the balance of power in the oil world for decades.

On one side of the English Channel, Sir Marcus confidently strode through business fresh off his "deal of the century" with Guffey. From his headquarters in London, Sir Marcus directed one of the most aggressive oil transport and sales operations in the world, with a guaranteed link to almost unlimited amounts of refined American crude for the next twenty years. Sir Marcus knew that Shell had become the darling of the oil world. He also knew that it was the ideal time to sort out his tiff with Royal Dutch. Confident in his own powers, he wanted to bring an end to Royal Dutch's price war in Asia. The job of convincing Deterding to do this fell to Lane.

Across the Channel at The Hague, Royal Dutch still suffered from the aftershocks of Kessler's abrupt death in Naples that previous December. Tapped to inherit his former mentor's responsibilities, Deterding presently stood untested as the company's "interim" manager. He had yet to achieve a significant breakthrough or strategic acquisition for the company. Inside Royal Dutch, he harbored the dream of consolidating all the oil producers in the Indies into a single, coordinated body. Before this could occur, though, he needed to bring Sir Marcus's Shell tankers to heel. His price war on kerosene was intended to soften Shell for negotiations. Their two companies did not have to be locked into a state of permanent conflict. All the same, the price war was intended to make Sir Marcus more pliable when forging an eventual peace in the Far East. Deterding therefore saw Lane as his key to making Sir Marcus see reason.

Shady Lane, middleman extraordinaire, stood between these two great companies as the ever-effective enigma whose agency escaped scrutiny. By early October 1901, he was working on a plan to align the interests and ambitions of Royal Dutch and Shell into a single marketing agreement. Ideally, this would allow both companies to cooperate on kerosene sales, pool their respective assets, and potentially even sell their products at predetermined prices. This concept was eerily similar to the "harmony" that Rockefeller had created through Standard. The major difference was that Sir Marcus and Deterding sought their peace deal as a *defensive* strategy against predatory pricing from 26 Broadway. Royal Dutch and Shell were still too small to go toe to toe with Rockefeller's behemoth by themselves. By working together, they could create a more effective rival to Standard and perhaps survive. That alone would be good for customers.

At least in principle, the rationale for a marketing agreement between Sir Marcus and Deterding had many benefits. Individually, each company possessed advantages that the other lacked. Royal Dutch was a large oil producer with few ships, no modern bulk tankers, and a relatively small retail business. Conversely, Shell was a small-time oil producer in possession of the world's largest fleet of bulk tankers and a vast distribution network across Asia, England, and parts of Europe. In concept, this was a win-win.

The basic dividing line was the question of who would control the marketing organization once it was up and running. When push came to shove, and oil from either Royal Dutch or Shell sailed to a given port, someone had to pick winners and losers—someone had to be in command. Sir Marcus saw himself as the obvious leader of this arrangement. Deterding hoped for a more equitable distribution of responsibilities. Lane was of a different mind altogether. He did not see the logic behind a low-scale marketing deal. What both companies needed was a full-scale merger. But since neither Deterding nor Sir Marcus were prepared to commit to that option, he toiled away on the marketing agreement.

Samuel and Deterding tossed offers and counteroffers at each other. As both executives considered their options, the gaps between their respective positions began to emerge. Aside from leadership, one of the biggest impediments to a deal was the time frame. Samuel was willing to sign a short-term joint-marketing agreement, perhaps lasting three years. Deterding wanted a long-term agreement, lasting for up to twenty years. The next notable sticking point was product. Whereas Samuel wished to limit the terms of their cooperation to just kerosene, Deterding wanted Royal Dutch and Shell to team up on everything: kerosene, fuel oil, and gasoline. Finally, there was scope. Samuel insisted that any arrangement with Royal Dutch had to be exclusive to Asia. This would allow him a free hand to expand in England and Europe. Deterding was willing to accept a deal that was exclusive to the Orient, but he balked at Samuel's demand to be the senior partner in the arrangement. The discussion moved in circles, and Lane got nowhere.

As with any peace deal, Sir Marcus and Deterding were both attempting to maximize their position in the postwar settlement. However, the existence of the price war alone was not enough to force Shell to make any deep concessions to end it. Something had to change in order to break the deadlock. That something occurred in the middle of October, when Sir Marcus boarded a ship for New York. His destination was 26 Broadway. His goal was to do the unthinkable: he wanted to make a separate peace with the enemy itself, Standard Oil.

On the surface, Sir Marcus's opening of negotiations with Standard might seem hard to fathom. After all, his organizing purpose since the early days of the *Murex* had been to break Rockefeller's monopoly, not to help it. Now he wanted to start a joint venture with Standard. Had the world turned on its head—again?

The explanation for Sir Marcus's abrupt about-face was twofold: he was simultaneously overconfident and blind to the true nature of his enemy. It was a dangerous combination. He falsely assumed that the strength of his tanker fleet and his long-term access to Texas crude put him on par with Standard. Nothing was further from the truth. Standard preferred its competitors to misjudge its true size. It achieved this by owning many of its "rivals" in secret and closing its books to outside scrutiny. Sir Marcus arrived in New York thinking that 26 Broadway would be keen to negotiate on equal terms. Instead, Standard saw the head of Shell as an aspiring prince of oil, not as a sovereign of equal status. As for his proposed joint venture, Standard did not venture jointly with anyone. Rockefeller's empire either purchased competing companies or destroyed them, and it often did both at once. The discussions in New York ended cordially but without a clear conclusion.

After returning from New York, Sir Marcus discovered that his trip to 26 Broadway had produced one undeniably positive outcome: he had put the fear of Rockefeller into Deterding. Seen from Royal Dutch's viewpoint, the very fact that Shell and Standard were talking at all was dangerous. If a deal between Deterding's two rivals ever materialized, the collective might of Standard and Shell would be unbeatable in the Far East. Royal Dutch might hold out for a time, but the power of its two greatest rivals would eventually be overwhelming. Deterding believed that he had to move quickly before Sir Marcus could conclude any arrangement with the Americans.

By November, Deterding was ready to offer up concessions to Sir Marcus. His driving mission was to intertwine the interests of Royal Dutch and Shell; only in this way could he protect Royal Dutch against the prospect of a Shell-Standard combination. It was Deterding's fear that put Sir Marcus in an immensely powerful position. The reality of Royal Dutch's situation was not as dire as Deterding assumed. The odds of a peace deal between Sir Marcus and Rockefeller were infinitesimally low. In the heat of negotiations, however, human perceptions are more important, and Deterding's perception of Sir Marcus's strength pushed him to the point of surrender.

Deterding's fear and the accidental power of Sir Marcus became the origin of the ill-fated "British-Dutch" agreement. In principle and in fact, the "British-Dutch" agreement was an undeniable victory for Sir Marcus. Under terms that Lane set down, Royal Dutch and Shell would remain independent companies but pool their resources. The price war would end. Sir Marcus and Deterding would coordinate their kerosene sales in the Orient. Shell would keep its free rein to expand fuel oil and gasoline sales elsewhere. If Deterding wanted to use tankers in the Shell fleet, Sir Marcus would make a hefty fee by loaning them to Royal Dutch. It was an exceptional deal for Shell. "British-Dutch" would make Sir Marcus a formidable power in Asia, maybe too powerful. But if Deterding wanted to preempt a combination between Standard and Shell, he needed to act—now.

On December 23, 1901, Standard returned to Sir Marcus with a gigantic offer. Instead of a joint venture, 26 Broadway wanted to pay Sir Marcus $40 million ($1.1 billion today) to own Shell lock, stock, and tanker. It was a hefty sum of cash, totaling twice the value of Shell's assets and twenty times its annual earnings. But the money had strings. Samuel would have to give up his control of Shell. He could become the nominal head of Standard's British subsidiary, the Anglo-American Oil Company, but 26 Broadway would call all the shots.[1]

Predictably, Sir Marcus and his brother Sam disagreed on their best course of action. Sam favored the comfort of cashing in his chips through the buyout. Conversely, his risk-taking older brother was cool to the idea. Nevertheless, the size of the offer made it hard to immediately dismiss. The poison pill was control. Sir Marcus, knight of the British Empire, did not wish to hand Shell over to the Americans. Since the *Murex*'s very first crossing of the Suez, he had seen Shell in patriotic terms. His company was a British enterprise, operating in the interests of the British Empire. If he accepted this enormous cash payment, Shell's British tankers would become Rockefeller's private navy. For a man who once promised the queen that his fleet stood "at all times, at Her Majesty's entire disposal," even this princely offer of cash might not be enough.

On December 27, Sir Marcus was pondering his options at the

Mote when Lane called him back to London. Deterding was ready to capitulate.[2] There could be no further delay in hammering out "British-Dutch." Tasked with formalizing the terms of Deterding's surrender, Lane spent the better part of that day drafting the agreement. He reached Sir Marcus just before the close of business in London.

By a peculiar coincidence, the timing of this event was particularly poignant. December 27 was the anniversary of the sudden death of Zijlker, the founder of Royal Dutch. Eleven years to the day after his death, Deterding was offering the company on a platter to Shell. Although not as tragic as Zijlker's passing, it was, all the same, a defeat for Royal Dutch. When one factored in the first anniversary of Kessler's death on the fourteenth, December was becoming a historically ominous month on Royal Dutch's calendar.

Outside, London was dark, cold and damp.[3] Inside, Sir Marcus's victory over Deterding was cheerier. The chairman of Shell affixed his signature to the "British-Dutch" agreement, after which a courier ferried the signed document across the Channel. After the sun was up the next morning, Deterding could countersign in The Hague. "I finally got Sir Marcus' acceptance of the memorandum this afternoon," Lane subsequently wrote Deterding. "In principle, it is exactly as you accepted it."[4]

The deal appeared to be all wrapped up. Lane had done his best to bring the two sides together. Sir Marcus had outmaneuvered Deterding—partially by accident—and emerged on top with nothing to do except to sit tight and let the gears of the "British-Dutch" deal run their course. Instead, he did something inexcusably foolish: he immediately sent a cable to New York formally rejecting the offer from 26 Broadway and calling off any future negotiations.[5] In an instant of transatlantic communication, all of Sir Marcus's powerful leverage over Deterding vanished. It would prove a terrible mistake.

When word of the "British-Dutch" agreement reached the House of Rothschild in Paris, it created ripples of panic. Was Deterding even aware of what he had done? "This contract," wrote a Rothschild executive, "in fact delivered the Royal Dutch, bound hand and foot, into the hands of Messrs. Samuel."[6] As far as the Rothschilds were concerned, Deterding had not signed up for a simple market-sharing agreement with Shell. He had altered the delicate commercial balance in the Far East, something that held potentially disastrous consequences for the Rothschilds. With Deterding in tow, Sir Marcus was about to go from being a cash-and-carry middleman for the Rothschilds to an oil powerhouse in his own right. Thanks to the pooling of resources with Royal Dutch, Shell could survive—perhaps even thrive—without oil from the Rothschilds. And even if Shell continued to buy kerosene in Batumi, it might eventually be in a position to curtail the Rothschild's own sales in Asia. In their view, the deal had to be stopped immediately.

Exactly how the Rothschilds helped to scuttle the "British-Dutch" agreement is unknown. Their role is betrayed through only a single letter from 1907, in which a Rothschild executive reminds The Hague about being saved from the "British-Dutch" deal, stating, "The Royal Dutch would have fallen completely into the hands of the Shell but for our intervention."[7] What form this intervention took is left unsaid. The remaining record goes blank until the start of the New Year, when Deterding came back a new man with a new strategy: what "British-Dutch" agreement?

On January 15, 1902, Deterding's board learned about the events of the previous weeks. Included in this rundown was a strange assertion that, as far as Deterding was concerned, Shell was "bound to the proposal" for "British-Dutch," but—somehow—Royal Dutch was not.[8] It was a disfigured version of reality, but one that Sir Marcus did not fight. Because he had foolishly surrendered his negotiating leverage over Deterding by calling off talks with Standard, he had botched his own coup. The great triumph of the "British-Dutch" agreement slipped through his hands. Worse still for him, the House of Rothschild now insisted on having a role in all future discussions between Royal Dutch and Shell. The one-on-one negotiation with Deterding was about to become a ménage-à-trois.

Over the next six months, all three sides—Deterding, Samuel, and the House of Rothschild—wheeled, dealed, and plotted to shape the peace between Royal Dutch and Shell. Once again Shady Lane was in the middle of the scrum. The reboot of negotiations was actually a gift to Lane. Throughout the entire process, he had held to the belief that Royal Dutch and Shell were wasting their time with a marketing agreement. Instead, an outright merger would be best for both companies. Did this mean that Lane had a hand in scuttling the "British-Dutch" deal? If he did, he left no fingerprints. All the same, the death of "British-Dutch" was in keeping with his overall goal. "There is no solution except the absolute amalgamation of the businesses," he claimed.[9] A joint marketing agreement would not work. Royal Dutch and Shell must become one.

The first significant breakthrough on the long road to amalgamation was the creation of the Asiatic Petroleum Company. As a company, Asiatic would be a model of compromise. Now that Deterding no longer feared a deal between Standard and Shell, his goals expanded. Under Royal Dutch's banner, he wanted to fulfill his original aim of forging an alliance between all crude producers in the Indies. Sir Marcus still wanted to end Deterding's kerosene price war in China. Meanwhile, the Rothschilds were eager to offload their Russian case oil into new markets. Remarkably, Lane found a way to satisfy everyone, but mostly at the expense of Sir Marcus.

Under the terms of the Asiatic agreement, all three sides would own a share of this new company. As co-owners, Royal Dutch, Shell, and the Rothschilds would manage their collective oil sales in Asia. Royal Dutch could consolidate producers on Sumatra and Borneo and ship oil on Shell's tankers. Royal Dutch would pay Shell handsomely for the shipments and end the price war in China. As for the Rothschilds, the sky was the limit for case oil, just as long as it did not tip the balance of supply and demand in the Orient. Originally Sir Marcus had been skeptical about including a third party, but by "joining hands with the Rothschilds," as he called it, Shell could guarantee its long-term access to Russian oil.[10] That offered its own appeal.

Through the forging of Asiatic, Lane had found something that all sides in the deal could support. The unfortunate trade-off for Sir Marcus was that he would be required to hand over day-to-day management of Asiatic to Deterding. Always sensitive to status, Sir Marcus nevertheless insisted on being named chairman of the company. Deterding agreed, then took the managing director's slot for himself. Sir Marcus could enjoy his title, but Deterding held the power.[11] With this arrangement, the basic structure of their future relationship was now in place. The rivals would at long last be partners, but Deterding would be first among equals.

On June 27, 1902, the parties formally settled the Asiatic deal. It was six months to the day since Sir Marcus signed the previous, abortive plan to create "British-Dutch." Now Asiatic would merge the financial and business interests—but not the actual companies—of Rockefeller's main rivals. "It is a matter of sincere congratulation to all concerned," the new chairman, Sir Marcus, informed his shareholders, "that the war which we have been engaged in with our Dutch friends has now ended, not only in peace, but in an offensive and defensive alliance."[12]

The Rivals

Any chance to truly savor the moment of the alliance proved fleeting. Just as the long price war with Royal Dutch ended, a new menace appeared on the horizon. There was something very wrong in Texas.

By the summer of 1902, crude production around Beaumont was humming along at an astonishing 17 million barrels annually.[13] Compared to the rest of the United States, the field at Spindletop singlehandedly accounted for 20 percent of all American crude production. The danger emerged when the petroleum holding tanks of Spindletop suddenly contained something new: salt water.[14] The prolific wells around Beaumont, flowing for less than two years, were now showing the initial signs of death in an oil field. The presence of salt water meant that Spindletop was drying up.

Unlike Royal Dutch's delayed reaction to saltwater incursion in Sumatra, Shell's agent in Texas immediately warned Sir Marcus by telegram. It was a shock of the first order. No sooner had Samuel tied off the conflict with Deterding then his diversification strategy in Texas began to unravel. A lot rode on Shell's "deal of the century" with Guffey. Sir Marcus had even commissioned four new tankers just to transport all the expected shipments from Texas. Without oil from Spindletop, Shell would be overly dependent on Russia and exposed to unexpected, disruptive shocks in the oil market. If any silver lining was to be gleaned from the news in Texas, it was that Shell's contract with Guffey went for twenty-one years—and a contract was a bond.

Beyond the worries in Texas, the future at home looked brighter. After more than a decade in the public spotlight, Sir Marcus was on the cusp of becoming the next Lord Mayor of London. This would be his greatest personal achievement to date. He was about to become the "merchant prince" of London. All that he had worked for was finally coming true. His worries in the oil business were about to seem very distant.

CHAPTER 12

The Echo of Applause

There were few jobs in the world for which Sir Marcus could have been a more perfect match. For more than a decade, the formerly obscure Merchant of Houndsditch had systematically transformed himself into one of the leading figures in the City of London. On September 29, 1902, his years of work in the public spotlight came to fruition when he won election as Lord Mayor of London. It was the "highest honor to which a London Merchant could aspire," he said.[1] This was no idle exaggeration. As head of the local government for the City of London, his new rank and responsibilities would be old, unique, and very grand. He reveled in every aspect of the honor.

Inside the single square mile of the City of London, only King Edward, son of the recently deceased Queen Victoria, held precedence over the Lord Mayor. Additionally, the office granted Sir Marcus an anachronistic set of honors and privileges, including the right to wear three colors of robe—scarlet, violet, and black—for occasions of either pomp or circumstance. At least on paper, the Lord Mayor could also stroll through the city brandishing one of four swords of his choosing. There was the sword of state for "supreme occasions;" the pearl sword for daily use; the black sword for funerals; and a fourth sword that no one ever bothered with because it hung on a wall in the Central Criminal Court. More mayoral equipment accompanied the swords, including possession of London's diamond scepter, its seal, its purse, its mace, and one of three literal keys to the City Treasury. Lady Fanny Samuel got to share in the honors as well. By virtue of being married to the new Lord Mayor, the Lady Mayoress won the privilege of being "attended by maids of honor" with the train of her dress "borne by pages" wherever she went.

The archaic holdovers of the Lord Mayor's office did not stop with its glittering baubles. By taking the oath of office that November, Samuel instantly became Admiral of the Port of London, "gauger of wine and oil, and other gaugable articles; meter of coals, grain, salt and fruit, and inspector of butter, hops, soap, cheese and other articles coming into the port of London." Mayorship likewise granted Sir Marcus the ability to come and go as he pleased from the Tower of London, while also making him governor of four hospitals, a trustee of St. Paul's Cathedral, and the city's coroner. "Needless to say," noted one contemporary, "these duties are performed by a deputy."[2]

As old and unique as Sir Marcus's new duties were, his inaugural procession through London was the most spectacular. Each year in November, for a single day, both the city and its pickpockets reveled in the distraction of the Lord Mayor's traffic-jamming parade. Nominally, the Lord Mayor's Show, as it is still called today, signified his first official trip from London's Guildhall to the Law Courts. When Sir Marcus assumed the office in 1902, many of the modern elements of this traveling public carnival were already coming into view. The practice of picking a theme was well established. Sir Marcus naturally chose the "development of British shipping," with an added emphasis on the newly signed Anglo-Japanese Alliance. There was also the now-familiar procession of floats and the martial grandeur of military bands, polished sabers, and civic costumes of every variety.

Interspersed between traveling models of British warships and steamers, Sir Marcus stacked his show with the cavalrymen of the Second Provisional Regiment of Hussars, the mounted band of the Royal Artillery, the bugle band of the London Rifle Brigade, and a mile of additional bands to accompany them. The one element that was clearly not missing from the show was sound: the new Lord Mayor's enthusiasm for music was a little too great. When the marching bands finally processed through London, they bunched up "so closely as to produce rather distressing effects in cacophony," remarked one observer. "However, the public was undoubtedly pleased."[3]

The main attraction of the parade, Sir Marcus himself, rode at the tail of this bugling snake. In a break with hallowed tradition, he did not proceed directly to the Law Courts that year. Rather, he redirected the entire route of the parade so that it swung past Houndsditch and processed right up the old Petticoat Lane (today Middlesex Street) in London's East End. Here in the heart of London's Jewish community, the cheers for Sir Marcus were loudest. Residents "welcomed the new Lord Mayor with a blaze of color" and erected a large triumphal arch under which the whole procession marched and played.[4] The East End loved Sir Marcus, and he returned its affection.

Later that evening, as waiters in black tails and starched dickeys served pheasant in his honor at London's Guildhall, Sir Marcus arranged for a less formal feast to be served to the public in the East End. This was smart political theater for the new Lord Mayor, a magnanimous gift to his neighborhood. The unorthodox route and generosity of his show conveyed a clear, calibrated message: he knew exactly from whence he came. Sir Marcus was not about to forget his roots.

After all, how could he? The offices of Shell were just a few blocks away from Middlesex Street, and Houndsditch was even closer.

Fresh into his post as Lord Mayor, Sir Marcus found that his organizing problem was time. His responsibilities to the city left precious little space on the schedule for conducting any actual business as chairman of Asiatic or Shell. Rather, his first weeks as Lord Mayor were packed with audiences with the King of Portugal at Buckingham Palace, dinner with the Royal Temple Yacht Club at the Hotel Cecil, public speeches, lunch parties, the dispensation of prizes, the selection of guest lists to fancy dress balls, return trips to Buckingham Palace, more prizes, and still more speeches. Even his cursory stopovers at Shell were unnervingly sparse. This fact is revealed in a diary he kept during his yearlong term. It would be one of his few personal documents that survived his death. By his own account, entire days passed in which Sir Marcus allocated only passing attention to Shell while the duties of Lord Mayor absorbed his main energy and focus.

By 1902, something fundamental had changed. Gone were the days when Samuel invested seventy-hour weeks in M. Samuel & Co. and micromanaged every conceivable aspect of Shell's business. As he transitioned to the gilded life of Lord Mayor, he still worked long hours, but few of them included the oil business. More alarming was the fact that he did not authorize anyone at Shell to stand in his place. This was the exact opposite approach from the one that Rockefeller created at Standard. Beginning around 1900, Rockefeller started to offload his day-to-day responsibilities at 26 Broadway onto managers like Archbold and Rogers. No longer a young man, he wished to spend more time on the golf course and less on the daily operations of the oil business. As Rockefeller began to decouple from Standard's tactical decision making, Archbold took over as head of the executive management team. Daily operations at 26 Broadway never lost their stride. In stark contrast, Sir Marcus loosed minions, rather than managers, upon Shell's offices at 16 Leadenhall. His army of clerks could file paperwork but do little else. Without Sir Marcus to manage Shell's direction, the company drifted out to sea.

It was for this reason that Sir Marcus's tenure as Lord Mayor marked the start of a significant turning point for Shell. Over the next three years, the company would suffer repeated setbacks and damaging reversals, some of them irreversible. The more surprising fact was that many of these calamities were self-inflicted. An astute executive would have put someone in place to captain the ship while he was away. Sadly for Shell, Sir Marcus was not that kind of individual.

Shady Lane saw the approaching danger. As a close friend of Sir Marcus's and a member of Shell's board from its early days, Lane could assess both the company and its chairman up close. After the Asiatic deal came into force, he began to closely scrutinize Shell's actual operations. What he found deeply distressed him. Shell's profits were turning into losses. Its market share was falling. Gigantic outlays of capital were wasted and shrugged off. This was not how a businesses survived, especially one that was constantly under Standard's threatening eye. Yet instead of jumping into action to save his floundering company, Sir Marcus was giving speeches and attending lunch parties. Lane foresaw a reckoning for Shell. Ever the agent of his own interests, he determined to be as far away from the company as possible when that day arrived.

On the evening of December 9, 1902, Sir Marcus was in the Mansion House, the official residence of the Lord Mayor, when he finally got around to reading a five-day-old letter from Lane. The note was his formal resignation from Shell's board. Only six months had transpired since the Asiatic deal, and at least at first, Sir Marcus did not believe it was a genuine resignation. He dismissed the idea and fired off a friendly message back to Lane. There was no need to resign. Old friends should stay. Shell would keep his counsel.

Lane's eventual answer proved devastating to Sir Marcus. In a damming indictment of Shell's management, he poured out his frustration with heartfelt honesty. "Unless some radical change be made in the policy and practice of the company, I could not afford to share the responsibility of the results," he wrote. "You are, and always have been, too much occupied to be the head of such a business." Lane saw what Sir Marcus could not: his old friend had once been fully devoted to Shell, but his attention had strayed. Shell needed to be managed as a global corporation, not as a hobby. "It is easy enough to have a quick perception of opportunities, and sound ideas of business in general," Lane continued, "but when a business is based on the continual sinking of vast capital, a profound study is necessary before entering upon it. . . . Business like this cannot be conducted by an occasional glance in one's spare time, or by some brilliant *coup* from time to time. It is steady, treadmill work." Sir Marcus was many things, but a treadmill runner was clearly not one of them. More alarming, Sir Marcus did not seem to be aware of the danger he faced from 26 Broadway. "The idea of creating widespread competition with the Standard . . . this is a policy that can be understood; but it is not one to be lightly entered upon," he cautioned. Unfortunately, that was how business was conducted at Shell. There was "no head or tail to its management. There seems only one idea: spend capital, create a great bluster, and trust to Providence. . . . It is just about as sensible as putting up a scarecrow in a wheat field to prevent the reaper's cutting."[5]

These were sobering, harsh, hurtful words. Unfortunately, Sir Marcus did not internalize them or alter course. Instead, he made copies of the letter and distributed them to the rest of Shell's board. Though this act, he showed himself to be overly emotional and unnecessarily defiant. He asked the remaining members of the board to read Lane's letter and to ratify his leadership of the company. The board duly endorsed Sir Marcus and rejected Lane's criticism. It was likely the worst of all possible outcomes. Not only had Lane's sage advice gone unheeded, but Lane felt betrayed by the airing of his private letter in public. The relationship between the two friends would never recover. Sir Marcus lost one of the best advisers he had ever known. All the while, the reaper sharpened her scythe. Lane's ominous forecast was about to come true.

At almost the same time that Lane was warning Sir Marcus about the "reaper's cutting," Shell's upstream supply of crude in Texas began to run dry. As oil production at Spindletop plunged, Guffey had none of its own oil to sell. In order to meet the minimum requirements of its contract with Sir Marcus, Guffey was forced to buy crude from other Texas producers at market prices. It was a terrible time to be caught short of oil. As output from Spindletop plummeted, the price of Texas petroleum rose from 5 to 35 and then 50 cents a barrel (around $13 today).[6] Locked into its long-term contract with Shell, the rising price of petroleum meant that Guffey lost money on every barrel it handed over to Sir Marcus. By the start of 1903, the "deal of the century" was becoming the blunder of the century—and there were still nineteen more years to go.

It was at this point that the Mellon family, the Pittsburgh bankers who had fronted the initial capital for Spindletop, stepped in to salvage the operation. It was "just about as bad a situation as I had ever seen," said William C. Mellon.[7] Acting on behalf of his uncles in Pittsburgh, Mellon's task was to find some way to stanch the financial hemorrhaging at Guffey Petroleum. The first order of business was to get Guffey out of the picture. The Mellons dutifully elevated the company's founder to the ceremonial post of "president" and pulled control of the company out from under him.[8] The next step was to incinerate the "deal of the century" with Sir Marcus. Breaking this gigantic contract was a rupture of all good commercial faith. Nevertheless, the Mellons felt that they had no other option. Losing money for the next two decades was madness. The deal with Sir Marcus had to go.

In the competitive business world that produced Sir Marcus, merchant traders could do many things. They could corner a market, exploit the difference in prices between two ports, and move "unmovable" regulations to make a profit. Kill or be killed, it was a highly permissible environment. One thing that merchants could never do—lest they singe their good names and reputations—was to break their contracts. The keeping of contracts was the basis of all commerce. When the Mellon family refused to honor Guffey's contract with Shell in 1903, they became the worst kind of commercial sinners. Rubbing salt in the wound was the importance of Texas oil for the future of Shell. Petroleum from Spindletop was crucial to Samuel's diversification strategy. Without it, Shell would be dependent on dockside oil purchases from the Rothschilds and whatever crude his company could suck from the soil of Borneo. Sir Marcus had no choice but to force the issue.[9] Shell's future depended on it.

On May 23, 1903, Shell served the Mellons with a notice of arbitration. This was a legal shot across the bow to the Pittsburgh bankers who were now running Guffey. Sir Marcus believed that he had a binding contract for oil and was determined to see that the Mellons honored it.[10] The Mellon family thought otherwise. In mid-July, they politely cabled a response to Shell's arbitration notice. They were ready to meet Sir Marcus in court if he wished. Alternatively, he could negotiate a settlement to the contract outside legal channels, like a gentleman. Luckily for Shell, William's uncle, Andrew Mellon, happened to be in England for the summer. Andrew Mellon was ready to talk.

Lane had always warned Sir Marcus about haste. In his desire to quickly ink the "deal of the century" with Guffey, Sir Marcus had glossed over the finer points of contract law. Lawyers in both America and the United Kingdom now had bad news for Shell. Whoever had drawn up the original deal had drafted a poor legal document. Amazingly, there were no terms that required arbitration in the event of a disagreement. All this crucial part of the contract said was that both parties agree to reach an agreement in the event of a dispute. It was legal gibberish. Sir Marcus needed to go into arbitration so he could control the forum and venue of the disagreement. The alternative was to march into a Texas court, where local biases and opinions made a jury decision about damages unpredictable. The lawyers for the Mellons had no doubt come to the same conclusion. They wanted a Texas jury of friends, supporters, and well-connected locals to decide the matter. Shell's vaguely drafted arbitration clause guaranteed them a crucial advantage.

The challenge for Sir Marcus was therefore in pressing his claim. Even if he could not force arbitration, he could still appear in a U.S. court, present the terms of his deal to buy oil at a set price for twenty-one years, offer proof that the Mellons had breached the agreement, and ask for damages in the amount of the harm suffered. Sir Marcus was ready to uphold his end of a bargain. The Mellons were not. Here was an open-and-shut breach-of-contract case. That was the easy part. Squeezing damages out of the Mellons was where things would get tricky. Since there was no telling how much—if any—money a *Texas* jury would award *British* Shell, the Mellons had made a cold-blooded calculation: no matter what Sir Marcus did, it was going to be much cheaper to breach the contract than honor it.

The Echo of Applause

Boxed into a tight legal corner, Sir Marcus opted to convene a summit with Andrew Mellon instead of gambling on a Texas jury. The first of these pivotal meetings commenced at the Mote on August 18, 1903. The stakes for both men could not have been higher. If Mellon kept to the letter of Guffey's contract, selling oil to Shell would bleed him dry. Without any oil from Texas, Sir Marcus's diversification strategy would become an expensive flop. Since Shell had no meaningful recourse, however, Mellon held all the cards.

When Mellon arrived at the Mote for the opening of his negotiations with Sir Marcus, the American banker comported himself as the perfect gentlemen. He graciously complimented the grounds of the estate, offered cordial conversation to Sir Marcus—and abjectly refused to budge on the contract. It was the most polite kind of hardball. Lacking a resolution on the first day, the summit spilled over into the next—this time back in London. Throughout these discussions with Sir Marcus, the perfectly polished American banker was abjectly unmovable. The financial hemorrhaging of the Guffey contract had left him with no alternative. The "deal of the century" had to die. It was far better for all sides to put that unfortunate document behind them.

From his side of the negotiation, Sir Marcus could find no openings or leverage. According to the best legal advice that money could buy, Shell's odds of winning damages through a court battle were low. Both Mellon and Sir Marcus knew this. The best offer that Mellon was willing to provide was a vague promise about possibly, maybe, delivering future volumes of oil to Shell. If this ever occurred, Shell would clearly have to pay more than 25 cents a barrel. It was the only compromise Sir Marcus would get. Just as Lane had warned, his strategy to "spend capital, create a great bluster, and trust to Providence" in Texas had failed in a spectacular fashion. Providence did not take his side on this occasion; nor did it mark the end of Shell's woes. In fact, they were just beginning. While Sir Marcus focused his attention on Texas, an even greater, more terrifying setback was burrowing its way to the surface in the Far East.

At the end of Sir Marcus's whirlwind year as Lord Mayor in September 1903, British foreign secretary Lord Lansdowne gingerly made a request of Shell's chairman. According to Lord Lansdowne, the Japanese government seemed to be making suspicious preparations in the Orient. It looked like Japan could be readying itself for a war against Russia. If so, Japan had not informed Great Britain of any such plans. The terms of the Anglo-Japanese Alliance expressly forbade such secrecy. If Tokyo was indeed preparing for war, it had to inform London. Lord Lansdowne wondered if perhaps Sir Marcus could help run this delicate issue to ground. Since the Lord Mayor was one of the best-informed men in London when it came to Japanese affairs, the foreign secretary asked Sir Marcus to provide additional information on Tokyo's intentions. If anyone could scare up some intelligence, it was the Lord Mayor. Naturally, Sir Marcus agreed to help. He tossed the question to a personal friend, the Japanese ambassador in London. The answer, delivered by letter, was *almost* assuring.

"I can almost assure you," wrote the ambassador, "that Japan will not aggressively go to war."[11] Almost? It was a curious choice of words. Moreover, had a country ever peacefully gone to war? Of course, the veil of diplomacy from the Japanese ambassador hid the actual course of events. Indeed, the Japanese Empire did plan to go to war with Russia. It also planned to aggressively strike in a surprise attack. The unexpected consequences of that conflict would endanger the very survival of Shell. When that occurred, Standard would be waiting.

CHAPTER 13

Reversals of Fortune

Inside the offices of 26 Broadway, there were many secrets. The perpetually guarded Rockefeller had fortified Standard with hidden facts ever since the earliest days of the company. Standard trusted in secrecy the way a besieged city trusted in its walls. They protected the American monopoly from three decades of attack by would-be competitors, from aggressive state legislative committees, and most especially, from meddlesome reporters. It was for this reason that one clandestine meeting in January 1902 was hard to comprehend. At long last, a journalist had breached Standard's protective bulwarks.

The unlikely incursion occurred inside the office of Hell Hound Henry Rogers, the second most powerful director at Standard. In the executive hierarchy of 26 Broadway, only John Archbold, Rockefeller's handpicked successor, outranked Rogers. If anyone knew where the corporate bodies were buried at Standard, it was Rogers. That was why his meeting with a rising star in American mass media named Ida M. Tarbell was so surprising. Rogers should have seen Tarbell as an enemy. At their very first meeting that January, he instead offered her unprecedented access to Standard's hidden history, its archives and business practices. True to form, he insisted that she keep their interactions secret.

It is difficult to pinpoint the precise reason for Rogers's open and remarkably candid revelations to Tarbell. Perhaps he felt slighted when Rockefeller promoted Archbold to the top position at Standard. Perhaps Tarbell flattered him, or he was intrigued by her wit. Maybe he just had a soft spot for talented underdogs. After all, it was Rogers who had personally financed Helen Keller's education, allowing her to become the first deaf blind person to earn a college degree. And it was Rogers who had saved Mark Twain from the poorhouse, when the first man of American letters could no longer keep his creditors at bay. A more compelling reason for Rogers was less high-minded: he wanted Tarbell to cleanse his reputation.[1] After word had broken that she was writing a history of Standard Oil, Rogers had asked Twain to broker an introduction. He had no clue as to the fury that Tarbell, a daughter of the Pennsylvania oil boom, harbored for Standard.

When Tarbell was thirteen years old, her father, Frank Tarbell, transplanted his entire family to the oil boomtown of Titusville, Pennsylvania. Home to the very first oil well in America, it was situated close by a legendary place called Pithole. Today the settlement of Pithole has disappeared, but its name stands as a warning to the brutal cycle of wealth creation and destruction caused by crude. It was in Pithole that petroleum flowed in such quantities that for a brief, prosperous moment in 1865, the town accounted for two-thirds of Pennsylvania's oil production. Previously worthless homesteads around Pithole were suddenly selling for $2 million ($30 million today).[2] As venture capital flowed into Pithole, fifteen thousand people followed, all looking to cash in on the petroleum bonanza. Counted among them was Frank Tarbell. Leaving Titusville for the town, Ida's father had hopes of making a fortune building wooden tanks for crude. His dream would end when the oil suddenly gave out.

After twelve miraculous months, Pithole's wells ran dry. The town's population was the first thing to collapse. The value of the local real estate market followed in lockstep. As the drillers, oilmen, and saloon-keepers of Pithole pulled up their stakes, Frank Tarbell had to improvise a retreat. He took advantage of the rock-bottom real estate market and purchased the three-story Bonta House, the finest hotel on the outskirts of Pithole, for $600 ($9,000 today). Afterward he systematically dismantled every timber, baseboard, and doorknob of the structure and transported it, along with his family, back to Titusville.[3] So much for Pithole.

It would be in Titusville where Ida grew up surrounded by the planks of the Bonta House hotel. As a child of the petroleum boom, she watched her teachers cancel class so they could speculate in the local oil exchange. She witnessed the outrage that erupted when Rockefeller's schemes to corner the refining sector or arrange kickbacks with the railroads leaked out. And she watched helplessly as her father struggled to resist Rockefeller's chokehold on the oil regions. "I used to see pointed out in the streets of Titusville men who had 'gone over to the Standard,'" Tarbell remembered in later years. "My father was an independent oil refiner, competing with the Standard, and not very successful in the contest."[4] Rockefeller did more than win against Ida's father. He broke him.

The sublime rationality of Rockefeller's ledger had a drawback. It disfigured the way he saw men like Frank Tarbell. Every dollar that independent refiners like Tarbell made without Rockefeller was a defeat. It created a ghost on Standard's balance sheet, since that revenue went into other pockets and not into the little ledger book in Rockefeller's pocket. Throughout his life, Rockefeller projected this grievance outward. He talked about "ruinous competition" as if it were a cataclysmic disaster. In one sense, this was true. Seen from Rockefeller's lofty position, the independents were enemies of the melodious,

rational "harmony" that redirected the wealth of the global oil industry to his company. Viewed from young Ida's lower position, the
struggle to resist Rockefeller looked very different. Her father appeared as a courageous, resourceful man who was ground down by the
unceasing attack from Standard. There was little that she could do to
help. Her only course was to watch, and listen, and memorize the
name of the man who was responsible for her father's defeat.

While Frank Tarbell waged his ultimately futile resistance against
Standard, Ida directed the bulk of her energy into learning. Getting
an education was one of the few respectable ways that a woman in the
late nineteenth century could rise on her own. By 1880 Ida achieved
two notable distinctions. She attained a bachelor's degree from Al-
legheny College, and she did so as the only woman in her graduating
class. Following a stint as a teacher and writer, she subsequently
packed her bags for a voyage across the Atlantic to Paris. There she
would continue her education at the Sorbonne.

After Tarbell arrived in Paris in 1891, she made the acquaintance of
an energetic magazine man named Sam McClure. Sporting an overgrown mustache and an incurable preference for floppy bow ties,
McClure was adept at spotting talent. The driven, highly intelligent
Tarbell immediately impressed him. He wasted little time in offering
her a job at his newly established magazine, a publication he modestly
called *McClure's*. The pairing of Tarbell's pen and McClure's magazine
would make history.

Hiring Tarbell proved to be a masterstroke for McClure. She wrote
in a crisp and precise style that offered a refreshing change from the
lumbering prose of her contemporaries. More than a mastery of
words, however, she had a perceptive eye for the dimensions of human greatness and weakness that was a defining trait of her writing.
At *McClure's*, her popular biographies of the French revolutionary

Madame Roland, and other notable figures such as Napoleon Bonaparte and Abraham Lincoln, all bore the hallmarks of her unique ability. During her time at *McClure's*, she had not forgotten about Rockefeller or what he had done to her father. Indeed, her greatest story was still unwritten. And so at the age of forty-five, her readership and influence at their peak, the daughter of Oildorado resolved to unpack the savage story of Standard Oil.

"Don't do it, Ida," Frank Tarbell said after hearing of his daughter's plan. "They will ruin the magazine."[5] Even in his old age, he still feared the reach of Rockefeller's power and the havoc he could wreak on his daughter's career. Ida was undaunted. Her determination to uncover the facts behind Standard extended all the way to its cryptic founder: John D. Rockefeller, America's richest man.

On the trail of Rockefeller, Tarbell and a gumshoe researcher named John M. Siddall quickly found themselves at a loss. The founder of Standard had scrubbed, buried, or erased nearly every fact that might be used against him. "I tell you this John D. Rockefeller is the strangest, most silent, most mysterious, and most interesting figure in America," Siddall wrote to her as they considered how thoroughly their quarry had covered his tracks.[6] Beyond superficial stories in the newspapers and antimonopolist screeds by his critics, little hard evidence surfaced on which to base an accurate biographical portrait.

Crisscrossing the country, Siddall tried to discover the man behind the legend by speaking with the people who knew him best. He found few who really knew Rockefeller, and none who would offer up anything especially insightful. Unlike Napoleon or Lincoln, who were already dead by the time Tarbell got around to them, Rockefeller was still very much alive. He had no desire to be scrutinized by the likes of Tarbell or anyone else. "This brooding, cautious, secretive man," as she called him, guarded his privacy as closely as Standard guarded its secrets. What little information she had turned up was circumstantial, speculative, or thin.

At this vexing stage in her investigation, a gentle inquiry arrived at the magazine's offices from Mark Twain. He wanted to know who at *McClure's* was snooping into the history of Standard. McClure ran breathlessly into Tarbell's office with the news. Mark Twain would provide an introduction to Henry Rogers. Was she interested in a meeting? The frustrated sleuth was absolutely interested. It was in this way that Tarbell quietly slipped into Rockefeller's corporate fortress.

Venturing through the mausoleum-like entrance of 26 Broadway, Tarbell did not know exactly what to expect from Rogers. When she finally stepped into his office, she was instantly impressed by the "handsomest most distinguished figure on Wall Street." His white mustache immediately caught her attention. "I remember thinking as I was trying to get my bearings, now I understand why Mark Twain likes him so much." The bond between Tarbell and Rogers was instant. Owing to their shared history in Pennsylvania's oil regions, the sharp journalist and the outgoing executive had a great deal in common. Surprisingly, he actually knew her father from the early days of Titusville. "Tarbell's Tank Shops!" he said with a flash of recognition. He speculated that he might just have seen a very young Ida Tarbell hunting for flowers along the banks of Oil Creek. The little girl had grown up.

Over the next two hours, Tarbell and Rogers engaged in a bizarre dance. She needed information but wanted to maintain the integrity of her investigation. He wanted to know what kind of story she was going to tell, and to possibly spin parts of it in his favor. As she would later surmise, he was particularly interested in how she might portray his old criminal indictment for a conspiracy to blow up a refinery in Buffalo. At the time, a grand jury investigation into the plot had garnered nationwide attention. And although he had eventually walked away without a conviction, he was eager for Tarbell to report his version of events.[7] As the two matched wits in his office, each took the measure of the other, but it was Rogers who pulled back the veil. In a seemingly magnanimous flourish, Hell Hound Rogers promised to provide Tarbell with "documents, figures, justifications, explanations, interpretations," anything and everything that would expand her understanding of Standard.[8] By the time the meeting was over, she had her source.

Through the winter, spring, and summer of 1902, Tarbell met clandestinely with Rogers at his home as well as at his office. During these interactions, he opened the archives of Standard to her journalistic eye.[9] Sometimes he spoke freely with her. At other times, he was oblique or even hostile. If he was hoping to gain an advantage from their meetings, he woefully misjudged the sharp mind of Ida Tarbell. The scale of the revelations that she acquired from him was without precedent. Never before had anyone, least of all a journalist, been granted such sweeping insight into the inner workings of Standard.

Unsatisfied with one source, Tarbell wanted more. The question was, who else would talk with her? John Archbold was out of the question. As Rockefeller's successor, he was too much of a company man to assist her. "I would never get the straight goods from Archbold," she believed.[10] By contrast, Henry Flagler, the closest approximation of a friend that Rockefeller had ever known, might be willing to give her something useful.

Thanks to Rogers, Tarbell arranged to sit down with Flagler. Their eventual meeting was the opposite experience of her time with Rogers. Far from being open about his activities at Standard, or for that matter about Rockefeller, he was wary, curt, and quiet. She asked her questions. He deftly evaded them. Their back-and-forth seemed futile until at long last his caution briefly slipped. "He would do me out of a dollar today, if he could," Flagler said of Rockefeller. Tarbell pressed on this opening, but the aging man of "vim and push" whom Rockefeller had known since his earliest days in Cleveland clammed up. As the interview came to a close, Flagler offered her one intriguing postscript about Rockefeller. "How often the reputation of a man in his lifetime differs from his real character," Flagler said. "Take for example the greatest character in our history. How different was our Lord and Savior regarded when he was alive from what we now know him to be."[11] John D. Rockefeller and Jesus Christ. In the mind of Flagler, the comparison was perfectly natural and appropriate.

By November 1902, eleven months after her initial meeting with Rogers, the first part of Tarbell's "History of the Standard Oil Company" was ready for the public. What she had initially envisioned as a four-part exposé on Rockefeller and Standard expanded into an all-encompassing nineteen-part series. As her series unfolded over the next two years, each new edition of *McClure's* exploded with fresh revelations about America's dreaded oil monopoly. If readers missed any part, they could eventually purchase the two-volume cloth-bound book set that included the entirety of Tarbell's reporting. In *McClure's*, Tarbell laid bare Standard's secret contracts, its nefarious kickback schemes, Rockefeller's "unholy alliance" between oil refiners and producers, and the creation of the Standard monopoly itself. This last item especially rankled 26 Broadway, which officially denied the very existence of such a monopoly.[12] After each new salvo, Tarbell fired off another with the ferocity and confidence of fact.

As readers eagerly read the disclosures in *McClure's*, Tarbell's reporting sparked a national sensation. Never before had anyone laid Standard so bare. "Her pen has made the name of Miss. Ida M. Tarbell a familiar household word throughout the land," wrote one reviewer.

Another called her work "an amazing account of petty persecution." It was, in the view of the modern oil historian Daniel Yergin, "the final revenge of the oil regions against their conquerors."[13] It was also the final severance of Tarbell's friendship with Rogers.

When the initial segments of the series hit newsstands, Rogers was supportive. It helped that Tarbell came down on his side of events in the case of the Buffalo refinery plot. She found no proof of his guilt in that specific intrigue. But she did not stop at that single conspiracy. As her series unfolded in full, she placed Rogers at the top of an even larger conspiracy to suppress all forms of competition in the American oil industry. Her broadsides against Standard were devastating; and in some cases, they specifically targeted Rogers. Never again would Hell Hound Rogers speak to Tarbell. For her part, she maintained a lifelong respect for him. In her estimation, he would always be "as fine a pirate as ever flew his flag in Wall Street."[14]

In the last installment of the series, Tarbell rendered her judgment on Rockefeller. She had spent years following his trail, dissecting his actions down to the smallest detail. The man she discovered in the process was neither a cartoonish monster nor a misguided do-gooder who had lost his way. Rather, he was a straight-up cheater. He was a man who "has systematically played with loaded dice, and it is doubtful if there has been a time since 1872 when he has run a race with a competitor and started fair." Swindler though Rockefeller was, Tarbell also saw him as a calculating strategist. Like a commanding general, he "views from a balloon the whole great field and sees how, this point taken, that must fall, this hill reached, that fort is commanded. And nothing was too small, not the corner grocery in Browntown, the refining still on Oil Creek, and the shortest private pipeline, for little things grow."[15]

Inside 26 Broadway, Tarbell's little exposé in *McClure's* had grown into a gigantic public relations disaster. The company's first instinct was to go on the offensive against her. Privately, Rockefeller seethed over her "poisonous twaddle."[16] But when asked what he wanted to say about her, he shot back: not a single word. Even if Rockefeller wished to publicly ignore Tarbell, Standard could not dismiss the damage she had caused. Her pen, it turned out, sparked a firestorm in Washington.

For years, domestic opposition to monopolies like Standard had been collecting in the American body politic like toxins in the liver. During the late 1880s, the "Ohio Icicle," John Sherman, led an unprecedented campaign against corporate combinations such as Standard from inside Congress. "The popular mind is agitated with problems that may disturb social order," he wrote, "and among them all, none is more threatening than the concentration of capital into vast combinations." At least initially, the federal government was wary of challenging Standard. Sherman pushed hard to change that fact. Ever so slowly, through his impassioned speeches, and through the scrupulous investigations of congressional committees, his assault on monopolies coalesced into a sweeping piece of legislation known today as the Sherman Antitrust Act.[17]

As a political force, Sherman's march to break monopolies of all sorts would prove unstoppable. When his antitrust law came before Congress in 1890, it passed unanimously in the House and encountered only a single vote of opposition in the Senate. Sherman had mustered a powerful countercharge to Rockefeller's war on competition. The antitrust act not only made Standard's basic business model illegal, it empowered the U.S. government to dismantle monopolies piece by piece. Worse yet for Standard, trustbusting was gaining even more traction at the state level. By the time President Benjamin Harrison signed Sherman's act into law on July 2, 1890, governors in

Kansas, Maine, Michigan, Missouri, Nebraska, North Carolina, Ohio, and Texas had already signed their own state-level prohibitions against monopolies.[18] Indeed, it was to be at the state level, not the federal, where the judicial hammer first fell.

In a historic decision on March 2, 1892, the Supreme Court of Ohio found against Standard in an antitrust action brought by the state's attorney general. The legal ruling excoriated Standard and voided Rockefeller's corporate trust, in part, because it represented an illegal monopoly. In practical terms, the decision meant that Standard's days as a monopoly were coming to an end—or so it seemed. Immediately after the decision S.C.T. Dodd, one of Standard's lawyers, told reporters that the verdict "will only give us some trouble."[19] This was no mere act of courthouse bravado. The trustbusters were trying to mount an attack, but Standard was already miles ahead of the Ohio Supreme Court, the U.S. Congress, and the unprecedented restrictions of the Sherman Antitrust Act. As a result of the Ohio ruling, Standard kept to the letter of the state's antitrust law while masterfully circumventing its intent. To accomplish this feat, Rockefeller and his fellow shareholders gathered in New York to formally dissolve their gigantic corporate trust on March 21, 1892. The bold act created sixty-four orphaned companies, each one representing a piece of the old Standard empire. Then came the masterstroke. The orphans immediately found homes in the waiting arms of twenty new companies, all of which were owned by shareholders of the now-disbanded trust. Rockefeller and his directors immediately appointed themselves as managers of these new companies, and—like a vanishing act on the gallows—Standard escaped its own court-ordered execution.[20] The trust was gone. Standard's monopoly continued.

On account of Rockefeller's corporate restructuring, the blow from the Ohio Supreme Court was not a fatal one. The anaconda of Standard merely shed its skin. What emerged was a fearsome, twenty-headed hydra. The formal incorporation of Standard's new firms replaced the old informal network of scattered companies and subsidiaries. One benefit of the change was a more efficient organization, since each component of Standard was now responsible for a specific function of the old trust. Standard of New Jersey, for example, positioned at the center of the operation, would oversee the U.S. market. Standard of New York would take control of international business. Additional entities, such as Standard of Illinois and Standard of Indiana, assumed similar roles on down the line.

Then came Ida Tarbell.

By the time *McClure's* ran the first part of her series in 1902, Standard's corporate reorganization appeared to have outfoxed the Supreme Court of Ohio and the federal government's Sherman Antitrust Act. The revelations that she scrawled over the pages of *McClure's* were more than an airing of Standard's dirty tricks and soiled laundry. The entire country suddenly discovered that Rockefeller and his directors were flouting America's legal system. Unless someone brought Standard to task, 26 Broadway risked becoming a law unto itself.

Immediately following the conclusion of Tarbell's series in November 1904, President Theodore Roosevelt began to consider a punitive federal expedition against Rockefeller's oil giant. Roosevelt had already tussled with the meatpacking and the railroad trusts. His next target was going to be the petroleum industry—and Rockefeller's monopoly in particular. While Roosevelt's lasting reputation as a trust-buster would be won, in large part, thanks to this attack on Standard, his own views on trusts were not black and white. During his first term in office, he had actually tried to take the middle ground on monopolies. He vacillated between impulses to regulate America's industrial giants and a desire to dismantle them entirely. As Tarbell whipped up opposition to Rockefeller's monopoly on the pages of *McClure's*, the option of simply regulating Standard became less attractive. It was politically advantageous for Roosevelt to make himself a public opponent of Rockefeller's. Tarbell had already done most of the legwork. The public wanted action. Adding Rockefeller to his collection of vanquished monopolists would score Roosevelt another political victory and demonstrate that all Americans could still expect a "square deal" in the United States. Big business did not get to make the rules in America. Government did that job. And so, before the aura faded from the Republican election victory in 1904, Roosevelt launched a full-scale federal investigation into Standard. Then as now, government did not do anything without formally investigating it first.

As 1904 drew to its conclusion, Standard closed the books on a very bad year. The trials and tribulations of Rockefeller's monopoly were many and growing. Yet even while 26 Broadway prepared to fend off the federal investigation, Standard was not entirely without hope. Standard's balance sheet was still in fine shape. Company dividends were at an all-time high. The threat from the White House was distant. The dangers to Standard's foreign rivals from war and revolution were drawing closer. It was time to celebrate. Rockefeller might have been a teetotaler, but on Broadway, the last hours of the year meant two things: getting fantastically snozzled and making one hell of a racket.

In the final hours of December 31, 1904, far below the executive suites of 26 Broadway, New York's most famous avenue descended into a cacophony of booze, bells, and bedlam. Every New Year's Eve for as long as anyone in Manhattan could remember, New Yorkers gathered at the steps of nearby Trinity Church to ring in the New Year. The countdown to 1905 played to form. The celebration began, as it always did, with a concert from the bells of Trinity's spire. That year the arrangement started with a rendition of "Evening Bells." Not that anyone in the assembled mob of celebrants could hear the bells. Up Broadway and down Wall Street, drunken revelers drowned out the music with horns: tin horns, brass horns, silver horns, big horns, and little horns—tens of thousands of horns, each one blowing with abandon. "The Trinity chimes haven't a chance," reported one witness. The police kept their distance from the intoxicated chaos, allowing the partiers to honk and wobble as they wished. There was only one rule on Broadway that night: "It matters not how hard you blow your horn so long as you don't knock the other fellow over the head with it."[21]

As with all previous New Year's Eve celebrations on Broadway, the mass of revelers and horns invariably spilled onto the avenue. People clogged the lanes from the park at Bowling Green, at the base of Standard's headquarters, all the way to Canal Street. New Year's Eve 1905, however, presented the drunken horn blowers with something new. They no longer owned the pavement. Passing caravans of automobiles now forced the revelers to the edges of the street. The vehicles paraded up one side of Broadway and rumbled down the other "with big touring cars clearing the way like snowplows in a blizzard."[22]

High above the clang of cars, horns, and drunks on Broadway, the bells of Trinity Church sounded their finale with a rendition of the song "Home, Sweet Home." Everyone on the street would have known the words by heart.

Mid pleasures and palaces though we may roam . . .

The bells chimed 1904 into oblivion,

Splendor dazzles in vain.[23]

CHAPTER 14

The Black City in Red

Baku had reached a precipice. After more than three decades of pumping oil from the sand of the Caspian, Russia's Black City was soaked in crude, new money, and ethnic tension. It was a place where Persian ruins, dazzling palaces, impoverished hovels, ethnic grievances, and the noxious "all-pervading smells" of petroleum mingled seamlessly along the Caspian coast.[1] Runoff from the badlands of oil had turned Baku's harbor and its surrounding waters an inky black. Some parts of the city center were little better. When the viceroy of India, George Curzon, visited the Black City at the turn of the century, he found a settlement of "chimneys and cisterns and refineries, with its acres of rails outside the station covered with tank cars, its grimy, naphtha-besprinkled streets, its sky-high telegraph poles and rattling tram cars."[2] What Lord Curzon did not know, when he looked upon this rattling, industrial mess, was that the Black City teetered on the edge of an abyss.

Across Russia's cities and vast frontiers, labor leaders and communist firebrands agitated against the tsar's autocratic rule. Years of stagnation and mismanagement had made the empire of Nicholas II a combustible pyre of inequality and excess. In the Romanov capital of St. Petersburg, Nicholas and his family distracted themselves with lavish costume balls as efficient servants "glided noiselessly" over the soft, plush carpets of the imperial residence.[3] Encasing Nicholas's twilight city of splendor was an inverted world of metalworking plants and low-wage factories. The industrial complex around St. Petersburg burned imported coal from Cardiff, Wales, and employed landless peasants who could no longer survive in their fields. The hours in these mechanized workplaces were hard and never-ending. "I did not live, I only worked," recalled one communist revolutionary of his time in the Kronstadt torpedo works.[4] The armaments from Kronstadt would soon be put to use. On the other side of the world from St. Petersburg, the rising power of Japan was steadily encroaching on the Korean Peninsula—an area that was nominally in Russia's imperial sphere. Japan wanted its own area of influence in the Far East. Thanks to the might of its modern navy and cutting-edge military equipment from the West, Japan intended to carve out that space from Russia.

At the start of 1904, shortly after Sir Marcus made his back-channel inquiries with the Japanese ambassador in London, rumors swirled that diplomatic talks between Russia and Japan were breaking down over the territorial status of Manchuria (today part of China) and northern Korea. Russia controlled these lands, and Japan wanted part of them. As offers and counteroffers sailed between St. Petersburg and Tokyo, statesmen postured and Japanese admirals readied their fleet. Gradually, the standoff approached a breaking point. On February 8, 1904, it broke without warning.

In a surprise attack, the Japanese military launched itself against Russia's Pacific forces, catching the tsar's units off guard. The Imperial Japanese Navy bombarded the Russian fleet at Port Arthur (today known as the Port of Lüshun). Ground troops landed farther up the Korean Peninsula, near Inchon. The Russo-Japanese War had begun. The conflict would end badly for the tsar.

The Black City in Red

Viewed from Nicholas's imperial offices in St. Petersburg, the war in the Pacific produced one disaster after another. Many of Russia's heaviest fighting ships in the Far East were damaged or sunk in early engagements with the Japanese navy. Over the course of the next year, the whole fleet at Port Arthur would be surrounded on land and sea.[5] As Japanese artillery rained down onto the port that December, still worse news erupted closer to home: the oil workers of Baku had walked off the job. This pivotal event signaled the opening of the tumultuous Russian Revolution of 1905.[6] It would cast Baku over the edge of its precipice.

Future Soviet history books would credit the mastermind behind this historic labor strike, the catalyst for the 1905 revolution, as Iosif Vissarionovich Dzhugashvili. He is better known today as Joseph Stalin. Under Stalin's later reign of terror, Soviet scholars erased and rewrote the past with such zeal, they transformed the recording of history into a dark art. Reimagined by Soviet propagandists, Stalin— the "Man of Steel"—became a visionary leader who inspired the workers of Baku to rise up against their capitalist oppressors.[7] Though thrilling stuff to imagine, the Soviets had created a completely false account of the event.

The real-life Stalin was not a rabble-rouser. In 1904 he was a quiet behind-the-scenes political organizer with limited experience, less charm, and no widespread following among the working class of Baku. In fact, young Stalin cut such a forgettable profile during the run-up to the revolution, his fellow travelers in Baku's communist underground hardly noticed him.[8] The memoir of one revolutionary that was not rewritten for propaganda purposes mentions "the still quite young Stalin" only once and then ignores him.[9]

The lack of attention paid to young Stalin was no surprise. Outshining him in the early political underground of Baku was a charismatic demagogue named Ilya Shendrikov. While Stalin's fellow Bolshevik communists obsessed over the esoteric nuances of Marxist philosophy, Shendrikov focused on winning practical labor concessions from the oil companies around the Black City. Benefits like a nine-hour workday, higher pay, and sick leave for oil workers were less ambitious than the Bolsheviks' fantasies of world revolution, but the right to stay home with the flu was more achievable. The practical ideas that Shendrikov spread around Baku found willing listeners among the Black City's oil workers. They began to rally around him in large numbers. His support grew so large by the end of 1904 that Stalin and his Bolsheviks were forced to grudgingly throw their support behind him.[10] Failing to do so would have put them at risk of irrelevance. Further, the Bolsheviks knew that if Shendrikov succeeded, they could always claim to have been part of his effort from the start.

On December 13, 1904, Shendrikov put his ambitious plan into action. Under his banner, Baku's oil workers walked off the job en masse. Never before had the Russian petroleum industry experienced such a widespread, coordinated action by its workers. Soon the oil industry was joined by others. Workers on a local railway organized their own strike.[11] By January, they were followed by railroad men in the distant Russian city of Saratov. Afterward, railroad car manufacturers as far away as St. Petersburg joined the effort.

As the number of labor strikes grew, so too did the size of public protests. When panicked guards outside the Winter Palace in St. Petersburg shot at a crowd of demonstrators in January 1905, even bigger strikes and rallies followed. The crack of tsarist rifles did not suppress the protests but instead incited larger ones. Across Poland, Finland, and the Baltic States, down through the Caucasus, and far east to Siberia, demonstrations proliferated. Soon they encompassed wider portions of tsarist society, including aggrieved middle-class professionals, students, and peasants. Their demands were also expanding, from ambitious labor reforms to the toppling of the tsarist autocracy itself.[12] Russian society was now in full revolt. The tsar's losses in the East may have primed the revolution, but the oil workers of Baku had slammed the plunger.

Down in the Caspian, the Black City seethed. During three days in February 1905, simmering distrust between Christian Armenians and Muslim Tatars (Azeris) erupted into widespread ethnic violence. Killings by one group spawned reprisals from the other, which seeded counterreprisals and fed an escalating cycle of assassinations, stabbings, and savagery. As blood begat blood, the brutality intensified. Roving bands of Tatars targeted the homes of Baku's wealthy Armenians, many of whom were successful oilmen. Their palaces became bunkers. The mobs turned them into death traps. Entire families perished together.[13]

One Armenian who refused to surrender to the mob was M. Adamoff, the manager of Baku's Naphtha Refining Works. Armed with a Winchester repeating rifle, Adamoff took up a firing position on his balcony and burnished his reputation as one of the best marksmen in the city. Inside his home on Arnianskia Street, thirty-nine members of his family had taken refuge. As waves of attackers tested the oilman's aim, the street around his house became a battleground.

During the first two days of the assault, Adamoff and his seventeen-year-old son kept the mob at bay. On the third day, the assailants sallied out in large numbers. They rushed Adamoff's house, smashed open the front door, and set his entryway ablaze with straw and kerosene. As flames climbed the exterior of his home, a bullet struck Adamoff in the head. The oilman vanished from his balcony, only to return minutes later with a bandaged skull and "aim that was not less deadly than at the start of the terrible siege." More bullets issued from the

Winchester. More attackers fell in the street. Finally, Adamoff's teenage son was shot by one of the attackers. The body of the youth tumbled over the edge of the balcony. Adamoff was next to be hit: this time a bullet struck him in the shoulder. After a pause, he answered the injury with another salvo of gunfire. The defense was growing desperate. His son dead, his home burning, Adamoff continued to fight, but his wounds were taking their toll. Sadly, the final moments of Adamoff were violent ones. "His movements becoming slow, the Tatars became more aggressive, and he finally received a fatal wound, which laid him low on the balcony," reported one chronicler of the carnage.[14]

After three days, the mob had at last silenced Adamoff and his Winchester. What came next was a deadly tragedy. All members of the Adamoff family perished once the assembled mob stormed their home, some by fire, others by gunshot. A few died in the basement, but most of the family was killed in the street.

Around Baku, ethnic strife continued for another day. The imposition of martial law on the fifth day following the outbreak of violence brought a merciful end to the killing. The residents of the Black City emerged from their hiding places to count the dead. The final tally totaled 126 Tatars and 218 Armenians, including Adamoff and his entire family.[15] Thanks to the spread of worldwide telegraph communication, the story of Adamoff's last stand at Baku raced around the globe in newspaper dispatches. For international readers, the death of the oilman became a vivid icon of the "Russian Butcheries" that winter in the Caspian. A wave of eulogies memorialized Adamoff. "By his death he left a name that should live in Caucasian history," wrote a British writer, adding that his name "should be honored by every friend of that ancient and oppressed nation—Armenia." Another simply stated, "He had in him the stuff of which heroes are made."[16]

Across the Caucasus, those who survived the fratricide grappled to understand it. At a mosque in Ganja, two hundred miles west of Baku, the Muslim intellectual Ahmad bay Aghaoghli lectured, "Even wild animals do not devour their own kind." For Aghaoghli, the cycle of killings and reprisals was all the more heartbreaking since "Muslims and Armenians had for centuries lived in peace before the coming of the Russians."[17] Unfortunately for Baku, the shattering of that tranquillity was just beginning.

Throughout the remainder of 1905, mayhem roiled the Romanov empire in violent spasms. That May the tsar suffered a new defeat when Japanese warships destroyed his Baltic Fleet off the coast of Korea. The Russian flotilla had sailed for seven months to reach the Orient; Japanese gunners annihilated the tsar's outdated warships in less than nineteen hours.[18] Closer to home, anti-Semitic pogroms erupted in Odessa; the crew of the Russian battleship *Potemkin* mutinied on the Black Sea; and in Baku, a new round of labor unrest prompted the Black City's dockworkers, typographers, porters, textile workers, and additional parts of its petroleum industry to walk off the job. By late summer, Russia's oil capital had ground to a standstill. Just as in February, conditions were set for a return of ethnic violence.[19] Only now the whole city would burn.

Hostilities between ethnic Tatars and Armenians burst forth in late August and early September 1905. Intending to quell the latest outbreak of violence, local tsarist officials dispatched armed Cossacks to suppress riots in Baku's outlying settlements. Rather than settling matters, the introduction of Cossacks merely expanded the existing two-way ethnic conflict between Tatars and Armenians into a three-way fight between Tatars, Cossacks, and Armenians. As Tatars gained the upper hand on Baku's outskirts, fleeing groups of Cossacks and Armenians began to stream back into the city center. That was when the sky around the Caspian began to glow.

When night fell on the evening of Sunday, September 3, the first visible signs of crisis could be seen from inside the Black City itself. Out on the horizon, the oil fields of the Nobel brothers were burning. The distant inferno was so large that it cast the entire night sky in a bizarre ambient light. Panic raced through the oil capital. The next morning most residents of Baku swarmed the train station as "the flight from the city soon became general."[20] All those who remained in the Black City after the sun set on Monday were treated to a dreadful, breathtaking sight. On Baku's immediate outskirts, an uncontrolled inferno feasted on the great oil refinery of the Bibi-Heybat field. This was the site of the spectacular 1886 gusher that had rained raw crude onto the downtown buildings of the city. Now the petroleum from that field was a meal for the flames. Nearby fires were also consuming Baku's lumberyard and most of the houses in its surrounding suburbs. Strong winds drove the blaze closer to the city.

Over the next three days, Baku descended into a chaos of "burning, shooting, killing and plundering." While violence raged in the middle of the Black City, its surrounding forest of 3,000 derricks and 300 oil storage tanks burned to the ground. Other rioters opened the earthen dams that contained Baku's huge reservoirs of petroleum. When these escaping lakes of oil were set alight, the torrents of crude created a literal flood of fire in sections of the city. Elsewhere in the oil capital, flames consumed the railroad station and the homes of more Armenians. It was like "hell let loose," said one survivor. "I thought the scene might well be compared with the last days of Pompeii. It was made worse than anything that could have taken place at Pompeii by the ping of rifle and revolver bullets, the terrific thunder of exploding oil tanks, the fierce yells of the murderers, and the dying screams of their victims."[21] After the slaughter had raged for almost an entire week, only a full-scale military intervention from tsarist troops based in Georgia was enough to suppress it. The fires of Baku could be extinguished, but there were not enough soldiers in the Russian Empire to halt the unchecked spread of revolution.

As Baku smoldered during September 1905, Russian diplomats managed to bring an end to the disastrous war with Japan.[22] This helped to stabilize the Russian Empire against immediate military threat in the Far East but did little to resolve its deeper domestic unrest. The pillars of Nicholas's reign were beginning to crack. The empire itself was now in danger.

Rushing into this crisis was one of the last capable individuals in Romanov Russia. His name was Count Sergei Yulyevich Witte. If anyone could avert a possible collapse of the empire, it was Witte. During the previous decade, he had served as the tsar's finance minister; helped to complete the Trans-Siberian Railroad; unsuccessfully lobbied to prevent Russia from becoming entangled in the war with Japan; and then successfully negotiated the ensuing peace treaty with the Japanese. Living in a society of stagnation, social rot, and political decay, where state appointments usually depended more on political connections than on competence, Witte insisted that the people who worked under him had to be qualified for their posts. Acting as a technocrat inside the confines of the tsarist autocracy, his efforts at reform often resembled those of a doctor whose patient refused any and all treatment. Only now Tsar Nicholas had no choice but to follow Witte's recovery plan.

As chairman of the tsar's committee of ministers, it was Witte who presented Nicholas with a fateful decision in the fall of 1905: bend to reform now, or watch the empire break. For the last of the Russian tsars, Witte's ultimatum was a painful one. Nicholas had been raised to believe that only God held more sovereignty on earth than himself. Accepting the proposal to give up some of that power was a crushing defeat. The only worse outcome would have been the end of his dynasty. That might very well have occurred if Nicholas had not agreed to Witte's harsh proposals for reform, which created an elected Duma (legislature) for Russia, established voting rights for all men (but not women), and relaxed restrictions on freedom of the press and association. It was the beginning of Russia's great experiment with popular government, and it would not last.

As Witte's reform package steadily defused the revolution of 1905, public order gradually returned to Russia. Unfortunately, Nicholas saw the resulting calm as an excuse to ignore the newly formed Duma. The war and riots of the previous year became a bad memory, nothing more. Tranquillity was restored. The postrevolution reform process was no longer necessary—or so the tsar thought. Nicholas instituted a sweeping crackdown on political freedom. He dissolved the Duma in July 1906, fired Witte, and sent Russia's revolutionaries into hiding, exile, or prison cells. The emergency reforms proposed by Witte ended before they could cure the ills of sickly Russia. Tsar Nicholas subsequently retreated into his self-contained world of luxurious illusion, and young Stalin tunneled deeper into the communist movement. There he waited. The opportunity for a new revolution—one that would finally destroy the empire—would come later.

When the Great War (World War I) fell upon Europe in eight years' time, Bolshevik revolutionaries such as Stalin would emerge from hiding and exile better organized, more militant, and far more adept at exploiting the opportunities that war and political turmoil provided. Without the release valve of Witte's reforms, public dissatisfaction with tsarist rule only grew stronger. The doomsday clock on Romanov rule began to tick. Once it hit zero in 1917, the free market oil industry in Russia would come crashing to an end. The Bolsheviks were no friends to men like Sir Marcus.

A more immediate result of the 1905 Russian Revolution was the introduction of a new concept into the oil business: country risk.[23] This was a fundamentally different kind of danger than the financial peril of a price collapse, or the threat that an innovative competitor might steal customers in a marketplace. For the first time, the world's oilmen had to consider the stability of an entire country when assessing their prospects in the petroleum business. What happened between naval fleets on the far side of Siberia could indirectly burn down an oil field 3,700 miles away in Baku. The chain of events that could produce such a disaster was immensely complex, hard to predict, and even harder to anticipate on the confines of a balance sheet. Nevertheless, the dangers of country risk are very real. Today the global oil industry is intimately familiar with this dynamic. Modern oil firms regularly make billion-dollar bets based on their best guess at the level of country risk in a given nation. In 1905, however, no one in the oil business had ever experienced country risk of this magnitude. Shell would soon be reeling from the consequences.

CHAPTER 15

The Warhorse and the Stallion

Amalgamate or die. This was the tough message that Robert Waley Cohen, a trusted employee of Shell, delivered to Sir Marcus in the months after the burning of Baku. Cohen had earned his stripes at Shell by toiling away in the ill-fated oil fields of Borneo. He had a degree in natural science from Cambridge, an understanding of chemistry, a respected family name, and—most important—the trust of Sir Marcus. It was partly on account of this trust that Cohen represented Shell's interests on the board of Asiatic. From his position at the intersection of Royal Dutch and Shell, Cohen held a commanding view of the global petroleum business and saw where it was headed. The ceaseless combat with Standard, the undulation of the oil market, the costly waste of capital in Borneo, the destruction of Russia's oil industry—all these setbacks had taken their toll on Sir Marcus's company. Shell was not going to prosper for much longer on its own.

Next to Royal Dutch, Shell was an emaciated warhorse parading alongside an oat-fed stallion. As Deterding paid his shareholders a whopping 73 percent dividend, Shell's investors were forced to accept a sickly 5 percent cut of the company's earnings. The future looked even worse. Shell's finances were slipping into the red. Sir Marcus's company carried much more debt than Royal Dutch, and its cash almost never exceeded 2 percent of the firm's assets. By comparison, Royal Dutch was flush with money. In fact, Deterding's cash position usually hovered at around 25 percent of company assets. While this fact insulated Royal Dutch against the cyclical ups and downs of the oil market, Shell had no such protection.

Amalgamation would at last bring together the great rivals of Standard Oil: Sir Marcus and Deterding. It would mean the survival of Shell, but at a tremendous cost. If Sir Marcus persisted on his own, his company faced a slow, certain death. There were no more tricks or coups or Spindletops to miraculously alter his prospects. Shell would experience a steady, unending descent into liquidation.

By early 1906, Sir Marcus gradually came around to Cohen's perspective. As chairman of Shell, it was Sir Marcus's opinion that counted most. The old model of forming a consensus with his younger brother Sam Samuel had atrophied. Sir Marcus was firmly in command of the company by virtue of his ownership stake. He called the shots at Shell. It was therefore on the older brother's shoulders that the fateful decision to amalgamate fell. Once he embraced the idea of a merger with Royal Dutch, his next course of action was obvious: he had to squeeze the best possible deal from Deterding. The trouble was that Sir Marcus's best days were in the past. Shell was no longer the most attractive prize in the oil business; nor could Sir Marcus wield the same kind of leverage that he had once held over Deterding. This negotiation was not going to be easy. Deterding had become a powerful force.

Thanks to the creation of Asiatic, Deterding now controlled a far superior marketing arm than he had back in 1902. This meant that Royal Dutch was no longer at a disadvantage when it came to selling kerosene in the Far East. It had even contracted its own, smaller cargo fleet to transport cases of illuminating oil from Sumatra to the ports of Asia. With respect to whatever advantages Sir Marcus held at sea by virtue of his larger tanker fleet, Royal Dutch could at least hold its own. Indeed, the crucial difference between Royal Dutch and Shell in 1906 was Russia. Deterding wanted to increase his upstream exposure to Russia; Sir Marcus wanted to be free of it. Coming so closely after the consuming inferno of Baku, it may have seemed odd that Deterding was so keen on Caspian oil, but his eagerness revealed a key insight into the organizing needs of both companies.

For Sir Marcus, the 1905 Russian Revolution had been a terrifying ride that he did not wish to repeat. The brilliance of his strategy—go big and go global—had always rested on Russia. This made Caspian crude the quicksilver of his successes but also the single largest source of Shell's current uncertainty. When Russian oil production temporarily went offline after 1905, Shell came close to being knocked out of the petroleum business. The more the company's revenue sank on account of its supply shortage from Russia, the greater its need for diversification grew. This made access to Royal Dutch's wells in the Indies an existential prize.

Deterding saw the oil world in a different light. For him, the rioting in Baku represented not disaster but a remarkable opportunity. Once the Black City was rebuilt and its oil production went back online, Royal Dutch could widen the range of its upstream petroleum supplies by shipping more product from the Caspian. The price that Deterding paid for his diversification would be to assume all the country risk that came with Russia. He was ready to ride that tiger. He was not afraid of a little—or in this case a lot of—uncertainty.

It was on the basis of these very different perspectives that Sir Marcus and Deterding began to discuss amalgamation in 1906. In the wake of the Russian Revolution, amalgamation made a lot of sense.

After five years of holding hands inside Asiatic, the uneasy courtship of these two rivals was coming to a close. Lane had long ago predicted this outcome, having always believed that amalgamation was the only possible solution for the two companies. At long last, the marriage of convenience was now coming to pass.

Together, Sir Marcus and Deterding approached the merging of their two companies through the avenue of a joint venture, but it was unclear exactly how they would share it. As an opening offer, Sir Marcus proposed that both companies split ownership of the new entity fifty-fifty, making Shell and Royal Dutch equal partners. However, Shell was not worth nearly enough to justify such a generous valuation and the ever-clever Deterding was several steps ahead of his would-be equal. "With Sir Marcus especially you must remember that he will always propose the most impertinent things," Deterding wrote in a letter to Loudon. "He has this principle: there are a lot of fools in the world, let us accept that there are in business 5 fools to each 100 persons. Well, then, consider them all to be fools. Ninety-five will reject a mad proposal with more or less contempt. But there is always the chance that you may meet a fool and he probably will accept. This argumentation is one of the biggest assets of his company."[1] Deterding dismissed the idea of a fifty-fifty split and counteroffered with a sixty-forty division. Instead of parity, Royal Dutch would own the controlling stake. Sir Marcus was appalled.

When Standard issued its buyout offer for Shell back in 1901, the issue of national ownership was a point of pride for Sir Marcus. The very idea of ceding control of his company to Royal Dutch was appalling enough, but the fact that it was not a British firm made it worse. "The property and interests of Shell would henceforth be managed by a foreigner!" he said.[2] Foreign ownership of Shell was a pill that Sir Marcus could not bear to swallow.

As Deterding's counteroffer remained on the table with no answer, Shell continued to burn cash. The longer Sir Marcus put off his decision, the more Shell's prospects dimmed. Ever so cautiously, he eventually accepted the idea of foreign ownership. He finally was able to say as much in a letter. "I should be prepared to leave the management to Royal Dutch, if you, Deterding, could give me some absolute guarantee that it would be in the interest of the Royal Dutch to manage the Shell properly." The Dutchman now had Sir Marcus where he wanted him. It was the inverse of their "British-Dutch" negotiation—all the power was in Deterding's hands. He could easily dictate terms and was inclined to only make a single promise. If Sir Marcus was so worried about protecting the interests of Shell, Royal Dutch would buy a quarter of his company. As a shareholder in Shell, Royal Dutch would be bound by a fiduciary duty to look out for the interests of Sir Marcus's firm. Take it or leave it. Deterding would give no more.

In actuality, Deterding's offer to purchase Shell's stock was not entirely a negotiation tactic. As he explained to the Royal Dutch board, "We are in our business far too dependent on the British government because we have to sell a large part of our products in English colonies." If the British government ever cracked down on non-British firms that operated in the colonies, Royal Dutch would be in a dangerous position. By owning a quarter of Shell, Royal Dutch could at least claim that it was a stakeholder in British interests and therefore partly British itself. That alone could be worth some political cover when push came to shove.

By March 1906, Sir Marcus and Deterding had come a long way toward full amalgamation, but Sir Marcus wanted more time. He asked to consider the latest Royal Dutch offer more thoroughly, but Deterding pressed his advantage. "I am at present in a generous mood," he said. "I have made you this offer, but if you leave this room without accepting it, the offer is off."[3] Check and mate. Sir Marcus could play for no more time. He at last conceded to the Dutchman.

Deterding was triumphant.

Following five years of reversals, shifty contract antics, and incomplete victories, the rivals to Rockefeller's empire would at last become one. On September 12, both companies inked an initial agreement to form a new joint venture. Asiatic would fall away. Thereafter the two companies would be known as the Royal Dutch/Shell Group. The only remaining hitch was with the Rothschilds.

In all the excitement generated by the negotiations between Deterding and Sir Marcus, no one had quite figured out how to dispose of the Rothschilds' third-party interest in Asiatic. The Rothschilds were happy to take a mountain of money in exchange for their trouble, £1.2 million to be exact. Alas, this kingly sum of cash was beyond Deterding's means. His eventual solution was to fold Asiatic into the amalgamated Royal Dutch/Shell Group, a headache that took more than two years to complete. As a result of this fix, the Rothschilds would continue to draw profits from Royal Dutch/Shell. They were, after all, going to become its single largest shareholders. Representing their interests on the new board of the group was none other than Shady Lane. It was an appropriate appointment: Lane had taken as much of a hand in its founding as anyone else.

There was no ribbon cutting, champagne toast, or formal speech to commemorate the creation of the Royal Dutch/Shell Group, which made it hard to fix a proper date for an anniversary. Instead, the group came into existence in a rather dull, businesslike fashion. Officially, the terms of the September agreement were set to take effect on January 1, 1907. Since the enacting documents for each segment of the group were signed in a piecemeal fashion, the whole process spilled over into 1907. In fact, parts of the deal were not finalized until 1908.

For this reason, the true birthday of Royal Dutch/Shell is best captured in a different kind of anniversary: the day Sir Marcus left his post at M. Samuel & Co.

In December, a mundane legal announcement began to appear in London's newspapers. It stated that "the partnership existing between Sir Marcus Samuel, Bart., and Mr. Samuel Samuel trading under the style of M. Samuel & Co. having expired by effluxion of time, Sir Marcus Samuel has decided to retire from business, and will do so from the 31st."[4] Sir Marcus was leaving the firm that had borne him to so many victories. With his departure went the animating force of the company. M. Samuel & Co. was to be a moribund memory.

After sealing the deal with Deterding and announcing his departure from M. Samuel & Co., Sir Marcus felt free to speak his mind with reporters. His bitterness at losing Shell to his rival wore no veil. "I am a disappointed man," he said.[5]

It was the end of a great, profitable run.

It felt like defeat.

CHAPTER 16

The "Fateful Plunge"

Partly out of self-consolation, and still deeply in love with the sea, Sir Marcus nursed his disappointment in business by purchasing a lovely toy: the 166-foot *Lady Torfrida*, one of the most gorgeous yachts of her age.

Sailing under the power of three pine masts and an auxiliary steam engine belowdecks, the *Lady Torfrida* was renowned as a "magnificent specimen of naval architecture and artistic decoration." Whenever he wished, Sir Marcus could take to the ocean without leaving behind any pleasures or comforts from land. His stateroom was "most artistically got up" in carved oak, "fluted pilasters and leather panels with beautiful designs of figure and flower subjects." There were additional staterooms for visiting guests, a saloon designed in the Louis XV style, accents of imitation ivory and gold throughout, and enough additional space for a maid, a valet, and eighteen other crewmen.[1] Some of the finest homes in England were not this luxurious.

In Sir Marcus's hands, the *Lady Torfrida* was a solace, a getaway, and a mobile home. He enjoyed every aspect of the experience. "Sir Marcus was a very keen yachtsman and loved it," recalled the ship's steward.[2] This was not, however, an enthusiasm that Lady Fanny

209

Samuel shared. After completing a four-month voyage to Norway and Scotland with her husband, Fanny refused to undertake any more long trips. Thereafter the *Lady Torfrida* made only short runs across the Channel or up the English coast. During these outings, Sir Marcus was a constant presence on the bridge regardless of the weather. There were no calls or distractions and often, no particular destination.

Back in London, there was cause for even more consolation—and even a few laughs. As Sir Marcus prepared to step down from his official chairmanship of Shell, the company's shareholders commissioned his portrait by the artist Sir Hubert von Herkomer. It was a fine gift for the man who had made them rich. In the painting, Sir Marcus sports round, well-fed cheeks. His pince-nez sits squarely above his famously soft mustache. He bears no hint of being a disappointed man. His eyes stare out from the portrait looking bemused by the whole experience. He also sits impatiently, a man who still has things to accomplish.

During a dinner reception at London's Savoy Hotel in 1908, the original architect of the *Murex*, Sir Fortescue Flannery—now a knight himself—presented the painting to Sir Marcus before an audience of Shell's shareholders. "We believe that he is retiring from business with what we hope is a sufficiency," Flannery deadpanned. The dinner erupted in laughter. "With care and economy," Flannery said, Shell's chairman might just have enough money to "live a simple life."[3] There was even more laughter. Sir Marcus was one of the wealthiest men in all of London. Thanks to his previous holdings in Shell, he now had a sizable ownership stake in the combined Royal Dutch/Shell Group. Under Deterding's command, Royal Dutch/Shell quickly began to reap enormous profits for Sir Marcus and his fellow shareholders. The simple life was going to be easy.

Richer than ever and freed of his managerial duties, Sir Marcus pursued his long-standing passion as an unrepentant public advocate for oil. The main target of his effort was the Royal Navy. For years now, parts of the Admiralty had steadfastly resisted the adoption of liquid fuel to power British warships. Sir Marcus saw this as the height of foolishness. "We have fallen on degenerate days," he lamented, "and the men at the head of affairs, however high-sounding their names, are mediocrities, never looking beyond tomorrow."[4]

One individual who saw far beyond tomorrow was Admiral John "Jackie" Fisher. It was Fisher who first conceptualized the maritime "keys" to the world, one of which, the Suez, Samuel had pried open with the *Murex*. Most recently, Fisher was fighting his own battle from within the Admiralty to force the Royal Navy's adoption of oil. The arc of Fisher's military career had put him on the leading edge of the greatest revolution of naval technology in centuries. By embracing that change, he had propelled his naval career through the Admiralty. It had also made him enemies.

When Fisher joined the Royal Navy in 1854, the Admiralty's fleets were still comprised of wood, rope, and sail. On his first day in the navy, at age thirteen, he boarded the hallowed HMS *Victory* to take his entrance examination. Hewn from six thousand trees, the *Victory* had served as Lord Nelson's flagship at the famous Battle of Trafalgar in 1805. It was aboard the *Victory* that Nelson had charged headlong into a line of French warships, unleashing half her 104 cannons in a point-blank broadside against the opposing French flagship.[5] By the time Fisher walked the deck of the *Victory*, almost fifty years later, Nelson's shadow, and the memory of his charge at Trafalgar, loomed over every officer in the Royal Navy. But much like Nelson's old warship herself, the tactics and technology that had triumphed at Trafalgar were relics.

As Fisher ascended through the ranks of the Royal Navy, his career epitomized the confluence of steam, speed, and steel that was reinventing British naval power. The technological transition was so dramatic that subsequent generations of vessels could no longer be called "ships of the line," the kind of wooden fighting ship that Nelson captained at Trafalgar. Nor could they accurately be considered "ironclads," for these new vessels were forged of steel. The Royal Navy was adopting a novel type of vessel that was so different, it required an entirely new name: *battleship*. In the later estimation of Winston Churchill, these powerful warships were like "gigantic castles of steel wending their way across the misty, shining sea, like giants bowed in anxious thought."[6]

The first of the Royal Navy's new giants was the HMS *Colossus*. Launched in 1886, she boasted a steel hull, a battery of four twelve-inch guns, five smaller six-inch guns, and no sails. Rather, she ran on coal. Inside the *Colossus*, a careful choreography of stokers shoveled low-efficiency coal fuel into her immense boilers. It was coal that powered her 7,500-horsepower engines. The coal, though, posed a problem.

The coal-burning "castles of steel" that Britain put to sea in the 1880s and 1890s were so heavily armored, they lumbered across the ocean at relatively slow speeds. This design philosophy collided head-long with Fisher's vision for a new kind of naval warfare. It was an unorthodox philosophy. Instead of building slow, armored ships, Fisher believed that "speed was armor." This was "because the speed enabled you to put your ship at such a distance that she couldn't be hit by the enemy, so it was the equivalent of impenetrable armor although you had none of it and your guns reach him when his could not reach you."[7] Alas, it was this unconventional opinion that many inside the Admiralty did not share with Fisher.

Seemingly everywhere he looked, the Royal Navy was trapped by outdated ideas from the days of wind and sail or distracted by the luxury of peace. Many of Fisher's fellow officers did not obsess over ways to modernize naval warfare or make the Royal Navy more deadly. Instead, they treated the navy as a "self-perpetuating . . . semi-aristocratic yacht club."[8] As one of Fisher's contemporaries recalled, "Polo and pony racing were much more important than gun drill."[9] Fisher thought otherwise. Even during peacetime, the crews under his command ran through endless gunnery practices and combat drills. Fisher's navy was no yacht club.

In 1892 Fisher scaled his first major height in the Admiralty by becoming the Third Sea Lord and Controller of the Navy. This promotion put him in charge of the design, construction, and repair of all vessels in the British fleet. While he saw the assignment as a chance to inject new thinking into the Royal Navy, he was aghast to receive a request from a member of the Admiralty's board to purchase sixteen sailing ships. This kind of request was indicative of the men whom Fisher called the "ancient admirals who believe in bows and arrows."[10] He wanted to eradicate the sail, not grant it artificially long life.

Instead of building sailing ships, Fisher oversaw the development of an entirely new breed of fast attack vessel. Similar to the battleship, this novel kind of warship was unique, so it too required a new name. He called it the "destroyer." It epitomized his concept that "speed is armor." Equipped with high-power engines and smaller, rapid-firing cannons, a destroyer could outrun what it could not outshoot. When Fisher first committed the Admiralty to this edgy concept, submarine technology was still in its infancy. In time, the Royal Navy would discover that his fast destroyers were the perfect hunter-killers of submarines. More than any other warship, Fisher's destroyers would inspire terror in the German U-boat crews that stalked England's waters during World War I.[11] Such was the benefit of speed.

The battleship proved to be a larger, more intractable issue. As successive designs of British battleships left their shipyards, they grew heavier and more powerful than the *Colossus*. They also continued to burn low-efficiency coal. Fisher thought this was folly. In any head-to-head fight between two battleships, a strategist could assume that the thickness of each vessel's armor, the size of their guns, and the marksmanship of their crews would all be equal. That meant the crucial difference in a fight between battleships was going to be speed. The captain with the fastest battleship would have the ability to pick when to attack, how to maneuver, and when to flee.[12] Fisher believed that high-efficiency fuel oil was an ideal way to grant England's battleships the added armor of speed. But the Admiralty's faith in coal bordered on religious devotion.

Despite the success of his innovations like the destroyer, Fisher found that many of his colleagues in the Admiralty were impervious to persuasion when it came to converting its battleships, let alone the entire Royal Navy, to fuel oil. His frustration eventually grew so great that he briefly considered retiring from the navy to become chairman of the private shipbuilder Elswick. "It's a place I should revel in," he said. Freed from the strictures of the Admiralty, he imagined himself "immediately set to work to revolutionize naval fighting by building on speculation a battleship, cruiser and destroyer on revolutionary principles—oil fuel, turbine propulsion, equal gunfire all around, greater speed than any existing vessels of their class, no masts, no funnels, etc."[13] The very fact that he entertained the fantasy of constructing a private flotilla on spec, just to prove the merits of oil, speaks to the intense resistance he encountered from the hyperconventional thinking of the Royal Navy. Thankfully for Britain, he did not retire. But he did forge a decisive partnership with Sir Marcus.

Fisher and Sir Marcus were natural co-conspirators. Their bond of commonality was based on the Orient, the empire, and oil. Much like Sir Marcus, Fisher had also risen from humble origins and spent many of his formative years in the Far East. As a young naval officer in China, he fought pirates on the Pearl River, attacked Chinese-held forts during the Second Opium War, and served as the second-in-command of the British flagship in Hong Kong, the HMS *Ocean*. Also like Samuel, Fisher's belief in sea power was absolute. "On the British fleet rests the British Empire," he said. "Only a congenital idiot with criminal tendencies would permit any tampering with the maintenance of our sea supremacy."[14] In tone, sentiment, and consequence, Sir Marcus would have heartily agreed. But the greatest glue for both men was their shared vision for the future. When they looked over the horizon, Sir Marcus and Fisher imagined fleets of British warships speeding across the oceans, all burning high-efficiency oil rather than coal.

The partnership between Sir Marcus and Fisher first bloomed into a friendship at the Mote. Starting in 1899, Fisher became a regular weekend guest at Sir Marcus's Maidstone estate. During his initial visit, their talk was rich in discussions about oil and naval strategy. In his study, Sir Marcus spoke to Fisher about the transformative potential of liquid fuel in maritime vessels. Fisher agreed but asserted that the strategic implications of oil were greater than he imagined. To demonstrate his point, Fisher grabbed items from Samuel's desk: a bronze paperweight, family photographs, an ink blotter, and a matchbox made from a horse's hoof. Using these articles, the old admiral laid out mock naval engagements to demonstrate how oil would fundamentally transform naval warfare.[15] The organizing concept was simple. As Fisher would later write, "The first of all necessities is *speed*—so as to be able to fight when you like, where you like, and how you like."[16] Oil was the ideal solution to speed. As for Britain's opponent in a fight, Fisher was convinced the enemy would be Germany. Even at this early date, fifteen years before the outbreak of World War I, Fisher anticipated the approaching conflict with the Kaiser. When war came, Fisher believed that oil would be crucial to Britain's victory at sea. Marcus was a zealous convert.

The first major test of the Royal Navy's transition to oil occurred on June 27, 1902. Following years of lackadaisical interest in petroleum, the Admiralty finally installed a new set of experimental oil boilers inside the battleship *Hannibal*. Now it was ready to test the concept of oil at sea. The trial of an oil-powered battleship was so momentous that both Sir Marcus and Fisher—as Second Sea Lord—traveled to the British naval base at Portsmouth, England, for the occasion. As the ship sailed out of the harbor in fine weather, a crowd of hundreds gathered on shore to watch the historic event. Aboard the *Hannibal*, six of the ship's boilers burned Welsh coal, as was obvious from the telltale trail of smoke that emanated from the battleship's funnels. The *Hannibal*'s two remaining boilers were idle, waiting to burn fuel oil. At the appointed moment, signalmen on land transmitted the historic order to switch from coal to liquid fuel. It was a heady event, representing the first time a British battleship would use oil for propulsion. The experiment was also an immediate flop. Upon making the switch, a choking black cloud of smoke and soot abruptly billowed from the battleship. The vessel became cloaked in a dark fog. This was absolutely *not* supposed to happen. Oil burners were supposed to be smokeless, but the *Hannibal* had become a smoke machine.

The failure was technical. Lacking any real-world experience with oil on a battleship, and having refused all offers of assistance from Shell, the Royal Navy had installed the boilers aboard the *Hannibal* incorrectly. The resulting black smoke was not typical for an oil-burning ship. Still, the smoke was hard to explain away in the face of Royal Navy skeptics who preferred to keep the fleet reliant on coal. It was a clear defeat for Sir Marcus and Fisher's cause, and the embarrassment ran all the way to Parliament. Several months later, when Secretary to the Admiralty H. O. Arnold-Forster was asked about the oil trial in the House of Commons, he endeavored to give the experiment the best spin possible. "The results obtained," he said, "though not unattended by difficulties, are considered promising."[17] This was true. But despite the promises of oil, the rest of the Admiralty deemed it far too risky to gamble its battleships on liquid fuel, let alone the entire Royal Navy. Oil would have to wait.

Coal still reigned supreme when, on December 2, 1906, Fisher unveiled the crowning achievement of his career. She was the battleship *Dreadnought*—the apex predator of her age. Encased in five thousand tons of armor plating, she bristled with ten twelve-inch guns, twenty-seven three-inch guns, and five tubes for torpedoes. In a single salvo from her main cannons, the *Dreadnought* could drop 6,800 pounds of high explosives onto a single point.[18] She was so deadly, nothing lived within the rage of the *Dreadnought* without the consent of her captain.

Outside the *Dreadnought* was a castle, but inside she possessed a weakness. Fisher's desired advantage of speed eluded him when it came to the otherwise fearsome battleship. On account of coal, the *Dreadnought* was not particularly swift. In the two decades that had transpired since the *Colossus* first put to sea, battleships had become larger, better protected, and armed to the teeth. All the while, their fuel source remained unchanged. Moreover, the *Dreadnought*'s coal-fired boilers required constant feeding and attention from stokers to shovel her low-efficiency coal, and an engine driver to constantly monitor her steam pressure. Burning coal, the *Dreadnought* could maintain a top speed of twenty-one knots, the same as competing German battleships. She was not fast enough to run down enemies or pick her battles.[19] Even worse, Fisher was running out of time to change things at the Admiralty.

By the time Fisher retired as First Sea Lord in January 1911, the top speed of British and German battleships remained dead even at twenty-one knots.[20] When it came to the velocity of capital ships, the arms race was stagnant. The unfulfilled dream of Sir Marcus and Fisher for a faster, oil-burning British fleet would require an additional champion before the Royal Navy took the "fateful plunge" into liquid fuel.[21] This would be the newly appointed First Lord of the Admiralty—the forceful and immensely opinionated Winston Churchill.

The first meeting of Fisher and Churchill was like the collision of two very chatty tornados. Back in April 1907, both men had joined King Edward VII for a short escape to the French resort town of Biarritz, 120 miles south of Bordeaux. This was the famed getaway of the rich and noble, a place where "sea-bathing," salt baths, fox hunting, and a tour of the casinos were all in a day's work. People watching was always on the agenda, either along the town's famous promenade—a favorite of the king—or down on the "marine boulevard" of the Côte des Basques.[22] Churchill had come mainly for the polo, but he ended up talking incessantly with Fisher for two weeks.[23] The friendship was instant. Fisher "fell desperately in love with Winston Churchill," he wrote. "I think he's quite the nicest fellow I ever met and such a quick brain that it's a delight to talk to him."[24] Even King Edward could not help but notice the blooming friendship. At Biarritz, Fisher and Churchill were "most amusing together," he said. "I call them the chatterers."

Two straight weeks with Fisher would have made an impression on anyone, but for Churchill, the gabfest in Biarritz was eye-opening. When he later took up his duties as First Lord in October 1911, one of his priorities was to squeeze every possible idea and strategy from Fisher's mind. He got all he could have hoped for and possibly more. His old friend proved to be a "veritable volcano of knowledge and inspiration," Churchill said. "I plied him with questions and he poured out ideas."[25] One of Fisher's favorite ideas was the marrying of oil and speed.

The timing of Churchill's interactions with Fisher was crucial. War was coming. After the Kaiser escalated his use of gunboat diplomacy in Africa during the summer of 1911, the German threat to Britain's overseas interests was becoming more real.[26] Like Fisher, Churchill now believed that Germany would eventually use its growing military machine against Great Britain. When that occurred, the Royal Navy would need every advantage at sea. The key to faster ships was oil, as Fisher well knew. His task was to convince Churchill of the same.

Hoping to bolster the case for oil, Fisher threw Sir Marcus into the mix. "I do so wish you will rub it in when you see Winston!" he wrote to him that fall. The fact that the entire Royal Navy did not run on liquid fuel was astonishing to Fisher. "It's the first time in sea history that the British Admiralty has not led the way!"[27] Sir Marcus was ready to help. "I am as heartsick as I know you are at the machinations of the permanent officials at the Admiralty," he wrote back to Fisher. "It will require a strong & very able man to put right the injury they have inflicted so far. If Winston Churchill is that man I will help him heart and soul—no one knows better than you what I have done & can do."[28] Fisher kept his confidence in Churchill but no one else in the Admiralty. "The present Admiralty officials are simply damn fools!" he wrote, venting to Samuel. "Timid as rabbits and silly as ostriches! I told Winston this."[29]

The hoped-for meeting between Churchill and Sir Marcus took place in early December 1911. It did not go according to plan. Although no exact record remains as to what was said, Sir Marcus apparently foozled the job. Perhaps Fisher raised Churchill's expectations too high; perhaps Sir Marcus "rubbed it in," at the old admiral's encouragement, with a little too much enthusiasm; perhaps both. Whatever was discussed, Churchill was decidedly unimpressed with Sir Marcus. This sent Fisher into damage control mode. "He is not as good at exposition," Fisher explained to Churchill in an apologetic follow-up, "but he began as a peddler selling 'sea' shells! Hence the name of his company and now he has six million sterling of his own private money. He's a good teapot though he may be a bad pourer." Fisher then got back on message. Whatever Sir Marcus had failed to get across, liquid fuel was plentiful; it could be distributed at scale; and as an added enticement, the Admiralty could save money. "East of Suez," he reminded Churchill, "oil is cheaper than coal!"[30]

Under Churchill, the Admiralty's questions about oil moved from the conceptual to the practical. If the Royal Navy was going to adopt liquid fuel, what were the costs, how much was available, and how secure were potential supplies? To find answers to these questions, First Lord Churchill determined he would need to convene a committee. When the Admiralty's subsequent departmental committee on fuel oil gathered in the final weeks of December 1911, the first witnesses it called were the old rivals Sir Marcus and Deterding. Now they were on the same side.

Sir Marcus was in prime form when delivering his testimony. "I took the bull by the horns and I had all the furnaces of our ships altered for burning liquid fuel," he declared. "And I want to impress upon you that we have never from that day to this had the slightest difficulty with our oil-fuel."[31] Like Shell, the Admiralty could doubtless expect the same. Indeed, it had no other choice. "The burning of liquid fuel in internal-combustion engines is coming," Sir Marcus warned, "and it is coming with far greater rapidity than any movement or improvement yet seen in the mercantile marine. . . . We can hardly imagine the revolution it is going to produce. It is going to scrap every steamer there is."[32]

The education of Winston Churchill was slowly paying off. By early 1912, the First Lord shared Fisher's views on Germany, and he was gradually coming around on oil. The former was a menace; the latter was a boon. But sizable obstacles impeded the Royal Navy's transition to a petroleum-burning fleet. Churchill may not have known it, but as First Lord he was grappling with the same problem set that Sir Marcus had once encountered on the shores of the Black Sea. Here again was the many-sided puzzle of distance, geography, risk, and technology. Greed would come later.[33]

"To build any large additional number of oil-burning ships meant basing our naval supremacy upon oil," Churchill would later write. "But oil was not found in appreciable quantities in our islands. If we required it, we must carry it by sea in peace or war from distant countries." Owing to the stakes, here was the puzzle of distance and geography writ large. Risk and technology, meanwhile, were intertwined. "The adoption and supply of oil as a motive power raises anxious and perplexing problems. In fact, I think they are among the most difficult with which the Admiralty has ever been confronted," Churchill would later tell the House of Commons in March 1912. "Oil is incontestably superior to coal, and if internal combustion engines of sufficient power to drive warships could be perfected . . . all those advantages of oil will be multiplied and some of them will be multiplied three or four times over."[34] Churchill was, of course, prepared to swallow the dangers of oil dependency in exchange for supremacy of the oceans. "If we overcame the difficulties and surmounted the risks, we should be able to raise the whole power and efficiency of the Navy to a definitely higher level; better ships, better crews, higher economies, more intense forms of war-power," he would later write, adding his famous epithet for oil: "Mastery itself was the prize of the venture."[35]

Mastery. As a young man, Rockefeller had pursued it as an unyielding obsession. He had even seized it—for a time—before Sir Marcus and Deterding began slicing away at Standard's monopoly. On the eve of war, Churchill grasped for the same mastery. Rockefeller and Churchill were two very different men, harboring divergent aims. Yet each one saw in crude a reflection of his own ambition. Both desired oil, as a substance, not for what it was but for what it could grant them. In Rockefeller's case, mastery was fortune. In Churchill's, it was supremacy at sea. Both looked at oil and saw themselves.

By April 1912, Churchill prepared to take the greatest leap yet in the naval arms race with Germany. On the drawing board, the Admiralty had scheduled the construction of a novel "fast" dreadnought. This new type of battleship was to be larger, better armored, and more lethal than any of her dreadnought sisters. But what type of fuel would she burn: coal, oil, or both? Churchill's committee on oil was no help. It punted on recommendations and proposed that a larger royal commission study the question of liquid fuel.[36] This was beginning to look like death by committee.

If Churchill wanted mastery over Germany at sea, he needed to proceed swiftly with the adoption of oil. The defenders of low-efficiency coal, however, preferred inaction. This new suggestion of a royal commission was Churchill's chance to break the Admiralty's deadlock, but he would need a reliable figure to lead it. Ideally, this would be an individual with an impeccable résumé and big personality— someone who could roll over the "timid rabbits" in the Admiralty.

Churchill clearly needed Fisher. "This liquid fuel problem has got to be solved," the First Lord wrote to Fisher, asking the old admiral to lead the commission. "I will put you in a position where you can crack the nut, if indeed it is crackable."[37] Fisher could not commit fast enough to the offer. He would ram that nut if necessary.

On July 30, 1912, the Royal Commission on Oil Fuel and Oil Engines got down to work. Once again Sir Marcus and Deterding were called as witnesses. After gathering some friendly testimony from the duo, Fisher wasted little time in producing his early findings that November. All doubts about oil were gone. His commission predictably concluded that there were "overwhelming advantages in favor of fuel oil."[38] Supplies of petroleum could be secured for the Royal Navy in great quantities. Shell's experiences in Asia showed that Britain could quickly establish a global system of oil storage and distribution for the fleet. As for supply, Fisher's royal commission conveniently discovered that Royal Dutch/Shell would sell the Admiralty all the fuel it could possibly burn.[39]

Fisher had delivered. From this point forward, British speed, armor, and firepower would hang on one word: *oil*. The birth of the oil-burning "fast" dreadnoughts signified an irreversible step in the Royal Navy's total conversion to liquid fuel. The few British destroyers and submarines that burned oil would join a new generation of capital ships. It was only a matter of time before the rest of the fleet fell in behind them.

On the morning of Thursday, October 16, 1913, the Royal Navy welcomed the first of its fast, oil-burning superdreadnoughts. The weather at Portsmouth harbor that morning was unusually beautiful—perfect for making history. An enthusiastic crowd of sailors and civilians assembled for the launch. After a quick snip of a ceremonial rope, the enormous hull of the superdreadnought HMS *Queen Elizabeth* slid down the greased wooden planks of her slipway. A deafening roar came up from the spectators as she began to roll. The Royal Marine Band piped up with a rendition of "God Save the King." When the gigantic mass of the warship's hull hit the water, the bow sent a heavy wave speeding across the harbor.[40] The future of the Royal Navy sloshed in its wake.

The *Queen Elizabeth* was an end and a beginning. As the world's very first battleship to run completely on oil, she marked a significant crossing point between the old age of coal and the new reign of crude. She was the emblem of Churchill's "fateful plunge" into oil. Capable of producing 58,000 horsepower,[41] her oil-burning engines represented a 673 percent increase in power over the first battleship, the coal-burning *Colossus*. Thanks to oil, the *Queen Elizabeth* embodied Fisher's mania for speed and firepower. She could reach a top speed of twenty-five knots, faster than her German rivals. And she could thank the energetic lobbying of Sir Marcus and Deterding for her high-efficiency liquid fuel. In the light of hindsight, the birth of the *Queen Elizabeth* seems almost inevitable. The steady advance of technology and the arms race with Germany meant that oil would eventually supplant coal as the Royal Navy's primary fuel. For the individuals who made this switch possible, the events leading up to the transition seemed far less certain.

Looking back at the decisive struggle to convert the Royal Navy to liquid fuel on the eve of World War I, Churchill gave immense credit to Fisher's foresight and preparations. "It was Fisher who hoisted the storm-signal and beat all hands to quarters," he wrote. "He shook them and beat them and cajoled them out of slumber into intense activity."[42] For his part, Sir Marcus dubbed Fisher the "God-father of oil."[43] It was a poignant title for an old sailor who began his first day in the Royal Navy on the deck of an oaken ship of the line.

The "Fateful Plunge"

On July 31, 1914, in the final hours of peace before World War I, Fisher wrote a letter to Churchill. Armies in Germany and Russia were mobilizing for the bloodiest conflict in human history up until that point.[44] Britain would shortly join the slaughter, and Fisher's thoughts were attuned to oil. "I have just received a most patriotic letter from Deterding to say he means you shan't want for oil or tankers in case of war—Good Old Deterding!" he wrote. "How these Dutchmen do hate the Germans! Knight him when you get the chance."

CHAPTER 17

The Colossus Falls

As the rest of the world approached the eve of World War I, a remarkable change began to occur in the world of oil. It was becoming a game of hunters and the hunted. The Standard Oil men were proving hard to catch.

For five days back in November 1905, a posse of process servers stalked the hallways of 26 Broadway. They held subpoenas for some of the richest and by now most infamous men in America. Down in Missouri, the state's brash attorney general, Herbert S. Hadley, had filed suit against Standard for violating local antitrust laws. As part of the case, a New York justice issued subpoenas for John D. Rockefeller, his nephew William G. Rockefeller, John Archbold, Henry Rogers, Henry Flagler, and a host of other executives at Standard. Attorney General Hadley wanted to get each man under oath for questioning. Like startled quail, Rockefeller and his fellow defendants abruptly vanished. More curious, none of the employees at Standard seemed to know the whereabouts of the top management at the world's largest oil company. Frustrated by the hunt, one unyielding process server named Max E. Palmedo opted for a new approach.[1]

On the morning of November 28, Palmedo waited in ambush outside 3 East 78th Street. Nestled between Fifth and Madison Avenues, the gorgeous Beaux-Arts mansion of Hell Hound Rogers was one of the most ornate and obvious hideouts one could find. Gothic Revival flourishes adorned the front door, large windows, and high gabled arch of Rogers's home. The limestone decorations were so impressive, they put the other stately residences on the street to shame. If Rogers was inside this lavish hiding place, all Palmedo had to do was wait for him to appear at the front door. It made sense in concept, but the strategy forced Palmedo to brave the foul weather outside. The first cold storm of the fall was rolling over New York that morning. In Albany, it was snowing. In Manhattan, rain soaked anyone who could not find shelter, and on 78th Street there was little to be found.[2]

Despite the elements, Palmedo's ambush paid off. Although Rogers had gone missing from 26 Broadway, he emerged from his home that morning. This was the same Rogers who once leaked Standard's secrets to Ida Tarbell, and his decision to aid her investigation largely accounted for his present predicament. He was a little older and grayer and was now under investigation along with the rest of Rockefeller's co-conspirators. In order to officially serve Rogers, all Palmedo had to do was physically touch the old Hell Hound with the subpoena. It should have been easy.

As Rogers shot from his front door into an awaiting car, Palmedo seized his chance. He leaped after Rogers, jumping onto the running board of his automobile as it started down the street. "Is this Mr. Henry H. Rogers?" Palmedo called out. Rogers stared speechless at the apparent madman who shouted his name while clinging to the moving car. Palmedo threw the subpoena at him through an open car window and showed the accompanying court order. True to his reputation, the Hell Hound tried to shove Palmedo off, but the deed was done. To the man who had once predicted, "We will see Standard Oil in hell before we will let any set of men tell us how to run our business," the subpoena was a greeting from Missouri's attorney general.[3] Welcome to hell.

Unfortunately for Palmedo, the dismount was less successful than the ambush. As he stepped off the speeding vehicle, he caught a snag. The car proceeded to drag the fearless process server for several feet before he broke free. Palmedo returned to his feet—thankfully unharmed. One subpoena down, only thirty-nine more to go.

One by one, Palmedo got his men. Among the last holdouts was William G. Rockefeller, the treasurer of Standard Oil. Palmedo went to great lengths to run down the location of this particularly elusive executive. His final break came by way of a tip from someone on William's household staff. At seven-thirty in the evening on Christmas Eve, William was walking down the steps of his home at 292 Madison Avenue, his arms full of wrapped Christmas presents. His wife strode beside him. The couple needed only to cross the short distance between the front doors of their apartment building and a car at the curb. It was more than enough space for Palmedo to pounce.

Owing to the fact that it was Christmas Eve, Palmedo likely caught William by surprise. "Are you Mr. Rockefeller?" he asked. "He replied that he was not in a rather gruff tone," Palmedo later recalled. "I was not in his way, but he gave me a push as he went to the auto. His wife stepped into the vehicle ahead of him. As he got in I touched him with the subpoena . . . afterward holding out, so that he could see it, the original order of the Supreme Court Justice directing him to appear at the hearing."[4] Not even the holidays were safe from Palmedo.

At the start of 1906, only one top executive at Standard still remained at large, the most elusive target of all: John D. Rockefeller. Seemingly overnight, the chairman of Standard had ceased to exist. At least, he could not be found anywhere in America. Newspapers openly speculated on his whereabouts. Was he hiding on Henry Rogers's yacht in Puerto Rico? Or was he perhaps bunkered with Henry Flagler down in Key West?[5] None of the rampant conjecture turned up any useful leads. Rockefeller had become a ghost, or so it appeared.

In an effort to stay one step ahead of his subpoena, he was in fact secretly traveling between his various properties up and down the East Coast. It was a humiliating existence for America's richest man. "As he decamped from one estate to the next," wrote one biographer, "Rockefeller was reduced to the degrading life of a fugitive." That is, an extremely well-protected and comfortable fugitive. Hired Pinkerton detectives stood watch for strangers on the grounds of Rockefeller's properties. All arriving cars and delivery trucks were inspected for concealed process servers. The attendants on John D.'s estates were sworn to absolute secrecy. William G.'s staff might have talked, but his uncle's people were bound to strict silence. As Rockefeller hid from his pursuers, paranoia took hold. He barely spoke on the telephone, having convinced himself that the lines were tapped. He kept a handgun by his nightstand. All business correspondence arrived in blank envelopes to evade prying eyes. The outside world gradually receded. Rockefeller's private world became a well-heeled prison. To set foot beyond the gates of his confinement would almost certainly result in a subpoena.

Aside from the indignity of hiding, life on the lam from process servers was annoyingly disruptive to Rockefeller's meticulously regimented routine. At sixty-six, the habits he had acquired over his lifetime were now calcified into an intensely repetitive cycle of rest, mild exercise, and digestion. He fastidiously held to the belief that if he kept to the exacting rhythms of his routine, he could live to one hundred. With this goal in mind, he scheduled his time down to the minute. Each day began without fail at the stroke of six. After rising, he read the newspaper for precisely sixty minutes and then walked the grounds of whatever estate he happened to find himself on that morning. Next came breakfast, which required exactly forty-five minutes to consume, followed by an additional thirty minutes of digestion and sixty minutes for morning correspondence. He then golfed until noon, ate lunch at midday, reserved thirty minutes for sitting and digestion afterward, and then retired to a couch for his beloved nap. At two-thirty p.m. on the nose, he attended to his afternoon letters, and when free to leave his estates, he devoted the remainder of the afternoon to driving. At five-fifteen, there was a short rest before dinner, which commenced, without exception, at the precise stroke of seven. Upon concluding the evening meal at nine p.m., he sat for more digestion, then devoted the final hour of the day to music or conversation. Sleep commenced precisely at ten-thirty p.m. without fail. Individuals who experienced Rockefeller's routine firsthand remarked on how weird it was. As his contemporary biographer William O. Inglis put it, there was "something bordering on the superhuman—perhaps the inhuman—in this unbroken, mathematical perfection of schedule. It was uncanny."[6]

While life as the "world's richest fugitive" circumscribed some of Rockefeller's daily habits, one comfort that he refused to part with was his cheese.[7] There were few culinary pleasures that he enjoyed more than cheese. He had eaten it at lunch for nearly the entirety of his life. Even on the run from process servers, he insisted on keeping his meals consistent. Although he took great pains to conceal his movements during late 1905 and 1906, he failed to realize that a telltale trail of cheese followed him everywhere he went. In the long history of treachery, this betrayer was one of the most pungent. Caesar had Brutus. Jesus had Judas. Rockefeller had his cheese.

Every day in February 1906 a special package of "suspicious cheeses" arrived from the New York Central Railroad at Rockefeller's sprawling property in Pocantico Hills, New York. A local taxi driver noticed the peculiar pattern and dutifully informed reporters. "Them cheeses," he said, "I would recognize anywhere, no matter whether it is day or night. . . . Rockefeller, in my opinion, is somewhere on his estate."[8] The trail of cheese was indeed a giveaway. Rockefeller was at that time hiding at Pocantico and ordering up cheese for lunch each day. The culinary ritual had unintentionally tipped the world to his location. As all eyes scrutinized Pocantico, Rockefeller could no longer remain hidden in New York State. He fled on a boat down the Hudson River, taking up residence at his estate in Lakewood, New Jersey. The process server Palmedo never did get to serve his final subpoena on John D. Rockefeller.

By August 1906, Rockefeller was tired of the lawsuits and wanted to resign from Standard. He believed he was becoming a human lightning rod for litigation. Ridding himself of corporate positions inside Standard might lessen the attacks. Archbold thought otherwise—both he and Standard's board repeatedly refused to accept Rockefeller's resignation. Rockefeller was long past the point where he could simply resign. "We told him that if any of us had to go to jail," Rogers said, prior to Rockefeller's attempted resignation, "he would have to go with us!"[9] There would be no slinking away.

Over the next three years, as Deterding consolidated his hold over Royal Dutch/Shell, Standard existed in two parallel worlds. In the commercial arena, it was the aggressor, inspiring fear in its competitors. In the legal arena, 26 Broadway was under siege. Attorney generals from across the country were pursuing it for violating local antitrust regulations. At long last, on November 15, 1906, the great assault by the federal government commenced against Rockefeller and his monopoly.

The field of battle would be the state of Missouri, where Attorney General Hadley was already pursuing the company under local antitrust laws. U.S. attorney general William S. Moody chose to file a suit in federal court against Standard there as well. The list of named defendants in the federal case was sweeping, including Standard of New Jersey, sixty-five subsidiaries, and most of the executive management team at 26 Broadway. It was the fight that Standard had expected.

In the time since the Tarbell series, the government's investigation into 26 Broadway had uncovered a vast network of illegality. It included complex kickback schemes with the railroads, predatory "cut to kill" pricing, corporate espionage rings, and the creation of bogus companies, as well as the operation of monopoly-controlled pipelines, refineries, and retail markets from the Atlantic to the Pacific. The net effect of this conspiracy was to eradicate all forms of competition across large swaths of the country. The federal government wanted nothing less than the total dismantling of Rockefeller's empire—this time for good.

The scale of Moody's suit was immense. It was so large that a court-appointed investigator required more than twenty-eight months just to gather evidence. During this period, even more legal cases against Rockefeller and Standard were mounted. At one point, 26 Broadway was fighting seven separate suits in federal court while simultaneously fending off state-level challenges in Texas, Minnesota, Missouri, Tennessee, Ohio, and Mississippi.[10] The greatest of these battles was Moody's federal suit in Missouri. Standard had already escaped one execution order from the Ohio Supreme Court back in the 1890s. The Justice Department wanted to ensure that 26 Broadway did not escape again.

On November 20, 1909, the federal government opened the first breach in the lines of Standard's legal defenses in Missouri. Coming almost three years to the day from the original filing of Moody's federal suit, a four-judge panel ruled in favor of the government. The federal court found that Standard Oil was indeed operating in violation of the Sherman Antitrust Act. The judges ordered that the company be dissolved. Immediately, 26 Broadway appealed the decision. Its final defense would be fought before the Supreme Court.

By the time the suit against Standard Oil reached the Supreme Court in 1911, it had grown to gigantic proportions. The case covered forty years of history, 1,374 exhibits, and 11 million words of testimony from 444 witnesses. Tipping the scales at 12,000 pages, the documentation filled twenty-one printed volumes. Among the many questions up for consideration by the Supreme Court was the precise English-language definition of the phrase *a restraint on trade*, the original prohibition in the Sherman Antitrust Act. Under the terms of the law, no company could impose a restraint on trade.

Arguing before the Supreme Court, Standard's lawyers stubbornly held their ground against the government's claims. The wording of the Sherman Antitrust Act was meaningless, they asserted, since every commercial contract was technically a "restraint on trade." More important, Standard's defense asserted that the federal government was acting far beyond its power by sticking its nose into the company's business affairs. Nowhere in the Constitution did the federal government have any authority to regulate the consolidation of capital. It was high legal drama at its finest. The stakes for the country could not have been greater.

A curious thing had occurred on Standard's way to the Supreme Court. The weight of the government's case against the company had grown larger than Rockefeller or his empire. Hanging in the balance was the future of America's young democracy. By agreeing to hear the suit against Standard, the Supreme Court took on more than mere questions about trusts and contracts—it was considering the very limits of federal authority in the United States. Was it possible for a gigantic company to grow so large that it became more powerful than Congress or the president? Was it in the public's interest to allow the federal government to meddle in business? A previous effort to enforce the Sherman Antitrust Act against a sugar monopoly had failed before the Supreme Court, with justices ruling that the government did not have enough authority to enforce antimonopoly restrictions against that particular trust.[11] Standard now wanted the Court to employ that same thinking to its case and apply a strict reading of the Constitution. As in their previous ruling on the sugar trust, Standard urged justices to restrict the scope of federal authority when it came to regulation of the oil industry.

If the Court agreed with Standard, the net effect would be to create a ceiling of power for Washington. Industrial titans who became large enough to soar above that low bank of clouds could exist beyond the reach of federal regulators. The flip side was equally dangerous. The Justice Department wanted the Supreme Court to allow Congress and the president the authority to regulate even the greatest of America's industrial titans. But did that power have any limits? If so, where precisely were they? The whole point of the Constitution was to curtail federal power. This allowed Americans the greatest amount of freedom to innovate, to get rich, and to implement the next big idea in business. Economic freedom was one of the things that made America powerful. Draping red tape around that freedom risked undermining it. So where was the balance to be found? What kind of American democracy would exist in the twentieth century and beyond?

As Rockefeller waited for the Court to hand down its decision, he vacillated between bitterness and gloom. Writing to Archbold in the interminable pause, he deemed the federal case "vindictive." He was also beginning to feel alone. The heady days of Oil Creek were a dim shadow. The adrenaline and excitement of Standard's early conquest of America were gone, and many of the men with whom Rockefeller had spent the bulk of his days at Standard were dead, dying, or very old. The obstinate Charles Pratt, who begrudged Rockefeller's victory over him, had died of heart failure inside Standard's offices back in 1891. Even Pratt's old comrade Hell Hound Henry Rogers had passed away since the subpoenas started to fly. In May 1909 Mark Twain had been traveling to meet Rogers in Manhattan. Since brokering the introduction to Tarbell, the first man of American letters had maintained his lifelong friendship with Rogers. Twain had just disembarked from a train in Grand Central Station when he learned of Rogers's death. "It is terrible. It is terrible," he kept saying upon hearing the news. "I can't talk about it. I'm inexpressibly shocked. I don't know what I shall do. It is terrible. I feel it very much."[12] When Standard convened a memorial service for Rogers at 26 Broadway, Rockefeller visited the company's offices for the last time.

In total, he counted more than sixty men whom he had outlasted. Among the living, Henry Flagler still clung to life, but the "vim and push" that Rockefeller had so admired in Flagler was gone. In the weeks before Rogers's death, Flagler announced his own retirement from business.[13] This left Rockefeller with Archbold, who was a creature of Rockefeller's own making but never really a friend.

The end for Standard Oil came at four o'clock in the afternoon on May 15, 1911. In his soft-spoken voice, Chief Justice Edward White nonchalantly informed the gallery of the Supreme Court that it had reached a decision in *United States vs. Standard Oil Company*. Word raced out from the room. Members of Congress dashed from their offices to listen to the verdict. The decision was nearly unanimous—all but one of the justices had voted to uphold the lower court's ruling that Standard was an illegal monopoly. The Court ordered that Rockefeller's empire was to be broken apart. Standard had a mere six months to comply, and its shareholders were forbidden from attempting to reconstruct the monopoly, as they had done in the 1890s. This time the order would stick.

Writing the majority opinion, Chief Justice White used the opportunity to extend his famous "rule of reason" over the Sherman Antitrust Act. By doing so, he established a lasting principle in American jurisprudence. The organizing concept was simple. Congress liked to put a lot of half-baked ideas into legislation. When the executive branch got around to enforcing those ideas, myriad unforeseen consequences could emerge. In the case of the Sherman Antitrust Act, White agreed that the motivation for the legislation was sound: monopolies hurt the public good. In its zeal to eradicate all monopolies, however, Congress had not thought through what it was putting down on paper. When applied literally, Sherman's law could have made all commercial contracts illegal. This made no sense, since a contract was "the essence of freedom from undue restraint on the right to contract."[14] Restricting that freedom was clearly not what Congress had had in mind when it passed the act. So what was to be done?

The answer was the "rule of reason." Instead of mindlessly applying a literal reading of Sherman's law, the Supreme Court gave itself extra room to consider the wider circumstances of the case. This flexibility would set the boundaries of modern antitrust law in America. It recognized the federal government's power to protect consumers from some monopolies but staked off safe ground for others. This is why natural monopolies like public utilities still endure in the twenty-first century, while other entities like Standard have gone extinct. When the cost of doing business requires massive capital investments up front, the first company that makes those investments typically locks down all the available customers in a market. Due to the huge capital costs required to duplicate that feat, potential competitors stay on the sidelines. This is known today as a natural monopoly.

In the twenty-first century, most people experience the delights of a natural monopoly when they deal with their water or power company. Because it can be economically unfeasible for multiple firms to attach competing water or power lines to every home and business in America, natural monopolies tend to emerge in these kinds of markets. In order to protect consumers against the excesses of a natural monopoly, government regulators usually exert close oversight over these fragile marketplaces, balancing the needs of supply and demand in the interest of the public good.[15] White's fix to the Sherman Antitrust Act made this possible. But who would draw the line between a natural monopoly and an illegal one like Standard? For White, that answer was easy. If there were ever a dispute between business and regulators, the courts would be the final arbiters of greed and the public good.

Standing in opposition to White, only one justice disagreed. Delivering a minority opinion in the Standard case, Justice John Harlan denounced White for putting "words into the antitrust act which Congress did not put there." He ridiculed White's reasoning, saying, "You may now restrain commerce, provided you are reasonable about it; only take care that the restraint is not undue."[16] Harlan was not opposed to White because he supported Standard Oil. On the contrary, he wanted to see far more aggressive enforcement of federal antitrust law. He was nevertheless outvoted. His more aggressive interpretation of the Sherman Antitrust Act did not attract followers on the bench. Instead, the majority of justices took the middle ground. As a result of the Supreme Court's verdict, the pendulum of government regulation began to swing against big business, if more slowly than Harlan would have liked. All the same, that pendulum would never again swing back to the permissive environment that gave rise to Rockefeller. The era of the colossal industrial titans was ending.

Back in New York, Rockefeller was playing golf with a Catholic priest when word of the Supreme Court verdict reached him. He read the verdict and put it away. "Father Lennon, have you some money?" he asked. The priest had none, but asked why. "Buy Standard Oil," Rockefeller said. It was a strange moment to be bullish on Standard. The founder of the world's most feared monopoly had just lost his empire. His life's work was about to be undone. So why was he handing out stock tips?

One reason for Rockefeller's confidence in the face of the Supreme Court decision was hidden behind his balance sheet. Owing to his overly cautious instincts in business, the individual segments of Standard were exceptionally well capitalized and stuffed with surprisingly valuable, often undisclosed assets. Brokers on Wall Street were sure to discover this fact when they got their first look at Standard's books and could assess its true might. A second cause for bullishness was the change in the risk profile for Standard. Years of perpetual antitrust litigation had cast a shadow over Rockefeller's corporate domain. Now that the legal war with the federal government was over, the future looked surprisingly bright. This positive outlook benefited from a third factor: the rise of mass automobile ownership. The motorcar was no longer an expensive hobby of the rich. As Americans raced into the 1910s, the cost of an automobile was falling. Consumers were snatching up new cars in record numbers. Each of these vehicles would need gasoline—something that Standard could provide in abundance.

The fourth, and perhaps most important, reason for optimism lay in the wording of the Supreme Court decision itself. The justices had not ordered that Standard be abolished; they insisted only that Rockefeller's old monopoly be broken into pieces. As the largest shareholder of Standard's stock, Rockefeller was about to become the largest owner of a great many companies. Standard of New Jersey would eventually become Exxon; Standard of New York would operate under the name Mobil; Standard of California would rise as Chevron; and Standard of Indiana as Amoco. Other segments of the old monopoly, such as Atlantic Refining, would become Sun Oil; Continental Oil would become Conoco; and Standard of Ohio would merge into BP.[17] The hydra's many heads would never die. Severed from the body of Standard, they would endure under new management and now-famous names.

True to the Supreme Court's order, the dismantling of Rockefeller's monopoly would be swift. In the span of a few months at the end of 1911, Rockefeller went from being a very rich man to a fabulously wealthy one. When the individual pieces of Standard were subsequently listed on the New York Stock Exchange, speculators on Wall Street climbed over one another to buy shares in the new companies. The stock prices of Standard's shattered remnants soared. During Standard of New York's first ten months of trading in 1912, its shares increased by 123 percent. Meanwhile, Standard of New Jersey's stock appreciated by a *mere* 65 percent. It was the great irony of Rockefeller's defeat. By forcing the "splendid happy family" of Standard to scatter, the Court unintentionally increased Rockefeller's net worth from an estimated $300 million ($8 billion today) before the breakup in 1911 to just below a billion dollars ($23 billion today).[18] At the time, no other human was in reach of the coveted billion-dollar benchmark.

As the wealth from the breakup rolled in, old habits died hard at 26 Broadway. In principle, the management of the old Standard monopoly was officially firewalled from owners like Rockefeller. But as the American financier J. P. Morgan wondered, "How the hell is any court going to compel a man to compete with himself?"[19] At least initially, the answer at Standard was: very poorly. Following Rockefeller's suggestion after the breakup, the executives of the disassembled companies gathered at the old monopoly's New York headquarters for a weekly meeting. This tradition echoed the daily directors' lunch that Rockefeller had once presided over during the peak of Standard's power. After the breakup, the informal gathering of company executives became a way of sustaining coordination between parts of the old empire. Just as before the breakup, the oil giant parceled off territories, and Standard's descendants refused to undercut one another's prices. Real competition took time, as did the departure of aging leaders like Archbold, who had known only one kind of monopolistic business. When the old guard stepped aside, elbows grew sharper, competitive impulses rose, and a new generation of executives eyed the creation of their own powerful domains. "It was felt all along the line—younger men were given a chance," said one of the new guard at Standard.[20] So too were the company's customers.

The colossus had fallen, though the smaller giants lived on.

CHAPTER 18

"We Must Take America"

During the four decades of its existence, Rockefeller's monopoly had dominated the petroleum business. Throughout the life-span of the monopoly, Rockefeller crushed his competitors and held his customers hostage with smooth efficiency. The might of the Supreme Court was enough to disband Standard but not to fully crack Rockefeller's petroleum monopoly. The best antitrust laws in the world mattered little if there was no competing, sizable alternative for consumers. Government regulation and powerful market forces had to combine. Without this convergence, the exploitation of consumers on the part of Rockefeller's old monopoly could continue in practice. Indeed, collusion and market coordination persisted even after the Supreme Court's breakup of Standard. For this reason the emergence of the Royal Dutch/Shell Group as a globe-spanning alternative to Standard became crucial. Customers needed a choice. Royal Dutch/Shell was beginning to provide it on a grand scale.

Much had changed since the early days of the oil war. When the *Murex* first transited the Suez in 1891, the sources of crude had been relatively few, the petroleum market was smaller, and global demand was centered on kerosene. Two decades later everything was backward. The Texas boom had inspired American wildcatters to sniff out new oil fields farther north in Oklahoma and out west in California. Additional crude reserves were flowing from distant places like Persia (today Iran) and Romania. Thanks to this diversity of upstream sources, the days when a single company could create a chokepoint on 80 percent of the world's oil was a thing of the past. The spread of the internal combustion engine likewise meant that demand for petroleum was growing larger and more diverse. No longer disregarded as a waste product, gasoline had become a best-selling commodity. Sales of gasoline in the United States surpassed kerosene for the first time in 1910. The trend would continue due to the permanent switch from coal to oil as the world's primary transport fuel. Helping to drive nearly all these changes in the marketplace for petroleum were the twin cylinders of Royal Dutch and Shell.

What had not changed in the oil business were the constant challenges of crude. As the planet sped into the second decade of the twentieth century, Deterding faced a familiar problem set. Daunting distances and imposing geographic barriers existed between Royal Dutch's wells in the East Indies and its consumers in scattered markets across the globe. The financial and country risks from political upheavals in Russia and China had not abated. And owing to the rise of fuel-hungry motorcars, the technological pressures to squeeze ever-greater efficiencies out of the refining process only intensified. Finally there was greed—the most implacable piece of the puzzle.

In 1910, Standard remained the largest oil company on earth. The Supreme Court verdict was still a year away, and Rockefeller's titanic monopoly was entrenched in the Americas, Europe, and the Orient. Even so, the combination of Deterding's Royal Dutch and Sir Marcus's Shell was producing an unprecedented alternative to 26 Broadway. Deterding now commanded an integrated petroleum company that could stand its ground against the American monopoly in some of the world's biggest oil markets. Standard's problem was distraction. While it fought off legal attacks in America, the monopoly missed its chance to deliver a knockout blow against Royal Dutch/Shell. It was a crucial respite. "If the Standard had tried three years ago to wipe us out, they'd have succeeded," Deterding confessed. "Now things are different."[1]

Always the peacemaker, Deterding felt the time was right to make friends with Standard. As the final breaking of Rockefeller's monopoly loomed over the horizon, Deterding believed conditions were ripe to negotiate an end to the warfare with 26 Broadway. The combined size and marketing power of Royal Dutch/Shell would bolster his negotiating position, or so he believed. Sir Marcus had made the same mistake back in 1901. He too had thought it was possible to negotiate with Standard as an equal. Instead, Standard had eyed Shell as an acquisition target. Now Deterding would try to succeed where Sir Marcus had failed. It was his turn to take an olive branch to 26 Broadway.

When Deterding arrived at the docks of Manhattan in 1910, the city was getting richer, rising higher, and traveling faster than ever before. New York Harbor had become the busiest in the world, annually churning through $1.5 billion ($38 billion today) in foreign trade each year, and New York's stock and commodities exchanges were now the most active in the world. Priming this economic pump was a mountain of money. Inside the vaults of New York's banks sat 36 percent ($1.5 billion at the time) of all the reserve currency in the United States. This supply of cash was so large, it equaled all the currency sloshing around the entire Austro-Hungarian Empire. The financial confidence that resulted from New York's cash surplus was pushing Manhattan to new heights—literally. The previous year New York's Singer Tower achieved the status of the world's tallest building. In

1910 the seven-hundred-foot Metropolitan Life Tower stole that lofty honor away. It would maintain the grand title for three short years, until the rising Woolworth Building reached an even greater height of 792 feet. Necks craned. The first golden age of the skyscraper had begun.[2]

As Manhattan's skyline pushed upward, New Yorkers were furiously digging underground. The old elevated locomotives still rattled overhead, but their days were numbered. The city's growing subway system was faster and more extensive than the elevated trains, moving travelers along more than one hundred miles of buried track in 1910.[3] At street level, the remaining horse carts and carriages that still plodded along were left to fight a losing battle against the invasion of automobiles. Traffic had never been more chaotic across the island. In fact, the only remaining place of real tranquillity was the sky, though this too was beginning to change.

In May 1910 pioneering pilot Glenn H. Curtiss brought all of Manhattan to a standstill with a record-breaking feat of aviation. Joseph Pulitzer's *New York World* had previously put up $10,000 in prize money ($250,000 today) for anyone who could complete the 150-mile journey from Albany to New York in an *aeroplane*. Curtiss aimed to win that prize in an aircraft of his own design. He had a powerful motivation to pull off the stunt: he desperately needed the money. In court, Curtiss was fighting a legal battle to break the Wright brothers' monopoly over all powered human flight, but it was bleeding him dry. If he could win Pulitzer's prize, he could sustain his fight to open the skies to innovation.

The stakes of Curtiss's flight from Albany were lofty. Ever since Wilbur and Orville Wright became the first humans to master powered flight back in 1903, they had zealously pursued legal action against anyone who tried to take to the sky in an airplane without paying them. Since the Wright brothers were the pioneers of a new technology, they claimed that U.S. patent law gave them a sweeping monopoly over every possible design for airplanes, even ones they had not invented. The brothers did not care that Curtiss had actually built a better aircraft, or that his innovation for controlled flight was superior to their outmoded technology; because they were first, Curtiss had to cough up royalties for the privilege of flying. Curtiss was hell-bent on fighting that absurd claim. What was the use of improving technology if someone else—in this case, the Wright brothers—got to profit from his own hard-won inventions? Today this same fight is being waged across the computer and software industries. In 1910 the battleground of intellectual property law was the sky.[4] Curtiss chose the morning of Sunday, May 29, to try to snatch Pulitzer's prize money and thereby continue the legal war against the Wright brothers.

The weather that morning was perfect for flying. The winds were mild. The sky was almost completely clear of clouds. As he prepared for takeoff, Curtiss donned a cork-lined life vest and put his legs into a pair of rubber fishing pants. The curious apparel was not so much to keep him alive, in the event of an emergency landing on the Hudson, as to keep him warm once he was aloft in the rushing air. Dressed for the flight, the mustachioed aviator took up position over the front lower wing of his aircraft. Behind him, a large, rear-mounted combustion engine siphoned gasoline from a ten-gallon fuel tank. The lightweight engine was the key to flight, and gasoline was its crucial element. When Curtiss accelerated the motor, his aircraft hurtled down a stretch of open land east of Albany. Ever so gracefully, the pilot and his flying machine climbed into the air.[5]

The race was on. Chasing Curtiss from ground level, *The New York Times* had chartered a special train to cover the event. Inside, it carried Curtiss's wife, a support team, and a pool of excited reporters. As the locomotive sped down the rails of the New York Central's Hudson River Line, its passengers hung out from the windows, noting every bob, dip, and swerve of the aircraft. Curtiss's wife waved a handkerchief at her husband. One of his assistants unfurled an American flag in the rushing wind. It was the first time in history that an airplane and a locomotive had traveled side by side. Together, Curtiss's Albany Flyer and the patriotic train made quite a scene. "It was like a real race," Curtiss recalled, "and I enjoyed the contest more than anything else during the flight." Only during the flight's two scheduled refueling stops did the train lose direct sight of its quarry. At the final refueling point in Poughkeepsie, Curtiss set down on the grounds of the New York State Hospital for the Insane. The irony was not lost on the hospital's superintendent. "Most of you flying-machine inventors end up here anyway," he quipped.[6]

On the final leg of the flight into New York City, the locomotive had difficulty keeping pace with the oil-powered airplane. Curtiss flew ahead, appearing like a small bird over the Hudson. As he edged closer to Manhattan, a crowd of thousands gathered to watch from New York's Riverside Drive. The buzz of the aircraft's engine drew even more people to the rooftops of Washington Heights. Seeing an airplane for the first time, observers struggled to describe the sight and sound of Curtiss flying overhead. "He appeared not unlike a gull floating with rigid wings on the breast of a gale," said one witness. "The drumming of the motor sounded like the belligerent humming of an angry wasp." Down on the Hudson, the constant armada of ships that surrounded Manhattan blasted their whistles and fog horns, giving the aircraft a "hearty, if inharmonious, welcome" to New York.[7]

Instead of flying directly to his original destination on Governor's Island, Curtiss made an abrupt turn and doubled back up the Hudson River. He found an open stretch of grass at the northernmost tip of Manhattan (today Inwood Hill Park) and brought the aircraft to earth. This was the moment when Curtiss technically made history. The aviator and his rubber pants were the first to complete what everyone at the time considered a "cross-country" flight. To modern air travelers, 150 miles seems like a short hop. In 1910 the crossing of this impossibly long stretch of terrain garnered wall-to-wall media coverage and front-page headlines.[8] The conquest of such a great distance by air proved the concept for all future long-distance airmail and passenger service. Curtiss's aircraft could do more than fly in circles like the Wright brothers' contraption. His gasoline-powered engine could take him practically anywhere.

After landing his aircraft on Manhattan proper, Curtiss found a telephone and called in his achievement to the *New York World* to officially claim Pulitzer's prize money. Then he inspected the flaps and wires of his aircraft. They were all in working order, so he sailed back into the air for a salutary victory flight around the island of Manhattan. It was a scene that New York would not soon forget.

By now, word of the flight had swept across the city. New Yorkers ducked out from church services. Some closed their shops. Curtiss gave everyone a show. Flying low over New York, he buzzed Grant's Tomb at two hundred feet and edged above the masts of passenger steamers and cargo ships moored along the Hudson River. He flew so low that the skyscrapers along New York's skyline rose above the height of his aircraft. Viewed from the air, he thought the spire of the Metropolitan Life Tower was an "awfully pretty thing on a Sunday morning." As the number of spectators swelled to the hundreds of thousands, New Yorkers thought much the same of him. In Battery Park alone, ten thousand people scurried to the waterline to catch sight of the Albany Flyer as it rounded the southern tip of Manhattan. Included among them was a photographer who captured Curtiss on film just as he buzzed above the Statue of Liberty. The camera froze him in time like a wasp in gray and silver amber.

The unusual sight of an airplane held aloft over Manhattan by gasoline was emblematic of petroleum's transformative power in the modern world. Oil was already fortified on earth. It was now beginning its conquest of the sky. The same year Curtiss made his historic flight from Albany, so many cars were racing across American roads that President Roosevelt's successor, William Howard Taft, felt confident enough to declare, "We are living in the automobile age."[9] Taft was right, of course, and Deterding wanted to be the one to fuel that age. What he did not want was an interminable war against Standard, which was why he had come to New York. By 1910 the incessant cycle of price wars and cease-fires with Standard was becoming tiresome. Deterding believed that a marketing agreement with the Americans was the best way to bring the mindless flare-ups of commercial warfare to an end. Small steps in this direction were already bearing fruit. After the amalgamation of Royal Dutch/Shell, for example, the company began to sell modest quantities of gasoline to Standard of California. As far as Deterding was concerned, there was no reason that cooperation on this limited scale could not become the basis for a more comprehensive deal with the Americans. Standard thought otherwise.

In the corporate culture that Rockefeller had created, 26 Broadway had no interest in cooperating. Up until the very moment when the Supreme Court issued its order to disband the monopoly, Standard sought to expand it even more. The company rejected Deterding's offer of a marketing arrangement and proposed to buy Royal Dutch/Shell outright for $100 million ($2.5 billion today). This was not what Deterding had come to discuss. The whole trip had been futile. "I am sorry to have to place on record that my visit to this city"—he swallowed his rage—"has been so useless."

Since there could be no agreement with Royal Dutch/Shell, Standard went on the attack. Even as it fought the government's allegations of predatory pricing in the run-up to the Supreme Court hearing, 26 Broadway unleashed a new round of price cuts against Deterding in August 1910. Over the next eleven months, Standard would end its existence in a final, furious fight against Royal Dutch/Shell. In addition to a price war, it abruptly canceled its contract to buy Deterding's gasoline shipments from the Indies and renewed its efforts to pump oil in Sumatra through a Dutch proxy company. Coming on the heels of his good-faith offer to cooperate, the ferocity of Standard's assault on Royal Dutch/Shell brought out Deterding's instinct for commercial slaughter. If Standard wanted a war, so be it. Royal Dutch/Shell had fought wars like this before, and this time Deterding would to take the fight to America.

Suddenly, a new strategy took hold across Royal Dutch/Shell: "To America!"[10] Over the next four years, from 1910 to 1914, Royal Dutch/Shell systematically laid the groundwork for an all-out expansion into the States. If Standard wanted to undercut prices in Europe or Asia, Royal Dutch/Shell would do the same in America. "We obviously had to dig ourselves in as traders on American soil," Deterding said. "Otherwise we would have lost our foothold everywhere else. Until we started trading in America, our American competitors controlled world prices. So to put an end to this state of things, I decided that we must take America."[11]

The invasion was easier said than done. It required a staggering build-out in the upstream oil fields and downstream markets of the United States. Although Royal Dutch/Shell could ferry petroleum across the Pacific on Samuel's old tanker fleet, it would also need to control its own petroleum production inside the United States. But Royal Dutch/Shell did not own any oil wells in the strategically placed fields of Middle America. To correct this weakness, Deterding dispatched company representatives on a quest to buy up as much crude production as possible. This meant venturing into the new frontier of petroleum: Oklahoma.

Back in 1901, the same year the Lucas well came in at Spindletop, drillers in Oklahoma had opened the first producing oil well at a place called Red Fork. The closest settlement to this small petroleum find was a clump of wooden homes and brick stores known as Tulsa. While the find at Red Fork was not a game-changer like Spindletop, it was enough to entice two wildcat drillers named Robert Galbreath and Frank Chesley to try their luck in a stretch of land south of Tulsa. There in November 1905 they tapped into the legendary Glenn Pool field, fifteen miles outside town. Shouting, "Oil! Oil! My God, Bob. We got an oil well," Frank Chesley announced the starting cry of the Oklahoma petroleum boom.

Since Royal Dutch/Shell was late to the bonanza in Oklahoma, it would have to make up for lost time with cash. Drawing on an infusion of capital from the House of Rothschild and other French and English bankers, Deterding's plan was to buy as many proven wells as possible in Oklahoma. He could then use this production to power the company's expansion into Standard's home market. He chose Sir Marcus's nephew, Mark Abrahams, to complete the task. On account of the merger, Abrahams now worked for the combined Royal Dutch/Shell Group. Abrahams agreed to undertake the assignment, but only if his wife, Roxana, could accompany him on the journey. Deterding had no objections.

Throughout his career, Abrahams had existed on the rough edges of the oil world. He had earned his first battle scars establishing Shell's oil production in the jungles of Borneo. For this thankless task, he became Samuel's whipping boy, receiving endless blows by letter and telegram from his uncle in London. It was never the fault of Abrahams that Shell's Borneo field did not gush with oil like Deterding's wells in Sumatra; Samuel vented frustration onto his long-suffering nephew all the same. For Abrahams, the trip to Oklahoma would be a chance to wipe the slate of Borneo clean—he would prove his worth. But he had no idea what conditions he would find in Oklahoma. Did the place even have banks? What about lines of communication? Whatever existed there, he was not going to be caught unprepared. Strapping $2,500 around his waist (worth $60,000 today), he packed a typewriter into his luggage and set out from New York with Roxana and a Dutch technical adviser in July 1912.[12] Their destination was Tulsa, which postcards called the "Oil Capital of the World."

When Abrahams arrived in Tulsa that summer, he found a city unlike anything he had encountered in Borneo. Instead of a jungle, Tulsa was an island of eighteen thousand people living in an ocean of grassland. Practically everything about the town was new, and nothing looked entirely finished. Fresh construction projects seemed to be going up in every direction at once. A few streets in the center of Tulsa were paved, but the rest were dirt. Telephone lines were strung in every conceivable direction. Merchants of all stripes were hanging out shingles, trying to cash in on Tulsa's expanding wealth from the oil trade. This was the civilized side of Tulsa. Down on the Glenn Pool, civilization was hard to find.

In the oil boomtown of Kiefer, just outside Tulsa, the streets were mud, the sidewalks were dirt, and the buildings were flimsy and small—the conditions Abrahams had no doubt been expecting to find when he left New York. What the boomtown lacked in conveniences, however, it made up for in crude. There was so much oil in the Glenn Pool field that Kiefer had attracted the now-familiar tribe of prospectors, gamblers, prostitutes, moonshiners, and con artists. Creatures common at every petroleum boom, they burrowed into the shelter of Kiefer's brothels and saloons, dreaming of oil and staining the floors brown with the spit of chewing tobacco.[13] Staked with his bankroll from Royal Dutch/Shell, Abrahams put everyone else in Kiefer to shame in terms of wealth. Naturally, Sir Marcus's nephew went on a buying spree.

As the new owner of several oil properties in Tulsa, Abrahams eventually needed to incorporate his acquisitions into a legal business entity. The question was what to call this fledgling company. It seemed that every conceivable name was already taken. Two competing tales exist as to how Royal Dutch/Shell's foothold in America acquired its name. One asserts that it was found in the back of an office dictionary. The other claims that Roxana Abrahams named the company after her namesake, the famed wife of Alexander the Great. Whatever the origin, the Roxana Petroleum Company would soon be a linchpin of the "To America!" strategy. Once Abrahams had done his work, Deterding boasted to Loudon: "At last we *are* in America."[14]

The timing of Deterding's invasion was fortuitous. Just as Rockefeller's shattered empire was reeling from the Supreme Court breakup, Royal Dutch/Shell systematically established one of the largest oil companies in America. During the frenzied peak of the effort from 1912 to 1914, Deterding's invasion strategy amounted to the largest foreign investment in the U.S. economy in the early twentieth century.[15] Aiding this expansion was the fact that Standard was no longer a monolith. Before the breakup, the size of the American oil giant dwarfed Royal Dutch/Shell. Afterward, the dismantled chunks of Standard were less invincible.

As the internal harmony between Standard's offspring entered a period of flux, Royal Dutch/Shell tenaciously stormed the U.S. oil market. In the midcontinent, Roxana Oil provided domestically produced crude. Simultaneously on the West Coast, Royal Dutch/Shell replicated Samuel's original expansion into Asia, establishing dockside receiving terminals in Seattle, Portland, Vancouver, and San Francisco. The group constructed an inland distribution network and registered a new marketing company to sell its product: Shell. In a breathtakingly short period of time, the bright red-and-yellow shell emblem of the Samuel family proliferated across America. On U.S. roads and rails, the shell suddenly graced tank cars, highway signs, and filling stations. Never had any of Standard's competitors executed an expansion of this size and ferocity. The growth of Shell in America was so aggressive that famed newspaperman William Randolph Hearst even dubbed it in jest the "yellow peril."[16]

Ultimately, "To America!" proved to be an enduring success. Rockefeller and his empire had turned consumers into hostages for four decades. Now the regulatory lance of antitrust law and the spur of competition had combined to topple the unbeatable greed of 26 Broadway. The combination of these two elements was essential for breaking Rockefeller once and for all. Fighting between themselves, the rival houses of Royal Dutch and Shell had never been large enough to go toe to toe with Standard in the United States. Only after Sir Marcus and Deterding joined forces did their combined strength make a real challenger out of the unified Royal Dutch/Shell Group. Had Deterding deployed the "To America!" strategy against the full might of 26 Broadway prior to 1911, his prospects for success would likely have been grim. This was why the collective efforts of John Sherman, Ida Tarbell, Theodore Roosevelt, and the Supreme Court were equally essential. The trustbusters weakened Rockefeller's monopoly. Free marketeers like Deterding provided a competitive alternative to it. Acting in tandem, the Supreme Court and Royal Dutch/Shell defined how the world would now travel, what it would burn along the way, and the price it would pay to get there.

CHAPTER 19

Wealth Beyond Measure

You cannot serve both God and money.

Matthew 6:24

Rockefeller wore retirement well. During the winter of 1914, just as Europe was proceeding inexorably toward war, the founder of Standard Oil began to detach himself from the world he had helped to build. Across the globe, his great petroleum empire was broken and destabilized. Standard's enemies, from small-time independents to the invading giant of Royal Dutch/Shell, had seized on the opening to expand outward from a growing list of oil fields in Texas, Oklahoma, California, Sumatra, Romania, and Russia. Had Rockefeller been a younger man, he might have fought the changing tide. At seventy-five, however, his greatest battles were behind him. He now turned his attention from oil to other passions. Chief among them were golf, God, fast drives in his motorcar, and flirtatious women. Down in Florida, he could indulge all four.

Rockefeller was no stranger to Florida. His first visit to the state had occurred back in 1883, during a trip to see Henry Flagler when he was on honeymoon in St. Augustine. Although Rockefeller initially resisted the temptations of the damp tropical air and ocean breezes, they proved irresistible to Flagler. Over the next thirty years, Rockefeller's longtime colleague devoted most of his wealth from Standard Oil to transforming the state from a swampy backwater into a playground for the rich. At the time of his death in May 1913, Flagler had dropped $18 million ($424 million today) into railroads, $12 million into hotels, and $1 million on a steamship line to Cuba.[1] Among his many investments in Florida, Flagler's most renowned accomplishment by far was the "Eighth Wonder of the World," a $10 million railroad built across the ocean to Key West. "Henry did a great job in Florida," Rockefeller later said of his old colleague. "Think of pouring out all that money on a whim. But then Henry was always bold."[2]

Only after the death of Flagler did the allure of Florida finally catch up to Rockefeller. What pushed him over the edge was golf. When he learned from the U.S. Weather Bureau that Daytona Beach received more sunshine every winter than the fairways of Augusta, Georgia, the tropical hook was set. The prospect of a longer golfing season was too tempting to pass up. During the winter of 1914, Rockefeller and his household staff occupied an entire floor in Flagler's famous Ormond Hotel, six miles north of Daytona. For the next four winters, Rockefeller would be a constant fixture at the hotel and a daily presence on the links of Ormond Beach.

When it came to golf, Rockefeller burned through money with uncharacteristic abandon. In one year alone, he spent an astonishing $27,537.80 (nearly $1 million today) just on golfing expenses. Golf was more than a pastime for him; it was an obsession, a hard-mastered skill, and practically the only time when he could safely socialize with others. As a biographer noted, "Golf brought out a native drollery that he had never allowed to flower before." On the fairway, Rockefeller's personality immediately lightened. His banter became playful rather than laconic, because the golf course made conversations safe. Whenever a social interaction with a golfing partner threatened to move beyond the realm of the superficial into the serious or personal, the game provided infinite off-ramps for pantomime humor or casual distraction. And of course, there was always the opportunity to best his opponents. "We should not rejoice in the downfall of others, but I slaughtered four men at golf on Saturday last," Rockefeller wrote his daughter. "This was very wrong, and of course I will never do it again."[3]

When Rockefeller was not golfing, he was on the road. As a younger man, he had thrilled at racing his horse and carriage down Euclid Avenue in Cleveland. Now in later life, his desire for speed manifested itself in daily drives in his automobile. Motoring in the back of his open-air Crane-Simplex touring car, he frequently timed how fast his driver could reach certain destinations. The setting of new records was a regular affair.[4] Like the golf course, the daily adventures on the road were a chance for socializing. After Rockefeller's wife died in 1915, he used such chances for the bountiful opportunities they offered to indulge in mischief with the opposite sex. Tightly nestled between two women in his backseat, the strictures of Rockefeller's Victorian upbringing loosened. With a blanket draped over their laps, Rockefeller "became notorious for his hot schoolboy hands" on these drives. While most of his female guests seemed to enjoy the attention, the sentiment was not universally shared. "That old rooster!" said one woman as she fled into an accompanying car. "He ought to be hand-cuffed."[5]

Florida was growing on Rockefeller, along with a gnawing sense of his own mortality. During his time away from the fairway and the road, he passed the winters in Florida strolling unaccompanied through Ormond Beach or "belting out hymns with gusto" in the

Ormond Union Church.[6] Throughout his life, his evangelical Baptist faith had defined his personality and outlook on the world. Nevertheless, he had no difficulty separating reverence for the divine from every other aspect of his life, particularly when it came to the annihilation of his business rivals. He took pains to create elaborate explanations for why his prosperity on earth was a sign of God's heavenly blessings and approval. As he approached his eighth decade of life, the monumental size of his fortune created a wrinkle in his conscience. His personal balance sheet was at odds with his devout Christianity. According to the teachings of Jesus, "It is easier for a camel to pass through the eye of a needle than for one who is rich to enter the kingdom of God" (Matthew 19:24). For the pious and aging Rockefeller, the enormity of his wealth presented a problem.

In 1918, that enormity was staggering. When *The New York Times* dug up his tax returns for that year, it discovered that he reported a taxable annual income of $33 million on an estimated net worth in excess of $800 million. This was after Rockefeller had already given away roughly $500 million to numerous charities and educational institutions like the University of Chicago. Inflation adjustments at these heights and long timescales can be difficult to frame in terms of contemporary purchasing power. In 2007, when journalists Peter W. Bernstein and Annalyn Swan attempted to compare Rockefeller's net worth to that of every other wealthy American, they discovered that Standard's founder was not merely a rich man—he was an unimaginably wealthy one.[7] At the peak of his fortune, his net worth would have amounted to roughly $357 billion today. Close on his heels was the second-richest American who ever lived, Andrew Carnegie, at an adjusted $328 billion. Rounding out third place was Cornelius Vanderbilt with a relatively paltry $197 billion. Compared to these blazing fortunes, Bill Gates's current net worth of $79.2 billion is a dim fire.[8]

No matter the size of his wealth, in the end, not even Rockefeller could take it into the great beyond. As he rounded out his seventies, the fate of his remaining fortune remained surprisingly unsettled. Holding on to his money until the end was one option, but this would ensure that the federal government took a sizable cut of any funds he could not spend before death. Worse, the federal noose of the inheritance tax was tightening. During 1916 and 1917, for example, Congress approved back-to-back increases in the death tax. There was no telling how high this and other taxes would go in the future. Since Rockefeller intended to reach his hundredth birthday, Congress would have ample opportunities over the coming years to allot itself ever larger portions of his money.[9] Whatever warnings about wealth Rockefeller found in the Bible, losing his fortune to taxes was a distasteful prospect for the aging titan. Adding to the urge to shed his riches sooner rather than later was his competitive nature. The world's second-richest man, Andrew Carnegie, was giving away his money at a fantastic pace. In the race to the top of the oil world, Rockefeller had soundly bested his fellow industrialist when it came to gathering money. Now in the twilight of their years, Carnegie was beating his old rival in an unofficial contest to give it all away. "The man who dies rich dies disgraced," Carnegie wrote decades earlier, explaining, "The day is not far distant when the man who dies leaving behind him millions of available wealth, which was free for him to administer during life, will pass away unwept, unhonored and unsung."[10] Carnegie held true to his word. In the early decades of the twentieth century, he surpassed Rockefeller in philanthropic giving, encouraging the popular perception that the second-richest man in the world (Carnegie) was the first in charity. Once

Carnegie threw down the gauntlet of charitable competition, the mighty Rockefeller looked like a greedy hoarder of cash by comparison.[11]

The final impetus to action was the raw power of compound interest and dividends. With each passing year, the Rockefeller fortune grew exponentially larger. Aiming to manage the disposal of this income rationally and to keep pace with Carnegie, Rockefeller had previously hired a Baptist minister named Frederick T. Gates to sort through the incessant requests from needy causes. But Gates's full-time efforts were insufficient. "Your fortune is rolling up, rolling up like an avalanche!" he warned Rockefeller in 1906. "You must keep up with it! You must distribute it faster than it grows! If you do not, it will crush you and your children and your children's children."[12] It was sage, persuasive council.

Following Gates's advice, Rockefeller began to divert large portions of his fortune to the newly established Rockefeller Foundation in 1909. This included an initial transfer of 73,000 shares of Standard Oil of New Jersey (equivalent to $1.3 billion today). Enlisting Gates, his son-in-law Harold McCormick, and his son John D. Rockefeller Jr. as trustees, the foundation would serve as the main vehicle for Rockefeller Sr.'s charitable giving. His transfer of wealth was so monumental that the Rockefeller Foundation is still a powerful philanthropic force after more than a hundred years of existence. Throughout the twentieth century, the foundation put Rockefeller's wealth to use in the fight against contagious diseases like yellow fever. More recently, it has deployed his remaining fortune (now totaling $3.4 billion in assets) to offset the impact of global climate change.[13] Similar to Alfred Nobel, who once used the money he earned from selling the weapons of war to promote peace, Rockefeller's oil wealth endures to mitigate changes in the atmosphere.

Breaking Rockefeller

While the creation of the Rockefeller Foundation helped to formalize the philanthropic outlays of Standard's founder, it did little to halt the unchecked growth of his total fortune. Once the bountiful shock wave of the Standard Oil breakup shattered Rockefeller's monopoly in 1911, his wealth grew faster than before. In the end, he jettisoned his money with the same ruthless efficiency with which he made it. The single largest transfer of family wealth in history began on March 13, 1917, when Rockefeller handed over 20,000 shares of Standard of Indiana to his son John D. Rockeller Jr. The next summer brought a gift of 166,000 shares in Standard of California, followed by chunks of Atlantic Refining and Vacuum Oil (now Exxon). Throughout 1919, Rockefeller's eldest son received an additional 100,000 shares of Standard of New Jersey. Rafts of interest-bearing federal and municipal bonds followed. John D. conducted each of these transfers with the demeanor of a mildly friendly ATM. "Dear Son," he wrote from Ormond Beach on February 17, 1920, "I am this day giving you $65,000,000 par value of United States Government First Liberty Loan 3.5 percent bonds. Affectionately, Father." Over the course of four gilded years, from 1917 through 1920, Rockefeller bequeathed a final $475 million to his children and $200 million to charity.[14] After the dispersal, he was an extremely well-off "pauper." His remaining reserve of $25 million allowed him to enjoy a comfortable existence as a migratory winter snowbird. Florida was becoming a new home away from home.

In 1918, during his fantastic wealth transfer, Rockefeller purchased a three-story house across the street from the Ormond Hotel. Around town, he relished the relative anonymity of being "neighbor John" to the beachside residents of Ormond. It was a polite fiction. Everyone knew their most famous neighbor by sight. The recently "poor" Rockefeller took pleasure in the everyman nickname just the same.

Ensconced in Ormond, he took to the life of a carefree retiree. He teed off each morning at ten-fifteen on the nose; he sang from the pews every Sunday; and during racing season, he made the short drive down to Daytona Beach to watch high-performance racecars burn their way across the hard-packed sand.[15] It was difficult to miss the beach races each winter. Flagler had first promoted them as a way to drum up tourism. The drivers came in droves and stayed—naturally— across the street from Rockefeller at the Ormond Hotel. By the time that he solidified his roots on the Florida coast, Daytona was billing itself as the "Mecca of motorists."[16] Rockefeller could count himself among the faithful pilgrims.

Sitting in a white wicker chair and draped in a light curtain to protect him from the sun and flecks of blowing sand, an increasingly frail Rockefeller watched new generations of motorcars roar across Daytona Beach.[17] Every season the old speed records seemed to fall. The beach track was a closed circuit, of course. The glory days of city-to-city contests like the Paris-Marseilles-Paris Grand Prix were long over. But the same desire to go faster and finish first remained unchanged. It fed, as always, on the unquenchable thirst for gasoline.

With the rising importance of racing at Daytona Beach, Henry Ford became a casual visitor to Ormond and a Rockefeller acquaintance. Rockefeller was by now deep into his meditations on God and eternity, but Ford gave little truck to such sentiments. Wishing Ford off one day, Rockefeller said, "Good bye, I'll see you in heaven," to which Ford wryly answered, "You will if you get in."[18] For his part, Rockefeller never lost his abiding faith in redemption. "Many folks believe I've done much harm in the world," he once said to the mayor of Ormond Beach, "but on the other hand I've tried to do what good I could and I really would like to live to be a hundred."[19]

On his final day on earth in 1937, one of Rockefeller's last acts was to pay off the mortgage of the Euclid Avenue Baptist Church in Cleveland. Later that day he suffered a heart attack. At some point in the early morning hours of May 23—two years, one month, and fifteen days shy of his hundredth birthday—John D. Rockefeller slipped into a coma and died in his bed.

CHAPTER 20

Legacies

S tanding in the middle of a war, one could almost see the future.
During the first week of August 1916, the world's first modern
oil tanker, the *Murex*, sailed into the warm harbor of Mudros Bay. Embraced by the rocky arms of Lemnos Island in the Aegean Sea, the low
hills around the bay had served as the staging area for Britain's disastrous invasion of Gallipoli the previous year. By seizing the narrow
opening of the Dardanelles between the Black Sea and the Mediterranean, the invasion was supposed to knock Turkey out of the war. Instead, it descended into a morass of trenches, sand, and bloodshed. At
the head of the Allied armada to force open the Dardanelles was none
other than the oil-burning *Queen Elizabeth*. The Royal Navy used her
massive fifteen-inch guns to pound Turkish fortresses on the coast. It
was an impressive display of her firepower and a feckless waste of her
speed. By deploying their super weapon against fixed emplacements,
the Royal Navy cast aside Admiral Nelson's hallowed maxim that "any
sailor who attacked a fort was a fool." Along the Dardanelles, all the
efforts of Samuel, Fisher, and even Churchill to endow the *Queen Elizabeth* with the benefits of oil were wasted. More foolishness followed.[1]

From the spring of 1915 until the winter of 1916, Gallipoli became a place of futile, mechanized killing. Existing on the edge of the fighting, Mudros Bay was the final place of tranquillity for soldiers who embarked for Gallipoli's beaches and the first spot of safety for the returning wounded. It was also the best point in the Aegean Sea to harbor and refuel warships. Had any of the remaining British forces around Mudros Bay happened to survey the bay on the morning of August 7, 1916, they would have glimpsed a historic sight. The bulk oil tanker *Murex*, now under charter to the Admiralty from Shell, was refueling the world's first aircraft carrier, the HMS *Ark Royal*.[2] Oil had gone to war.

The *Murex* and the *Ark Royal* were trailblazers. Thanks to Flannery's self-contained, go-anywhere pump for moving petroleum on and off his tanker, vessels like the *Ark Royal* could take aboard fuel anywhere in the world—even while at sea. Shell helped to make this possible. As the Great War raged across Europe, Shell became the principal supplier of gasoline to the British Expeditionary Force and the sole supplier of aviation fuel to British aviators.[3] This fuel now supplied the *Ark Royal*'s Sopwith biplanes, which launched from the deck of the experimental carrier. Viewing the *Murex* and the *Ark Royal* together in Mudros Bay that August, an observer could catch a glimpse of things to come.[4]

For the first time in human history, the British Sopwiths that burned Shell's oil during the war allowed an admiral to peer over the horizon and project power beyond the range of his naval guns. And while the *Ark Royal*'s aircraft were not yet capable of turning defeat into victory in the Dardanelles, they were the technological forerunners of the sophisticated supersonic fighters that launched from decks of carriers in the twentieth and twenty-first centuries. Anchored side by side at Mudros Bay, the *Ark Royal* and the *Murex* were changing modern warfare, one gallon at a time.

Legacies

Like so many vessels of her time, the *Murex* would not survive the war. By the end of her service life, she had seen the world. She had made history in the Suez, crisscrossed the waters of Europe, Asia, and the Pacific, and all the while made Sir Marcus a tidy fortune in shipping oil. The innovations of Flannery's original design had kept her dangerous cargo from exploding, twice rescued her after running aground, and endowed future generations of tankers with a legacy of safety. Unfortunately, Flannery's efforts could not make the *Murex* invincible against a torpedo.

On December 21, 1916, the *Murex* was on a return voyage to Mudros Bay. She was sailing ninety-four miles from Port Said when German U-boat captain Gustav Siess caught sight of her in the water.[5] Siess and the crew of his U-73 were fast making a name for themselves. The previous month one of their mines had sunk the last sister ship of the *Titanic*, the HMHS *Britannic,* off the coast of Greece. Now the U-73 would send another historic ship, the *Murex*, to the seafloor. Her death came without warning. When the U-73's torpedo struck her outer skin, it blasted a twenty-square-foot hole into her side. Although the damage was fatal for the *Murex*, only one crew member died as a result of the attack. The rest of the tanker's crew made it back to shore in Egypt.[6]

After the Allied victory over Germany in 1918, Sir Marcus began to withdraw from all formal responsibilities in the oil business. He delivered the official announcement of his retirement from the board of Royal Dutch/Shell at the group's annual meeting on July 20, 1920. Quelling the murmurs that erupted from the news, Sir Marcus was gracious. "The weight of this gigantic business must be carried by younger soldiers," he said.[7] That turned out to be Sir Marcus's son Walter Samuel, whom the board swiftly approved as chairman of Shell. After stepping aside, Sir Marcus returned to long voyages aboard the *Lady Torfrida*. His luxurious yacht was no longer the consolation for a "disappointed man," as after Deterding's triumph over Shell. That sting lasted about as long as it took for Deterding to double Shell's gross annual income from £556,000 in 1908 to £1.2 million in 1912 (roughly $162 million today).[8] Instead, these trips became well-deserved holidays to the beaches of Biarritz, France, and still longer journeys to explore the Mediterranean. On the deck of the *Lady Torfrida*, Sir Marcus nourished his lasting love of the sea.

In the final years of his life, when he was not aboard his yacht, Sir Marcus cycled between showers of honors and praise and recurring bouts of sickness. On May 25, 1921, his hard-fought struggle with the Royal Navy ended in a triumphant—and unsurprising—victory. It was on that day that the Admiralty officially declared the full conversion of all future British warships to liquid fuel. One of Sir Marcus's former directors at Shell, the Scotsman Sir Reginald MacLeod, immediately fired off a letter to his old chairman. "I want to congratulate you on the Admiralty decision announced yesterday that all the King's ships are to burn oil," MacLeod wrote. "What a triumph for your judgment and far-sightedness! And how rapidly things have moved since 1913 and 1914, when the Admiralty turned a nearly deaf ear to all your proposals!"[9] The praise was well deserved and the triumphs just beginning.

Less than two weeks after the Admiralty issued its decision on oil, Sir Marcus attained his long-coveted peerage as a full baron. On June 4 it became official. Sir Marcus Samuel would thereafter be the Baron Bearsted. This time there were no battleships to be hauled from the mud. The peerage was granted on account of Samuel's "eminent public and national services, and [as] a generous benefactor to charitable and scientific objects."[10] After a lifetime of steady ascendancy, the son of Marcus Samuel, Sr., had at last vaulted into the upper reaches of the British social hierarchy. "You can't think what pleasure it gives me to put 'The Honorable' on my children's envelopes," Samuel said to a friend as he drafted a letter. The good name of Samuel was now officially an honorable one.

After 1921 more honors followed, along with bouts of sickness. In his final years, the Honorable Marcus Samuel retreated to a private life and was forced to make use of a wheelchair. He reemerged into public view to receive an honorary degree from Sheffield University and a similar honor from Cambridge. The next summer Samuel's crowning achievement arrived. On the occasion of the king's birthday in 1922, Samuel finally became the First Viscount Bearsted.[11] The well-wishes and letters rolled in like a tide. Lord Esher, a reformer in his own right at the War Office, added a slight twist to the congratulatory surge. "Dear old Jackie F. who adored you, always said you ought to be a Duke, as you were such a great patriot!" he wrote.[12] Perhaps if Samuel had lived longer, he would have become a duke. All the same, only a handful of nobles in England outranked the new Viscount Bearsted by the end of his life. Fewer still could match his bankroll—such was the bounty of oil. As for Sam Samuel, he too got to taste the good life and finished out his career as a member of Parliament. Always the bachelor, Sam never did marry or have children.

On October 8, 1925, Samuel's estranged friend Shady Fred Lane died quietly, away from the public eye. There was little ceremony or official mourning over Lane's death. After spending a lifetime in the background of the oil business, he had intentionally shunned the spotlight. Few people had ever heard of him, and fewer still commemorated his passing, which is a great pity. Lane's contribution to the development of the modern energy market was equal in significance to Samuel's. Without his insight and Samuel's friendship, the erstwhile Merchant of Houndsditch would not likely have forged his initial deal with the House of Rothschild for bulk Russian oil, pried open the Suez, or come close to capturing Royal Dutch "bound hand and foot" during the ill-fated "British-Dutch" negotiations. After the rupture of Lane's relationship with Samuel in 1902, the two remained professionally close but were never again friends. The oil business forced them to be allies. Lane was, after all, the Rothschilds' designated representative inside the combined Royal Dutch/Shell Group— a giant that he had personally helped to construct.

The end came for the First Viscount Bearsted and his wife, Fanny, a little more than a year after Lane's death. Samuel and Fanny had spent most of their lives together. A natural symmetry linked them in death. On January 16, 1927, they were both ill and resting in separate rooms of their home at 3 Hamilton Place in London. Against the stern objections of her family and medical attendants, Fanny tried to force her way up the stairs to see her husband. Her assembled platoon of nurses urged her to return to bed—she was deemed too sick to move around. After failing to see her husband for a final time, she suffered a stroke on the spot and died. At the time of his wife's passing, Marcus had already slipped into a coma. Within twenty-four hours of Fanny's death, he too was dead. The next day was to be their forty-sixth wedding anniversary. Much like the many experiences they shared in life, the couple shared a funeral service and a humble burial plot. Today only a plain granite tombstone in the Jewish Cemetery at Willesden marks the final resting place of the First Viscount Bearsted and his beloved wife.

As for Deterding, he finally did get the knighthood that Fisher had recommended to Churchill at the outset of the war. On January 6, 1921, just five months before Sir Marcus became the Baron Bearsted, Deterding became a Knight Commander of the Most Excellent Order of the British Empire. The "To America!" invasion that he oversaw during the 1910s had, by now, steadily expanded outward into Latin America. By the 1920s, Royal Dutch/Shell was pumping oil from the United States as well as from new petroleum discoveries in Mexico and Venezuela. These upstream supplies proved crucial when it came to meeting the planet's rising demand for motor fuel. In America alone, car ownership had risen from 3.4 million vehicles in 1916 to 23.1 million by the end of the 1920s. No longer a waste product or even a luxury item, gasoline was becoming essential to modern life. Together, gasoline and fuel oil accounted for 85 percent of total oil consumption in 1929. The transition from kerosene was complete. As the oil historian Daniel Yergin nicely framed it, "The 'new light' had given way to the 'new fuel'" of gasoline.[13] This would be one of the lasting and most powerful legacies of Marcus Samuel, the little known merchant from Houndsditch, and the outsize aspirations of the un-proven "interim" manager, Henri Deterding.

But by far the most amazing aspects of the war to break Rockefel-ler's monopoly are those that still endure. In the twenty-first century, the streets around Houndsditch are very different from the way they were when Marcus Samuel and his family knew them. The chaotic melee of merchants, anarchists, and street vendors of the late nine-teenth century has given way to salad shops, cell phone stores, chain coffee houses, and the White Horse Pub and Grill—the current occu-pant of M. Samuel & Co.'s old address at 31 Houndsditch Street.[14] The old England of agriculture, aristocracy, and landed money has been replaced by trendy yuppies, $2 million apartments, and the egg-shaped silhouette of London's iconic Gherkin skyscraper.

Standing a block from Houndsditch, the Gherkin towers over the former site of M. Samuel & Co. In Samuel's day, the merchants and traders who populated the neighborhood exemplified the global eco-nomic transition from sail to steam. Now the tenants of the Gherkin tell a new story about the unfolding revolution of digital business and finance. The Gherkin houses the international wings of *Fortune* Global 500 finance and insurance companies, two of the largest law firms in the world, a subsidiary of the ICE derivatives exchange, and ready-made offices for new startups and entrepreneurs that have yet to make it big. Samuel would feel right at home.

One point of overlap between old and new is mass immigration. Although the heart of the East End has shifted slightly eastward— away from swanky Houndsditch—this dynamic region of London is still a place for arrivals and departures. Instead of the Jewish families who came from eastern Europe at the end of the nineteenth century, the wider East End has become home to waves of immigrants from South Asia, West Africa, and the Caribbean. Even now the displacement of old working-class families can be the source of sporadic social frictions in East London, an angst that Samuel would have understood.[15] As for Shell, today Royal Dutch/Shell has become unrecognizably larger and more powerful than either the First Viscount Bearsted or Sir Deterding might have ever imagined. In 2014 the company was ranked second only to Walmart on *Fortune*'s Global 500 ranking of the world's largest corporations. Generating $460 billion in revenue each year, the amalgamated forces of Samuel's Shell and Deterding's Royal Dutch now stand slightly ahead of Sinopec, China's oil and gas behemoth, and China National Petroleum (CNPC). It is a sign of the interlocking connection between oil's past and our present. At a fundamental level, little has changed in the energy world since the *Murex* first slipped through the Suez Canal at the end of the last century. The United States remains the world's largest consumer of hydrocarbons, and the energy balance of the planet hangs ever so delicately on those who can feed the insatiable need for fuel in the Far East.

Legacies

Standard too still exists today, though it is known by other names. When Exxon and Mobil joined together in 1999, they not only completed the largest industrial merger in history up until that time, they reunited two of Rockefeller's long-estranged siblings. After the former Standard of New Jersey (Exxon) and Standard of New York (Mobil) united, they undid part of the Supreme Court's ruling to break apart the old Standard empire. At the time of the merger, Exxon and Mobil were actively competing against each other in forty American states. Even so, the dead hand of John Sherman reached out from beyond the grave. After an eleven-month review, the federal government imposed a variety of stipulations on the merger so that the combined power of ExxonMobil would not run afoul of antitrust restrictions. "Because Exxon and Mobil are such large and powerful competitors, and because they now compete in several product and geographic markets in the United States, the Commission insisted on extensive restructuring before accepting a proposed settlement," said then Federal Trade Commission chairman Robert Pitofsky. "This settlement should preserve competition and protect consumers from inappropriate and anticompetitive price increases."[16] After almost eighty years, fear of a comeback from Rockefeller's multiheaded hydra still held sway over the federal government. But Standard was never—quite—dead.

CHAPTER 21

The Enduring Puzzle

Ιt was a new kind of coup. In the final days of August 2010, the Russian gas tanker *Baltica* was sailing east to China and making history. Stretching more than a football field longer than Shell's *Murex*, the *Baltica* was ferrying seventy thousand tons of natural gas from the Russian port of Murmansk to the Chinese city of Ningbo. These facts alone were not spectacular. In the twenty-first century, as in Samuel's day, Russia remains a major supplier of energy to China. What made the trip special was the course the *Baltica* took to reach its destination. For the first time since British explorer Sir Hugh Willoughby tried—and failed—to cross the Arctic's frozen Northeast Passage in 1533, that summer the *Baltica* became the largest energy tanker to successfully complete the shortcut to China across the High North.

Conditions that year were unprecedented. The High North was melting—fast. The summer sea ice had retreated from 40 percent of the Arctic's international waters. By making the historic crossing through the Northeast Passage instead of heading south through the Suez Canal, the *Baltica* shaved almost six thousand miles off a typical journey to China. Changes in climate have now made energy shipments across

272

the High North a regular occurrence during the summer months.[1] Yet the *Baltica*'s destination, and its cargo, hinted at a larger transition in how the world might adapt to a changing climate.

Next to the United States, China has emerged, in the early twenty-first century, as the most energy-hungry country on the planet. It is a place where 291 million tons of imported coal goes up in smoke each year; where car-crazy consumers buy 20 million new automobiles annually; where smog blots out the sky in many cities; and where traffic jams can sometimes last for days. The 20 million new cars that hit China's roads every year join 154 million private cars that are already clogging the country's highways. A surge of this scale is without precedent. Never before "in the history of humanity have we seen such an explosion in demand for cars," said one General Motors executive. "This thing is going to run for decades."[2] And since almost all those automobiles are burning gasoline, China must find slightly more than 10 million barrels of oil every day just to keep their engines humming. The good news is that China is able to pump around 4.5 million barrels a day on its own; the bad news is that the remaining shortfall has to come from the global pool of available crude. China's need for energy is great, and the hydrocarbons it burns eventually return to the atmosphere in the form of greenhouse gases. That makes China's energy problem the world's problem.[3]

Scanning the twenty-first-century energy horizon, China's fuel demands are fundamentally the same as those of nearly every other country in the world. In meeting the planet's need for power, the remarkable thing about the modern energy market is that the same challenges of distance, geography, risk, technology, and greed that Marcus Samuel and Henri Deterding overcame to break Rockefeller's monopoly still exist today. In three modern examples stretching from China to Europe and the United States, this problem set is still waiting to be solved. The encouraging part is that the past holds powerful lessons for some of the toughest energy problems of today: the quest for low-carbon energy substitutes, the persistence of market-killing monopolies, and the hangover of anachronistic regulations.

In China, the demand for carbon-heavy fuels is large and getting larger. But what if there was a way to quench China's thirst for these fuels without burning more oil (or even coal)? The answer to that question is unfolding right now in the southwestern Chinese province of Sichuan. Thanks to a revolutionary innovation, one developed in the energy fields of the United States, China has the potential to produce mind-boggling amounts of lower-carbon natural gas from shale rock. This fuel source is just like the natural gas that powers homes, factories, and vehicles in the United States. In fact, so much shale gas is potentially available in the world that the twenty-first century stands at the threshold of a new, revolutionary change in transportation and power generation. If successful, this crossover could be so great, it would resemble the transition from coal to oil that served as the backdrop for Royal Dutch/Shell's fight with Standard a century earlier.

The first wave of this revolution is already unfolding in the United States. The old, reliable, and proven technology of hydraulic fracturing (fracking) combined with new, unconventional advances in horizontal drilling is bending the structure of the U.S. economy to a new kind of energy abundance. In just ten years, America's production of lower-carbon shale gas increased by a stunning 1,900 percent (from 2 billion to 40 billion cubic feet per day). Thanks to the onrush of domestically produced shale gas, American imports of natural gas have since fallen to their lowest levels in decades.[4] For consumers, the availability of this resource has made life less expensive and, in many cases, far more prosperous due to lower energy costs and new high-paying, highly skilled industrial and commercial jobs. More important for the world's energy balance, the United States has begun to replace large parts of its carbon-intensive coal and oil economy with natural gas alternatives. Not only does natural gas produce fewer greenhouse gases and other pollutants like nitrogen oxide and sulfur dioxide when burned, the wealth of supply has made it cheap, and for consumers, cheap is good.

Across the United States, the economic incentive for using natural gas instead of higher-carbon fuels like coal and oil has begun to alter how Americans work, play, and breathe. Right now entire fleets of commercial vehicles are being retrofitted to run on natural gas from the U.S. shale boom. Even tiny engines, such as those used by fishermen and leisure boats, are burning natural gas instead of oil. The biggest change, however, is in the atmosphere. As American power generation has swapped out coal for natural gas, the air itself has been getting cleaner. In the United States, total emissions of choking sulfur dioxide and nitrogen oxides have fallen to their lowest levels since the Clean Air Act Amendments were passed in 1990.[5] The federal government set the regulatory bar; technological innovations made shale gas plentiful; and the competitive forces of the free market cleaned the air. This is what a revolution in energy looks like. Even better, it can happen in carbon-hungry China, which is why provinces like Sichuan matter.

In the quest for shale gas, China started out with big ambitions. Given the country's underlying geology, scientists calculated that it could hold the largest technically recoverable reserve of shale gas in the world—almost twice as large as in the United States. The future seemed bright for China until the drillers hit a reality check: the underground shale rock in the country's largest field in Sichuan proved harder to reach than in the United States. This made the recoverable amounts of Chinese shale gas potentially less plentiful and more expensive to extract.[6] While Chinese leaders hurried to dampen expectations on their future production, even these revised projections were impressive. By 2020, China will have enough shale gas to meet the annual consumption rate of Spain—Europe's fifth-largest economy.[7] That is no small feat, but expanding beyond this level will be tough. If China is going to create its own lower-carbon shale gas revolution and thereby free up more energy for the rest of the world, it will need to extract more of this resource from hard-to-reach places. This is where technology and greed, two crucial dimensions of the eternal energy puzzle, come into play.

Cost constraints are not new to shale gas; neither is the pressure of competitive innovation. At the outset of the U.S. shale boom, American firms faced high production costs and formidable geological headaches as well. What changed was a flurry of competition. The free market race for shale gas in America encouraged enterprising drillers to push down well costs and achieve impressive feats of innovation in the field. This was not magic—it was competition. It is also where China faces the greatest difficulty. Competition to extract shale gas in China is soft. The country's large state-owned companies, CNPC and Sinopec, dominate the Chinese shale gas industry to the exclusion of others. All remaining competitors face uphill battles when staking their own claims to Chinese shale gas plays. Meanwhile, foreign companies, which have the technology and know-how to improve China's shale production, face substantial government constraints when operating inside the country. This prevents them from entering the Chinese market and developing its shale gas resources in force.[8]

In policy terms, China can be a master of its own energy future, but it will first have to widen the available space for competition. This is especially true when it comes to implementing market-oriented reforms in the shale gas industry. Chinese leaders can still achieve their goal of pumping more lower-carbon shale gas into the domestic economy, but they will need to remove man-made obstacles aboveground in order to fully tap the potential of their shale gas resources below. This means embracing competition. As the experiences of Marcus Samuel and Henri Deterding show, breaking the grip of energy giants is not easy. But when it happens, the introduction of competitive forces can benefit customers, especially in China.

In the European Union, the need for energy is equally great, although its dilemma is slightly different than in the case of China. Much as Rockefeller held his customers hostage in the past, today a large and powerful monopoly holds dominion over nearly 100 million people from the Baltic Sea to the Black Sea. This monopoly is Russian, not American, and it is backed by the full commercial and military might of the Kremlin. Known as Gazprom, Russia's modern-day monopoly sells nearly all the natural gas destined for America's partners and allied countries in central Europe and the Baltic States. As a result, energy consumers in Austria, Bulgaria, the Czech Republic, Estonia, Finland, Hungary, Latvia, Lithuania, Poland, and Slovakia all are dangerously dependent on the Kremlin's gas monopoly to heat their homes and power their economies.[9]

It is difficult to imagine that, in the twenty-first century, cosmopolitan Europeans would be forced to cut down trees in their public parks just to stay warm in the winter. In 2009 this was precisely what occurred when Russia's monopoly shut off all the natural gas to Ukraine as part of a hardball negotiation over prices. Located at the tail end of the gas pipelines from Russia, Europeans became the accidental victims of Russia's winner-take-all energy politics. And while the EU's overall energy grid has somewhat improved since 2009, exposed states like Bulgaria and many of its neighbors in east-central

Europe are still vulnerable to future shut-offs from the Kremlin's monopoly.

In the hands of Russia, what was old is new again in Europe. As a monopoly supplier to large swaths of the EU, Russia's Gazprom has allegedly taken pages from Standard's old playbook, deploying monopoly pricing power to overcharge consumers and restrict the rise of free market competitors. Unlike Standard, however, the Kremlin has gone one step further by using energy as a politically motivated weapon against its neighbors.[10] Rockefeller could never have dreamed of wielding the kind of geopolitical power that Russian president Vladimir Putin enjoys today. In fact, Russia's grip on Europe is so strong, it once seemed that European regulators might not be able to break the Gazprom monopoly inside the EU. At long last, however, this is beginning to change.

On September 27, 2011, antitrust inspectors from the European Commission launched surprise raids against Gazprom and its affiliates in twenty locations across ten European countries.[11] It represented the most aggressive use yet of the EU's antitrust powers against Russia's feared energy monopoly. The raids netted officials reams of documents and computerized data related to the company's business practices. After combing through these records, European officials found enough evidence of wrongdoing to open a formal investigation of Gazprom in 2012. Then in April 2015, the EU pushed into uncharted territory. In a historic legal filing, it initiated a formal antitrust case against Gazprom. Not since Teddy Roosevelt launched the federal antitrust case against Standard have the stakes for breaking an energy monopoly been higher.

Like the U.S. federal government's famous suit against Rockefeller and Standard, the EU alleged that Gazprom had been running an illegal monopoly: dividing up markets, restricting access to pipelines, and using price discrimination to abuse its customers. In proceeding against Gazprom, the European Commission set down a bold marker. It asserted that "all companies that operate in the European market—no matter if they are European or not—have to play by our EU rules."[12] This might seem obvious, but it was not until the commission began to stand up to Gazprom that such a thing became possible. Now, though, the battle must be fought to the finish, and the EU must win it.

The main test for Europe will be in applying the right lessons from the past. Will the EU's assault on Gazprom be like the Ohio Supreme Court case, where Standard wriggled out of its own court-ordered execution? Or will it model Attorney General Moody's suit, which forced the final breakup of Rockefeller's monopoly? One of the prime lessons to be gleaned from the long-ago battles against Standard is that monopolies are terribly hard to kill. The Kremlin is unlikely to willingly abandon the immense leverage it wields over its energy-dependent neighbors. It will almost certainly seek to dodge the EU's efforts in court. The regulatory struggle to lift Gazprom's siege of Europe's east-central energy markets could therefore become a war of attrition instead of a single, decisive battle. Europe must be prepared for such a fight.

An additional but no less important lesson from the past is the need to provide viable commercial alternatives to Gazprom. Even if the EU can bring the Kremlin's energy monopoly to heel on the regulatory front, downstream consumers in Europe will still need to diversify their gas purchases away from Russia. In east-central Europe, a great many of these alternative shipments are likely to come in the form of liquefied natural gas, and many of them could originate from the United States.

Currently, a bipartisan effort is under way in the U.S. Congress to ease restrictions on American natural gas exports to allies in Europe. If successful, America could achieve a historic and powerful symmetry in the never-ending struggle against monopolies. Whereas Deterding's "To America!" strategy once helped free U.S. consumers from the dominion of Standard, the bounty of the American shale gas boom could now do the same for Europeans through U.S. exports. In the case of Gazprom, it is a fight worth winning together.

The final dilemma linking energy's past with our present can be found in the United States. Whereas the EU is struggling to enforce its own laws to promote energy competition, the legacy of regulatory overreach from the past is dulling America's competitive edge on the domestic front. The poster child of this challenge is an anachronistic oddity known as the Jones Act. In the twenty-first century, few Americans have even heard of this law. All the same, it affects their daily lives—often for the worst.

Back in 1920, U.S. senator Wesley Jones pushed through a seemingly patriotic law, officially known as the Merchant Marine Act of 1920. It was positively decked in red, white, and blue. The legislation stated that any ship that carried goods *between* any two ports in America had to be built in America, owned by Americans, and crewed by Americans, and it had to fly the American flag.[13] It seemed like an awfully pro-American piece of legislation. But look closer, and it becomes clear that Jones's law had less to do with patriotism than with eliminating competition.

By getting his bill signed into law, Jones was working to prevent companies from undercutting the price that unions in his home state of Washington charged to ship goods to Alaska. This was a good old-fashioned case of raw economic protectionism—all the rage in the 1920s. It surfed on the wave of expanded federal powers that trust-busters like John Sherman, Ida Tarbell, and Teddy Roosevelt had won to regulate industry in America.[14] Only instead of using the hammer of federal authority to protect competition, Senator Jones built a wall against it.

In the century since the Jones Act has been on the books, the global economy has become unrecognizably different. All the while, however, the protectionism of his law has remained trapped in time—creating absurd results. It is on account of the Jones Act that U.S. farmers purchase grain from Argentina instead of from other American farms—because the law increases domestic shipping costs, making it less expensive to import commodities from overseas.[15] The Jones Act is also why foreign vessels were initially slowed down when trying to assist in the cleanup of the 2010 Deepwater Horizon oil spill. In 2014 it even forced the Department of Homeland Security to interdict an emergency shipment of road salt between Maine and New Jersey. Highway officials desperately needed the salt to keep New Jersey's roads open during a dangerous snowstorm. But the Jones Act was indifferent to this need, and since the vessel carrying the emergency cargo was not built in the United States or employing Americans, the federal government refused to let it set sail for New Jersey. The government viewed protecting the Jones Act as more important than keeping New Jersey's highways safe for Americans to drive on.[16]

Imagine how American drivers would react if Congress forced them to buy third-rate automobiles because that seemed like the only way to keep Detroit's struggling car industry alive. While the challenge from foreign automakers was a tough one in the 1970s and 1980s, dauntless American manufacturers learned to adapt—and even thrive—against their competitors. The U.S. auto industry did not go extinct on account of foreign competition; it learned how to build better cars. As a result of this transformation, American drivers can now choose from more high-quality vehicles at competitive prices.

But when it comes to the sea-lanes, the Jones Act is working to strangle the same competitive forces that are great for consumers and that help to maintain America's economic edge. Even worse, it is wreaking havoc on America's domestic energy market.

One result of the U.S. fracking revolution has been a rebirth of America's oil might. The very same technological innovation that kicked off the shale gas boom has reopened the spigots of American crude. Just as shale gas rose to new heights over the last decade, the production of crude from "tight oil" increased from less than 0.5 million to more than 4.5 million barrels of oil a day by 2015—a sum equal to China's total daily output.[17] The onrush of this additional petroleum was great for drivers, who saw gasoline prices plummet, and even better for the U.S. economy. Instead of buying oil from foreign producers, fracking is saving Americans $107 billion each year (at current prices) thanks to increases in domestic petroleum production. The bad news is that the protectionism of one long-dead senator continues to enjoy a stranglehold on oil transportation in the United States, causing a gigantic and wholly unnecessary burden on Americans.

Under the terms of the Jones Act, there are only eleven crude oil tankers left in America that are allowed to move oil between U.S. ports, and it's expensive to use them. If energy companies want to ship petroleum from the Gulf Coast to the East Coast by sea, the tab will typically run between $5 and $6 per barrel. Meanwhile in nearby Canada, where the anticompetitive Jones Act does not hold sway, the cost is $2 per barrel. Due to the higher price of shipping oil by sea from one side of America to the other, many drivers on the East Coast end up burning gasoline from Nigeria and Saudi Arabia instead of filling their tanks with domestic U.S. oil.[18] The Jones Act's artificial restrictions on tankers can make it more economically efficient to use oil from Africa and the Middle East than from elsewhere in the United

States. In other cases, the Jones Act forces U.S. companies to send domestic crude on long overland rail journeys through American towns and cities. This is more expensive than shipping oil in tankers. It is also riskier. The Jones Act does not care.

The dangers of railroad shipments of petroleum started to become apparent just as the American oil industry hit its stride in the early 2010s. Because the Jones Act had effectively blocked sea-lanes between American ports, companies began to flood the U.S. railroad network with crude. One unforeseen consequence was that oil spills hit an all-time high. In a single year (2013), railroad accidents dumped more crude oil onto American communities than in the previous forty years combined.[19] While this means that 99 percent of all petroleum trains arrive at their destination without incident, the statistics are likely cold comfort to American towns and cities that must now endure a record number of spills, derailments, and oil fires each year—all because the economics of the Jones Act forces the use of railcars instead of petroleum tankers.

Back in Washington, one person has made it a mission to do away with the Jones Act. He is John McCain, the war hero turned senator who most people remember as the fellow whom Barack Obama beat to become president in 2008. McCain has railed against the absurdities of the Jones Act and even introduced legislation to do away with its outdated restrictions. It may seem surprising, given the obvious harms the law creates, but McCain's campaign against the Jones Act has found few supporters. One reason is a basic knowledge gap about the law itself. Some incorrectly assume that the Jones Act is still a patriotic "buy America" effort. Another factor is the powerful lobby that has been built up to sustain the law's protectionist rules. In the century of its existence, the Jones Act has insulated a small ecosystem of economic interests against the threat of outside competition, which makes it difficult to undo. "I would like to see the Jones Act repealed," said McCain. "But I don't think that's likely. I don't think I would get 20 votes if I were to bring it to the floor."[20] Just as Marcus Samuel learned when he tried to pry open the Suez, powerful lobbies can emerge to eliminate competition before it has a chance to stand on its own. Sadly, this is the case with the Jones Act. It long ago ceased to be a "buy America" law and became instead a "break America" law. Until Americans pressure Congress to change it, they will continue to suffer from its economy-busting effects.

Spanning the breadth of the planet, from the gas wells of Sichuan to the oil fields of America, these three examples demonstrate how the past remains indelibly linked to the present. In the modern era, few can trace the lineage of the mammoth supertankers lying at anchor off Houston or Shanghai back to the disjointed streets around Houndsditch. Few car owners think of Marcus Samuel's flash of inspiration on the shores of the Black Sea when they fill up their tanks. Even fewer recall Sailor Town when they glimpse Shell's ubiquitous yellow-and-red logo along the highway. But these are enduring monuments to Samuel's daring risk, Deterding's ambition, and Rockefeller's defeat. The race to reach Asia faster—and at scale—was a departure point for all of these legacies: the modern supertanker, the creation of the first globally competitive marketplace for oil, and the first time that the Far East altered the world's energy scales. It will not be the last.

When it comes to energy, the end really has no end. Booms and busts, oil and gas, titans and rivals—the same challenges that Samuel and Deterding once faced have never changed. Even after the last drop of oil is pumped on planet earth, probably in the next century and possibly in Iraq, the enduring elements of distance, geography, risk, technology, and greed will persist. Those who can solve this equation stand to make their own fortunes and legacies. In the process, they too will shape the balance of their own energy age. These individuals may not know it, but they will be treading in the footprints that Marcus Samuel, the First Viscount of Bearsted, left behind many years ago—when China seemed so very far away and the docks of Batumi smelled like crude.

Acknowledgments

O ne of the most tragic parts of this story occurred shortly after January 17, 1927, the day Marcus Samuel, the First Viscount Bearsted of Maidstone, died. As he took his final breath, one of the most remarkable lives of the late nineteenth and early twentieth centuries drew to a close. By the time of his death, only a handful of British nobles outranked the former "Japan merchant" from Houndsditch; fewer still could match his bankroll. Unfortunately, his death also initiated an egregious blow to history.

Acting on instructions issued before his passing, Samuel's family promptly burned his archive. This willful fire devoured Samuel's letters, business correspondence, and nearly every other record that he deemed fit to keep during his lifetime. Fueling the flames were notes from friends and rivals and the details of decisions both historic and mundane, as well as incalculably valuable evidence of Samuel's own flaws and virtues. As the documents burned, the fire also erased many of Samuel's memories, impressions, embarrassments, boasts, and mistakes. Part of his humanity vanished with the paper trail. This story was lesser for it.

By issuing the burn order, Samuel left a clue about himself. As a product of his time, he conformed to the highest standards of gentlemanly etiquette. Private things were not to be shared. It was not the business of strangers what friends or associates revealed to one another. In the interests of decorum, Victorian sentiment regarded paper intimacies as things best snatched from the fingers of postmortem voyeurs. History seeks to know the inner confessions and impressions of the people who shaped the past and present, but Samuel's burn order reveals that he did not view himself as the sort of person whom history might find interesting.

During his life, Samuel was certainly aware that his accomplishments were significant. After all, he had been the first to put the modern oil tanker to use, the first to breach the impassable geographic barrier of the Suez Canal with bulk petroleum, and the first oilman to successfully blitz Rockefeller's unassailable monopoly in Asia. Nevertheless, the intentional destruction of his archive shows that he did not fully grasp his historic importance. Thankfully for later generations, the flames did not burn every record. In fact, a great deal about Samuel and the fight against Rockefeller survived.

At its core, the research for this book represented a search for the scraps that escaped Samuel's bonfire. By helping to uncover the people and events that toppled the world's most feared monopoly, this narrative owes a deep debt to the scholarship and insights of Ida Tarbell, F. C. Gerretson, Robert Henriques, Daniel Yergin, and Ron Chernow. Each one of them would likely find cause to disagree with the others, but it is on their jostling shoulders that this story stands.

In writing this book, I owe the deepest of debts to my editors at Penguin, Kathryn Court and Sarah Stein. Both worked tirelessly to help bring this story to life. My wonderful literary agent, Michelle Tessler, was likewise essential. Through several false starts, her enduring patience and sage advice have made all the difference in the world.

Acknowledgments

An author could not ask for a better agent. Equally crucial were the editing skills of Charlotte Easter Earl. This story has greatly benefited from her deft touch with language and keen sense of narrative structure. Larry Hirsch and Wess Mitchell at CEPA deserve special thanks for their endless inspiration and support throughout the entire project. Additional thanks for the enthusiastic inspiration of Ambassador Keith Smith as well as to Svante Cornell, who provided firsthand insight into the BTC convoy described in the introduction. Research assistants Bart Bachman, Klaudiusz Magierowski, and Jason Gusdorf contributed background research and offered their tireless enthusiasm on some of the toughest assignments. Lastly, I was immeasurably aided by my parents Christopher and Patricia Doran, as well as a cadre of family, friends, and colleagues who helped propel this work to completion. Without them, none of this would have been possible.

Notes

Chapter 1: The King of Broadway

1. "Shrouded in Fog," *Evening World,* September 26, 1889.
2. Chernow, *Titan,* p. 45.
3. Rockefeller, *Random Reminiscences*, p. 73. On the ledger, see Chernow, *Titan,* pp. 49–50. On double-entry bookkeeping, ibid., p. 55.
4. Rockefeller, *Random Reminiscences*, p. 81.
5. Chernow, *Titan,* p. 66.
6. Ibid., p. 320.
7. Sweetser and Ford, *New York City,* p. 23.
8. *Mayor of New York v. Manhattan Ry. Co., 143 N. Y. 1*, New York Supreme Court Appellate Division—First Judicial Department, Papers on Appeal from Final Decree of Supreme Court, New York County, pp. 3:1239–1886, folios 3715–5658, New York County Clerk's Index no. 28346, 1923.
9. On the effects of the elevated roads, see *"Moss et al. v. Manhattan Ry. Co. et al.," The New York Supplement,* p. 46.
10. Costello, *Our Police Protectors,* pp. 367–68.
11. On the hotel's denizens, see "Sixteen Jewellers Swindled," *Sun,* July 25, 1885; "From Steward to Laundry Chief, Jacob Van Riper Accused of Getting Credit for the Hotel Royal and Taking the Cash," *World,* October 28, 1887. Front-page suicides include "Bet Heavily on Cleveland, Suicide of One of the Marshals of the Business Men's Parade," *Sun,* November 14, 1888. On the hotel's cuisine, see "Hotel Royal," *New York Daily Tribune,* June 9, 1884. And on the end of the hotel, see "A New York Horror, A Hotel in Flames and People Perish by the Score," *Lewiston (ME) Evening Journal,* February 8, 1892.

Notes

12. Sweetser and Ford, *New York City*, p. 49.
13. Chernow, *Titan*, pp. xxi–xxii.
14. Rockefeller, *Random Reminiscences*, p. 11.
15. On the assigned seats at lunch, see Chernow, p. 223. The "drink every gallon" boast is quoted in Yergin, *Prize*, p. 52. Archbold's remark on demagogues is quoted in Chernow, *Titan*, p. 279.
16. Tuchman, *Guns of August*, p. 38.
17. Twain, *Autobiography*, p. 522.
18. Chernow, *Titan*, p. 174.
19. The Standard Oil Trust was the legal corporate entity for Standard's business operations in the 1880s. The name is used interchangeably with *Standard*, *Standard Oil*, and *26 Broadway*. On the trust dividends, see ibid., p. 260.
20. Quoted ibid., p. 153.
21. On the whiskey barrels, see Yergin, *Prize*, p. 28.
22. Ibid.
23. The term *well borer* wouldn't catch on until 1901. The same for *driller*. The two terms are used interchangeably throughout this narrative. Ibid., p. 87.
24. Quoted in Bone, *Petroleum*, p. 58.
25. Chernow, *Titan*, p. 82.
26. McCully, *Ida Tarbell*, p. 20.
27. Wright, *Oil Regions*, p. 107.
28. Chernow, *Titan*, p. 95.
29. U.S. Energy Information Administration, "U.S. Crude Oil First Purchase Price," May 1, 2015.
30. On Standard's definition of peace, see Tarbell, *History of Standard Oil*, p. 363.
31. Quoted ibid., p. 111.

Chapter 2: The Merchant of Houndsditch

1. On Victorian sex worker prices, see Walkowitz, *Prostitution*, p. 265.
2. Cook, *Holiday Tour in Europe*, p. 115.
3. On Sailor Town, see Henriques, *Bearsted*, p. 17; Hare, *Walks in London*, pp. 318-348; "The Greatest Seaport in the World," *Naval Journal* 64 (August 1892).
4. U.K., *1851 Census*, Aldgate, London, HO 107/1546.
5. Five minutes, to be exact. "Documents Reveal Contents of the First Telegraph Message Between India and England," *Economic Times*, February 21, 2012.
6. Henriques, *Bearsted*, pp. 38–40.
7. Heckford, *Practical Sailing Directions*, pp. 109–12.
8. On Singapore's population, see Vincent, *Land of White Elephant*, p. 104, and

292

Seward, *Seward's Travels*, pp. 296–98. On goods for sale, see Balfour, *Cyclopædia of India*, p. 398.

9. On Calcutta's exports, see Robert Knight, "Export of Grain in Famine," *Statesman* (1880), p. 529. By comparison, today the whole of the United States only exports around 3 million tons of rice. U.S. Department of Agriculture, "U.S. Rice Exports by Type," *Rice Yearbook 2015*, March 31, 2015.

10. On the famine intervention, see Temple, *Men and Events*, p. 360.

11. Henriques postulates that Marcus could have taken an additional exploratory excursion to Calcutta after arriving in Singapore. But what Marcus did with the information regarding the Calcutta famine is more important, hence its focus in this narrative.

12. Henriques, *Bearsted*, p. 42.

13. Temple, in *Men and Events,* notes that a great deal of the rice eventually came from Burma (p. 395). But the amount delivered by M. Samuel & Co. was cataloged in the parliamentary investigation into the famine. U.K. House of Commons, "Papers Relating to the Famine (East India)," *Accounts and Papers of the House of Commons*, session 5·February–13 August, vol. 54 (1875).

14. U.K. House of Commons, *Accounts and Papers*, p. 96; Henriques, *Bearsted*, p. 42.

15. Dickens, *Dictionary of Thames*, pp. 26–27.

16. Leslie, *Marlborough House Set*, p. 290.

17. "The Derby," *Baily's Magazine of Sports & Pastimes* (1889), p. 53.

18. Tuchman, *Proud Tower*, pp. 39–47.

19. On land ownership, see *Return of Owners of Land*; Tuchman, *Proud Tower*, p. 31.

20. For the curious, all beheadings are counted after 1066 and include Queens Jane and Mary I and King Charles I. As for madness, it seems that George III was mad after all, or at least suffered from porphyria. Peters and Wilkinson, "King George III and Porphyria," pp. 3–19.

21. Bujak, *England's Rural Realms*, p. 45.

22. Ibid.; Tuchman, *Proud Tower,* pp. 39–47.

23. Quoted in Arnstein, "Survival of Victorian," p. 228.

24. Trollope, *Way We Live Now*, p. 113.

25. Berger, *Legacy of Jewish Migration*, p. 111.

26. Endelman, *Jews of Britain*, p. 158.

27. Henriques, *Bearsted*, p. 25.

28. Rappaport, *Queen Victoria*, p. xiv.

29. Endelman, *Jews of Britain*, p. 156.

30. Wasson, *Born to Rule*, p. 22.

Notes

Chapter 3: The Insider

1. Carlisle, "Coal Oil," p. 251.
2. On U.S. exports, see Howard Page, "Review of Testimony—Industrial Commission." In *Pure Oil Trust vs. Standard Oil Company: Being the Report of an Investigation by the United States Industrial Commission* (Oil City, PA: Derrick Publishing Co., 1901), p. 494.; Henriques, *Bearsted*, p. 90. On the *Sviet*, see "Tanks Steamer," *Institute of Petroleum Review*, vol. 21 (1967), p. 89.
3. The name "Black City" is used in this narrative to describe all of Baku and its immediate suburbs. This encompasses the refining portion of Baku, known to its residents as "Black Town." On the Nobel brothers, see Tolf, *Russian Rockefellers*, p. 47.
4. Most Baku wells produced between 6,500 and 43,000 barrels a day. Madureira, *Key Concepts in Energy*, p. 58. See also "Oil at Baku, Gusher that Spouts 11,000 Tons of Petroleum Daily," *Los Angeles Herald*, December 15, 1886.
5. MacMillan, *War That Ended Peace*, p. 177. MacMillan also uncovered Kennan's wonderful description in Kennan, *Siberia and Exile System*, p. 55.
6. The steam tanker *Gluckauf*, built by Armstrong Whitworth & Co., was technically the first made-to-order bulk tanker, having also been completed in 1885. See Forbes and O'Beirne, *Technical Development*, p. 527. Unlike previous Branobel tankers like the *Zoroaster*, which had merely been retrofitted with oil tanks, the Nobels built the *Sviet* around the tanks. On the *Sviet*, see *Marine Engineer and Naval Architect* 7 (1886), p. 218.
7. *The Derrick's Hand-book of Petroleum: A Complete Chronological and Statistical Review of Petroleum Developments from 1859 to 1899* (Oil City, PA: Derrick Publishing Co., 1899), p. 1024. On early tankers, see Spyrou, *From T-2 to Supertanker*, p. 56.
8. Villari, *Fire and Sword*, p. 29.
9. On Palashkovsky and Bunge, see Vassiliou, *A to Z of Petroleum*, p. 79.
10. On the railroad as a common carrier, Gerretson, *History of Royal Dutch*, p. 1:108. For maritime shipping costs to England, see ibid., p. 1:32.
11. On "Shady" Lane, see Jones, *British Oil Industry*, p. 19.
12. On "cut to kill," see Rosenbaum, *Market Dominance*, p. 22–23. For skepticism about the practice, see Olien and Hinton, *Oil and Ideology*, p. ix. For Tarbell's view, see Tarbell, *History of Standard Oil*, p. 2:31.
13. Yergin, *Prize*, p. 42.
14. Henriques, *Bearsted*, p. 80.
15. Samuel's office is described in Yergin, *Prize*, p. 65. For the staff, see Jonker et al., *Royal Dutch Shell*, p. 1:23.
16. The syndicated loan would come in 1897. Henriques, *Bearsted*, p. 159.
17. Quoted ibid., p. 56.

18. Flannery recalled discussing plans for a new kind of oil tanker with Samuel as early as 1888, meaning that plans could have been considered but not executed. The catalyst was Samuel's Batumi visit. Henriques, *Bearsted*, p. 66.
19. On the Channel monopoly, see Black, *Riviera*, p. 273.

Chapter 4: Rascality of All Descriptions

1. For cuisine *à l'Orient*, see Cars and Caracalla, *Orient Express*, p. 27; and Foxwell and Farrer, *Express Trains*, p. 105.
2. "Suggest Modifications to the Interstate Commerce Law," *American Law Review* 25 (1891), p. 121.
3. On the route and the struggles between coal and oil, see Winchester and Allen, *Railway Wonders*, p. 371.
4. On procrastination, see Baedeker, *Southern Germany*, pp. 175–226. The "quarrels" are noted in Waugh, *House of Wittgenstein*, p. 130, and "suicides" in Morton, *Nervous Splendor*, chap. 7. Strauss's "vanished splendor" is observed in Baltzell, *Complete History of Music*, p. 464.
5. Villari, *Fire and Sword*, p. 46.
6. LeVine, *Oil and Glory*, chap. 2; Gulbenkian quoted in Hewins, *Mr. Five Per Cent*, p. 21; Villari, *Fire and Sword*, p. 51.
7. In a single year, from 1889 to 1890, oil fell from 30 kopeks per pood (36 pounds) to 19, with no end to the decline in sight. By 1891, the Russian price would hit 1 kopek per pood, making oil all but free. Gerretson, *History of Royal Dutch*, p. 1:109.
8. Man, *Attila*, p. 114.
9. "Baku Petroleum," *Littell's Living Age* 66 (1889), p. 255.
10. Marvin, *Region of Eternal Fire*, p. 197.
11. The 3 million tins are mentioned in Hidy and Hidy, *History of Standard Oil*, p. 259. For total demand, see Gerretson, *History of Royal Dutch*, pp. 2:114–21.

Chapter 5: It Can't Be Done

1. Williams, *Tales of Foreign Settlements*, pp. 194–95.
2. On Kobe through foreign eyes, see *Chronicle & Directory for China, Japan, Corea, Indo-China, Straits* (Hong Kong: Daily Press, 1892), p. 51.
3. Ibid.
4. Henriques, *Bearsted*, p. 60.
5. Ibid, p. 53.
6. For diplomatic reports of the plan, see U.S. Bureau of Foreign Commerce, *Bureau of Statistics Monthly Consular and Trade Reports* 41, nos. 148–51 (1893).

Notes

Chapter 6: The Carnivorous Snail

1. MacMillan, *War That Ended Peace*, p. 120.
2. Eighty percent of all traffic through the canal was British. See Henriques, *Bearsted*, p. 106.
3. Rothschild and Rothschild, *"You Have It,"*, p. 20.
4. Henriques, *Bearsted*, p. 90.
5. "Obituary. Sir James Fortescue Flannery. 1851–1943," *Journal of the Institution of Civil Engineers* 21, no. 2 (1943), pp. 124–25.
6. Flannery shared the patent for the design with a civil engineer named Stephen H. Terry. See *Steamship: An Illustrated Monthly Scientific Journal* 6 (August 1894), p. 43.
7. "Launching a Big Fat Greek Supertanker," season 1, episode 1 of *Superships*, directed by Red Regan (2008).
8. Henriques, *Bearsted*, p. 91.
9. As early as December 1, 1891, Lloyd's was already conferring with the Canal Company as to what its needs were regarding the safety of bulk tankers. Ibid., p. 106.
10. Lodwick and Gulbenkian, *Gulbenkian*, p. 111.
11. On the debate over shipbuilders such as Gray being elected to Lloyd's management committee, see *Transactions of the North-East Coast Institution of Engineers and Shipbuilders* 6 (1890), p. 49.
12. C. T. Bowring & Co. learned first, in June 1891. See Henriques, *Bearsted*, pp. 89–92.
13. On "Hebrew inspiration," see Yergin, *Prize*, p. 67. On the letters from Russell & Arnholz and from the Mellons, see Henriques, *Bearsted*, pp. 100–2.
14. For evidence as to why it was Standard, see ibid., p. 121.
15. Ibid., pp. 109–14.
16. Ibid.
17. Henriques, *Bearsted*, p. 118.
18. The *Conch*, the *Clam*, the *Elax*, the *Bullmouth*, and the *Volute* would be constructed in West Hartlepool. Sunderland would produce the *Turbo*, the *Trocas*, and the *Spondilus*. Newcastle upon Tyne would produce the *Cowrie* and the *Nerite*. Ibid., p. 119.
19. The *Murex* had set sail from West Hartlepool on July 26, 1892. Ibid.
20. On oil consumption, see U.S. Energy Information Administration, "International Energy Statistics—Total Petroleum Consumption," 2015. On debt, see Sudeep Reddy, "Number of the Week: Total World Debt Load at 313% of GDP," *Wall Street Journal*, May 11, 2013. On tanker traffic, see Suez Canal Authority, *Suez Canal Traffic Statistics, Monthly Number & Net Ton by Ship Type, Direction and Ship Status*, 2014.

Notes

Chapter 7: The Royal Crown

1. On Zijlker, see Gerretson, *History of Royal Dutch*, p. 1:58.
2. On *sumatras*, see Wing-Huen Ip, ed., *Advances in Geosciences: Solid Earth (SE) Ocean Science (OS) and Atmospheric Science (AS)* (Hackensack, NJ: World Scientific, 2007), p. 9:112.
3. Yergin, *Prize*, p. 73. On skimming the wax, see Gerretson, *History of Royal Dutch*, p. 1:128.
4. Ibid., p. 1:90.
5. Another important sponsor was Zijlker's brother, Dr. D. de Ruiter Zijlker, who sat in the lower house of the Dutch parliament. Ibid., pp. 1:93–97.
6. Jonker et al., *Royal Dutch Shell*, p. 1:23.
7. Literally the "Royal Dutch Company for Exploitation of Oil Wells in the Dutch Indies." Ibid., pp. 1:23–29.
8. Ibid.
9. Poley, *Eroïca*, pp. 95–98.
10. Gerretson, *History of Royal Dutch*, p. 1:129.
11. Specifically oil from Telaga Tunggal well no. 1. Ibid., p. 1:132.
12. Each tin equaled 2 gallons. Jonker et al., *Royal Dutch Shell*, p. 1:29.
13. Henriques, *Bearsted*, p. 146.
14. Poley, *Eroïca*, p. 129.
15. For descriptions of Pangkalan Brandan, see Gerretson, *History of Royal Dutch*, pp. 1:140-143; and U.K. Hydrographic Department of Great Britain, *China Sea Directory: Pilot Guide* (London: Admiralty Hydrographic Office, 1896), p. 1:78.
16. Gerretson, *History of Royal Dutch*, p. 1:140.
17. Ibid., p. 1:144.
18. For the light as a landmark for shipping, see Jonker et al., *Royal Dutch Shell*, p. 1:27.
19. Quoted in Yergin, *Prize*, p. 76.
20. Gerretson, *History of Royal Dutch*, p. 1:110.
21. Ibid., p. 1:36.
22. Jonker et al., *Royal Dutch Shell*, p. 1:33.
23. Cameron and Bovykin, *International Banking*, p. 455.
24. On the share price fluctuations, see Jonker et al., *Royal Dutch Shell*, p. 1:47.
25. Ibid., pp. 1:35–36.
26. Forbes and O'Beirne, *Technical Development*, p. 65.
27. Henriques, *Bearsted*, pp. 236–37.
28. For the cables, see ibid., p. 230. On production and stock, see Gerretson, *History of Royal Dutch*, pp. 2:95–96.

Notes

Chapter 8: The Hidden Map

1. The description of colonial life in Sumatra is drawn from R. W. Egerton Eastwick, "Deli, in Sumatra (Notes of a Holiday Visit by an Idle Official)," *Fortnightly Review* 54 (1893), pp. 634–45.
2. E. B. Andrews, "Petroleum in its Geological Relations," *American Journal of Science*, ser. 2, 42 (July 1866), pp. 33–43.
3. On early theories, see Forbes and O'Beirne, *Technical Development*, p. 16.
4. One exception was White himself, who used his anticline theory to identify a small oil field in West Virginia in 1885. When recommending where to place a well, geologists had previously only found a trickle of oil. See Frehner, *Finding Oil*; Lucier, *Scientists and Swindlers*.
5. On being eyed by tigers, see Eastwick, "Deli, in Sumatra," pp. 634–45.
6. Gerretson, *History of Royal Dutch*, p. 1:137.
7. Ibid., p. 1:94.
8. A. J. Studer. "The War in Acheen and Its Effects on Commerce," in *Reports from the Consuls of the United States on the Commerce, Manufactures, Etc., of Their Consular Districts*, no. 35 (Washington, DC: Government Printing Office, 1883), p. 352.
9. Gerretson, *History of Royal Dutch*, pp. 1:235–38.
10. On navigating the Perlak, see U.K. Hydrographic Department of Great Britain, *China Sea Directory: Pilot Guide* (London: Admiralty Hydrographic Office, 1896), p. 69.
11. Quoted in Gerretson, *History of Royal Dutch*, pp. 1:115–37.
12. Ibid.
13. Ibid., p. 1:136.
14. None of these issues posed any lasting problem. Royal Dutch benefited from Loudon's speedy decision, and the concession was eventually transferred to the company without a hitch. Ibid.
15. On paper science, see Jonker et al., *Royal Dutch Shell*, p. 1:51.
16. Yergin, *Prize*, pp. 119–21.
17. Ibid.
18. Ibid.
19. Ibid.
20. In the creation of Shell, Marcus received 7,500 shares of the new company, while Sam received 4,500. These shares had special voting rights of five to one over other shares, ensuring that the brothers controlled the company. Shell officially came into existence on October 18, 1897. Gerretson, *History of Royal Dutch*, p. 1:198.

Notes

Chapter 9: The Knight in the Mote

1. "Mote Park," *Gardeners Chronicle* 4, September 29, 1888, p. 349.
2. Yes, Shell misspelled the original name *Pectan,* and it was not a tug, as is often misreported, but a tanker. Henriques, *Bearsted,* p. 228.
3. Ibid., p. 229.
4. Ibid., pp. 300–23.

Chapter 10: The Deal of the Century

1. Acting independently of Benz, his fellow inventor Gottlieb Daimler achieved the same breakthrough at nearly the exact time. Bird and Daimler, *Gottlieb Daimler,* p. 51.
2. Boesen and Grad, *Mercedes-Benz,* p. 15; Bouzanquet, *Fast Ladies,* p. 11.
3. A single pound of coal produces ~1.6 x 10^7 joules. The same measure (in this case a pound) of gasoline produces ~2.2 x 10^7 joules, or 37.5 percent more energy.
4. On gasoline as the "under dog," see Albert L. Clough, "Sweet Are the Uses of Adversity," *Horseless Age* 10, no. 5 (1902).
5. The type of fuel used on steam cars was as varied as their design. A common example, such as the model built by the Lancashire Steam Motor Company, burned unrefined petroleum. Others burned kerosene and gasoline. Some steam cars, such as the de Dion-Bouton model, burned coal or coke. Hasluck, *Automobile;* Karl Ludvigsen, "Steam Cars—Full Throttle at Last?" *Steam Automobile* 11, no. 2 (1969).
6. Bloomfield, *World Automotive Industry,* p. 57.
7. "A Horseless Epoch," *San Francisco Call,* May 19, 1895.
8. Douglas-Scott, *History of First Ten Years,* p. 77.
9. It was even more impressive given the rain. Smil, *Creating Twentieth Century,* p. 135.
10. Jarrott, *Ten Years,* p. 9.
11. For comparison, late-twentieth-century Formula One cars boasted engines of 1.5 to 4.5 liters.
12. Yergin, *Prize,* p. 86.
13. Linsley, Rienstra, and Stiles, *Giant,* p. 29.
14. Hinton and Olien, *Oil in Texas,* pp. 25–27.
15. Ibid.
16. The parishioner was George Carroll. Ibid.
17. Ibid.
18. Ibid.
19. U.S. Energy Information Administration, "U.S. Field Production of Crude Oil," June 30, 2015.

20. Yergin, *Prize*, pp. 85–87.
21. Ibid., p. 86.
22. Hinton and Olien, *Oil in Texas*, pp. 36–37.

Chapter 11: The Rivals

1. On Shell's earnings, see Howarth, *Century in Oil*, p. 57. The terms of the offer are in Henriques, *Bearsted*, pp. 376–79.
2. Yergin, *Prize*, p. 122.
3. "The Weather, London," *Sheffield Independent*, December 27, 1901; "The Weather," *Yorkshire Post and Leeds Intelligencer*, December 27, 1901.
4. Henriques, *Bearsted*, p. 377.
5. Ibid., p. 373.
6. Ibid., p. 378.
7. Ibid.
8. Ibid., p. 382.
9. Yergin, *Prize*, p. 122.
10. Henriques, *Bearsted*, p. 399.
11. Lane became deputy managing director, representing the Rothschilds. Jonker et al., *Royal Dutch Shell*, p. 1:75. On Deterding being in command, see Henriques, *Bearsted*, p. 398.
12. Henriques, *Bearsted*, pp. 400–3.
13. U.S. production topped 88 million barrels in 1902. See U.S. Energy Information Administration, "U.S. Field Production of Crude Oil," April 29, 2015.
14. Hinton and Olien, *Oil in Texas*, pp. 41–44.

Chapter 12: The Echo of Applause

1. Yergin, *Prize*, p. 124.
2. On the honors and grandeur, see Amyas Clifford, "A City of Strange Customs," *The Living Age, 7th. ser., vol. 4 (Boston: Living Age, 1899)*, pp. 4:621–24.
3. "Our London Letter, Lord Mayors Show," *Gloucester Citizen*, November 11, 1902.
4. "London Lord Mayor's Show, A Visit to the Ghetto," *Edinburgh Evening News*, November 10, 1902.
5. Henriques, *Bearsted*, pp. 437–40.
6. On oil prices, see Hinton and Olien, *Oil in Texas*, p. 41; on Guffey, see Yergin, *Prize*, p. 88.
7. Mellon and Sparkes, *Judge Mellon's Sons*, p. 277.
8. When the Mellons subsequently merged Guffey Petroleum with Gulf Refining, they created the Texas petroleum giant Gulf Oil. Hinton and Olien, *Oil in Texas*, p. 48.

9. On additional reasons to force the issue, see Yergin, *Prize*, p. 89.
10. Shell delivered thirteen claims on May 23, 1903. See Henriques, *Bearsted*, p. 463.
11. Ibid., pp. 472–73.

Chapter 13: Reversals of Fortune

1. On Rogers's motivations, see Weinberg, *Taking on the Trust*, p. 214–18.
2. Brady, *Ida Tarbell*, p. 31; Yergin, *Prize*, p. 31.
3. Yergin, *Prize*, p. 102.
4. "The Historian of Standard Oil," *Current Opinion* 37, no. 1 (July 1904), p. 28.
5. Brady, *Ida Tarbell*, p. 207.
6. Chernow, *Titan*, p. 450.
7. Archbold was likewise indicted. See Tarbell, *History of Standard Oil*, pp. 2:88–104. On the absence of convictions, see Weinberg, *Taking on the Trust*, pp. 214–16.
8. Yergin, *Prize*, p. 104.
9. While Rogers provided information, he was not always forthcoming when it came to evidence. McCully, *Ida Tarbell*, p. 137; Yergin, *Prize*, p. 104.
10. Weinberg, *Taking on the Trust*, p. 214.
11. Tarbell, *All in Day's Work*, p. 219.
12. Tarbell, *History of Standard Oil*.
13. The three quotations are from "Historian of Standard Oil," *Current Opinion*, p. 28; "Literary Notes," *Friends' Intelligencer* 61 (1904); and Yergin, *Prize*, p. 102.
14. Tarbell, *All in Day's Work*, p. 211.
15. The "loaded dice" quote is from Yergin, *Prize*, p. 105; "little things grow" is from Tarbell, "John D. Rockefeller," p. 245.
16. Chernow, *Titan*, p. xxi.
17. Rogers et al., "Antitrust in Formative Era." On the Sherman Antitrust Act, see Peritz, *Competition Policy*, p. 5.
18. On the vote, see U.S. Congress, Act of July 2, 1890, *Enrolled Acts and Resolutions of Congress, 1789–1992*, General Records of the United States Government, Record Group 11, National Archives. For the state lawsuits, see Hinton and Olien, *Oil in Texas*, p. 20.
19. Gerretson, *History of Royal Dutch*, p. 1:25.
20. Ibid., p. 1:261; Rosenbaum, *Market Dominance*, p. 22–27.
21. "Ushering in New Year," *New York Tribune*, January 1, 1905.
22. Ibid.
23. John Howard Payne, "Home, Sweet Home," *Yale Book of American Verse*, ed. Thomas Raynesford Lounsbury (New Haven, CT: Yale University Press, 1913), p. 34.

Notes

Chapter 14: The Black City in Red

1. Herbertson, *Asia*, p. 33; see also Henry, *Baku*, p. 157.
2. Curzon, *Persia and Question*, p. 66.
3. Rappaport, *Four Sisters*, pp. 68, 301, and 302.
4. On the metalworking industries, see Massie, *Nicholas and Alexandra*, p. 419. On working conditions, see Babushkin and Bobrovskaya, *Ivan Babushkin*, pp. 7–8.
5. "Admiral Alexieff Murders a Young Russian Officer After Port Arthur Fight," *Los Angeles Herald*, February 18, 1904.
6. Williams, "1905," pp. 62–69.
7. Ulam, *Stalin*, pp. 263–65; Wolfe, *Three Who Made*, pp. 432–34.
8. Rappaport, *Joseph Stalin*, p. 265.
9. Zelikson-Bobrovskaia, *Twenty Years in Underground*, p. 113; Wolfe, *Three Who Made*, p. 432.
10. Ulam, *Stalin*, pp. 64–65.
11. The strike by the oilmen in Baku was eventually successful, as they won a collective bargaining agreement on December 30, 1904.
12. Fitzpatrick, *Russian Revolution*, p. 33; Frankel, *Crisis, Revolution, and Russian Jews*, p. 61.
13. Williams, "1905," p. 48; Cornell, *Small Nations and Great Powers*, pp. 55–56; Altstadt, *Azerbaijani Turks*, p. 41; and "War Is Raging in Southern Russia," *Minneapolis Journal*, February 24, 1905.
14. Henry, *Baku*, pp. 159–60.
15. For the death toll, see Cornell, *Small Nations and Great Powers*; Van der Leeuw, *Storm over Caucasus*. On the end to the killing, see Altstadt, *Azerbaijani Turks*, pp. 45–46.
16. "Russian Butcheries," *New York Tribune*, February 24, 1905; "Baku's Streets Littered with Mutilated Dead," *San Francisco Call*, April 2, 1905.
17. de Waal, *Caucasus*, p. 52.
18. Busch, *Emperor's Sword*, p. 179; Vego, *Joint Operational Warfare*. p. V–76; "Events of the War, 1904–1905," *A Diary of the Russo-Japanese War*, Kobe, Japan: Kobe Chronicle Office, 1904.
19. Altstadt, *Azerbaijani Turks*, p. 43.
20. "Tartar and Armenian Turn Upon Cossacks," *San Francisco Call*, September 8, 1905; "Baku Terror Stricken," *New York Tribune*, September 8, 1905.
21. "Baku Terror Stricken"; "Tatars in Control of City of Baku," *Brooklyn Daily Eagle*, September 10, 1905; Yergin, *Prize*, p. 131.
22. This was thanks in no large part to the intervention of Theodore Roosevelt. Ericson, *Treaty of Portsmouth*.
23. Prior to the burning of Baku in 1905, the only other notable example of country risk was the Boxer Rebellion, which temporarily suspended Shell's

kerosene sales in China. Relative to the shutdown of Russian oil in 1905, the Boxer Rebellion was a footnote, hence its location here. Henriques, *Bearsted*, p. 322.

Chapter 15: The Warhorse and the Stallion

1. Henriques, *Bearsted*, p. 492.
2. Yergin, *Prize*, p. 126.
3. Gerretson, *History of Royal Dutch*, p. 1:346.
4. "The following changes," *Economist*, January 4, 1908.
5. "Rich but Disappointed," *Dundee Evening Telegraph*, January 8, 1908.

Chapter 16: The "Fateful Plunge"

1. "The Steam Yacht 'Lady Torfrida,'" *Engineering* 50 (August 8, 1890), p. 158.
2. Henriques, *Bearsted*, pp. 493–94.
3. Ibid., p. 627.
4. "Rich but Disappointed," *Dundee Evening Telegraph*, January 8, 1908.
5. Adkins, *Nelson's Trafalgar*, pp. 128–34; Fisher, *Memories and Records*, p. 1:142.
6. Massie, *Dreadnought*, pp. 390–91; Churchill, *World Crisis*, p. 1:225.
7. Fisher, *Memories and Records*, pp. 1:107–8.
8. Winton, *Jellicoe*, p. 13.
9. Massie, *Dreadnought*, p. 397.
10. Fisher, *Memories and Records*, p. 1:107.
11. Larson, *Dead Wake*, pp. 133–45.
12. Massie, *Dreadnought*, p. 468.
13. Ibid., p. 445.
14. Fisher, *Fear God and Dread Nought*, p. 1:166.
15. Henriques, *Bearsted*, p. 283.
16. Fisher, *Fear God and Dread Nought*, p. 1:166.
17. U.K. "H.M.S. Hannibal—Oil Fuel Trials," *Parliamentary Debates*, March 11, 1903 (London: Wayman and Sons, March 11, 1903), p. 377.
18. Massie, *Dreadnought*, pp. 468–98; Jane, *British Battle Fleet*, p. 150.
19. Massie, *Dreadnought*, p. 837.
20. During the building program of 1910–11, which was Fisher's last year before retirement, the designed speed of Britain's King George V class of dreadnoughts was equal to that of Germany's Kaiser Class (twenty-one knots). Massie, *Dreadnought*, p. 908.
21. Churchill, *World Crisis*, p. 76.
22. Cook, *Cook's Handbook*, p. 192.
23. de Mendelssohn, *Age of Churchill*, p. 1:323.

24. Fisher, *Fear God and Dread Nought*, p. 2:114.
25. Manchester, *Last Lion*, p. 1:438.
26. On the crisis of Agadir, see Churchill, *World Crisis*, pp. 26–44.
27. Henriques, *Bearsted*, p. 530.
28. Churchill and Gilbert, *Winston S. Churchill*, pp. 1926–1927.
29. Henriques, *Bearsted*, p. 531.
30. Ibid., Churchill and Gilbert, *Winston S. Churchill*, p. 1927.
31. Henriques, *Bearsted*, p. 532.
32. Ibid., p. 537. On Samuel's lobbying efforts, see "Samuel, Pioneer of Fuel Oil," *Petroleum Age* 8, no. 3 (1921), p. 69.
33. Greed later bloomed in Britain's "completely nineteenth-century colonial attitude" toward Iran. Kinzer, *All the Shah's Men*, p. 109.
34. Churchill, *Churchill Speaks*, p. 251.
35. Ibid., p. 219.
36. Yergin, *Prize*, p. 140.
37. Yergin, *Prize*, p. 157.
38. Ibid.
39. Churchill did not wait for the commission to issue its report before initiating plans to lock down supplies of oil in Persia. Fisher's commission can therefore be seen as offering political cover to the First Lord for a decision he had already made. On the commission's findings, see Rasor, *Churchill Annotated Bibliography*, p. 157.
40. "Queen Elizabeth," *Taunton Courier and Western Advertiser*, October 22, 1913; "Launch of the Queen Elizabeth," *Aberdeen Journal*, October 17, 1913; "Oil-Driven Battleship," *Nottingham Evening Post*, October 16, 1913.
41. Jane, *British Battle Fleet*, p. 191.
42. Churchill, *World Crisis*, p. 50.
43. Fisher, *Memories and Records*, p. 1:123.
44. For the final hours of peace amid Germany's *Kriegsgefahrzustand*, see "The Crisis of 1914," Keegan, *First World War*.

Chapter 17: The Colossus Falls

1. "Oil Probe Ended," *Pittston Gazette*, March 28, 1906; "Subpoena for H. H. Rogers," *Sun*, November 29, 1905.
2. For comparison to Number 3's neighbors, see a 2007 *New York Times* article, which reproduced "the original architectural rendering of the homes now numbered 10 through 20 East 78th, which were built in 1887," from Columbia University's Avery Architectural and Fine Arts Library. The article cites the home's original owner as Edmund C. Converse, but by 1905 it was home to Rogers. See Christopher Gray, "Where Historic Town Houses Still Hold Court," *New York Times*, December 23, 2007. For the weather on the

day in question, see "The Weather Report," *New York Daily Tribune*, November 29, 1905; "Rain to-day," *Sun*, November 28, 1905.

3. Chernow, *Titan,* pp. 523, 520.
4. "Unwelcome Xmas Gift for W. G. Rockefeller," *New York Times*, December 27, 1905.
5. Chernow, *Titan*, p. 523.
6. Ibid., pp. 502–4.
7. Ibid., p. 523.
8. Ibid.
9. For Rockefeller's resignation attempts, Hidy and Hidy, *History of Standard Oil*, p. 322. The "jail" quote is from Nevins, *John D. Rockefeller*, p. 438.
10. Chernow, *Titan*, p. 538.
11. *United States v. E. C. Knight Company*, 156 U.S. 1, 43 (1895).
12. "Death of Charles Pratt," *New York Times*, May 5, 1891; "H. H. Rogers Dead from Apoplexy," *New York Tribune*, May 20, 1909.
13. "Flagler's Faith in State of Florida," *Ocala Banner*, May 14, 1909.
14. *Standard Oil Company of New Jersey et al. vs. United States,* 22 U.S. 1 (1911).
15. On utilities, see Nauges and van den Berg, *How "Natural" Are Natural*, p. 2. On antitrust and competition, see Hartman, Mersky, and Tate, *Landmark Supreme Court Cases*, p. 21.
16. Chernow, *Titan*, p. 558; Flynn, *God's Gold*, p. 445.
17. Yergin, *Prize*, p. 94.
18. For Rockefeller's net worth, see Winkler, *John D. Rockefeller*, p. 157; Chernow, *Titan*, pp. 555–56.
19. Winkler, *John D. Rockefeller*, p. 157.
20. Chernow, *Titan*, p. 558.

Chapter 18: "We Must Take America"

1. Quoted in Gerretson, *History of Royal Dutch*, p. 3:303.
2. On the port and the cash, see "Surprising Facts About the Second City of the World," *New York Daily Tribune*, May 1, 1910. The skyscrapers are described in Landau and Condit, *Rise of Skyscraper*, p. 354.
3. "Fourth Avenue Branch Is Made the 'Goat' by Offer of Interborough," *Evening World*, December 10, 1910.
4. Lawrence Goldstone, "The Wright Brothers and a Patent-Law Dogfight," *Wall Street Journal*, April 8, 2014; Goldstone, *Birdmen*, pp. 206–16.
5. Seth Shulman, "The Flight That Tamed the Skies," *MIT Technology Review*, September 1, 2002.
6. Ibid.
7. "Curtiss Flies from Albany to New York," *New York Tribune*, May 30, 1910.

8. By way of comparison, the distance Curtiss traveled was six times as long as Louis Blériot's crossing of the English Channel the previous year. Tobin, *To Conquer Air*, p. 339.

9. Benjamin Briscoe, "Autos Within Easy Reach," *New York Times*, January 23, 1910.

10. Gerretson, *History of Royal Dutch*, p. 3:307.

11. Beaton, *Enterprise in Oil*, p. 58.

12. Yergin, *Prize*, p. 128.

13. Franks, *Tulsa*, p. 40.

14. Yergin, *Prize*, p. 128.

15. Wilkins, *History of Foreign Investment*, p. 287.

16. Priest, "'Americanization' of Shell Oil," p. 190.

Chapter 19: Wealth Beyond Measure

1. "H.W. Flagler Dies in Palm Beach Home," *Sun*, May 21, 1913.

2. Standiford, *Last Train to Paradise*, chap. 8; Winkler, *John D. Rockefeller*, p. 241.

3. Chernow, *Titan*, pp. 610, 402.

4. Winkler, *John D. Rockefeller*, p. 243.

5. Chernow, *Titan*, pp. 634–35.

6. Today it is known as the Ormond Beach Riverside Church. *Daytona Beach News-Journal*, October 30, 2012; Chernow, *Titan*, p. 611.

7. "Financier's Fortune in Oil Amassed in Industrial Era of 'Rugged Individualism,'" *New York Times*, May 24, 1937. When comparing fortunes, Bernstein and Swan considered the overall size of Rockefeller's wealth against inflation-adjusted GDP, then translated the resulting percentage into contemporary dollars. See Bernstein and Swan, *All the Money in the World*.

8. For Rockefeller, Carnegie, and Vanderbilt, the figures provided by Bernstein and Swan have been updated into 2014 dollars, from 2006 dollars used in the original calculation.

9. This concern proved accurate. During the 1930s, federal income taxes rose from 55 to 63 percent on the top bracket and the estate tax spiked from 40 to 65 percent. Chernow, *Titan*, p. 672.

10. Fosdick, *Rockefeller Foundation*, p. 5.

11. Chernow, *Titan*, p. 563.

12. Fosdick, *Rockefeller Foundation*, p. 3.

13. Ashvin Dayal, "The Need for Climate Change Resilience," Rockefeller Foundation, August 27, 2014.

14. Ernst and Rockefeller, *Dear Father, Dear Son*, p. 99; Chernow, *Titan*, chap. 32.

15. Chernow, *Titan*, p. 611.

Notes

16. "Daytona Abounds in Attractions for Winter Colonists," *Sun*, December 14, 1919.
17. On Rockefeller at Daytona, see Chernow, *Titan*, p. 611.
18. Brands, *American Colossus*, p. 621.
19. Chernow, *Titan*, p. 671.

Chapter 20: Legacies

1. James Penn, ed., *Mediterranean Pilot* (London: Taylor, Garnett, Evans, 1908), p. 4:98. On forcing the Dardanelles and the *Queen Elizabeth*, see Erickson, *Gallipoli*, p. 17. On the foolishness, see Van der Vat, *Dardanelles Disaster*, pp. 161–71.
2. U.K. HMS *Ark Royal* Logbook, December 1914 to December 1916, entry for August 4, 1916.
3. Henriques, *Bearsted*, p. 595.
4. Hobbs, *British Aircraft Carriers*, pp. 19–21.
5. Alternatively Sieß.
6. On *Murex* and *Britannic*, see Herzog, *Ritter der Tiefe*, pp. 196–97. On the sinking of the *Murex*, see "Three Big Ships Sunk," *Daily Mirror*, January 6, 1917; "Shipping Losses," *Manchester Evening News*, January 5, 1917. Today the *Murex* rests at the bottom of the Mediterranean Sea at 32°20′ N, 31°00′ E. Jan Lettens, "SS Murex," wrecksite.eu.
7. Henriques, *Bearsted*, p. 636.
8. Ibid., p. 651.
9. Ibid., pp. 638–39.
10. "King's Birthday Honors," *Western Times*, June 4, 1921.
11. "Birthday Honors," *Hull Daily Mail*, June 3, 1925.
12. Quoted in Henriques, *Bearsted*, p. 643.
13. Yergin, *Prize*, p. 208–9.
14. If you visit 31 Houndsditch, try the chunky chips.
15. Dench, *New East End*; "Buried like Kings," *Economist*, December 21, 2013.
16. U.S. Federal Trade Commission, "Exxon/Mobil Agree to Largest FTC Divestiture Ever in Order to Settle FTC Antitrust Charges; Settlement Requires Extensive Restructuring and Prevents Merger of Significant Competing U.S. Assets," November 30, 1999.

Chapter 21: The Enduring Puzzle

1. On the decline in sea ice, see "The Northeast Passage Opens Up," *New York Times*, October 17, 2011. On High North shipping, see Chester Dawson, "Arctic Shipping Volume Rises as Ice Melts," *Wall Street Journal*, October 29, 2014.

Notes

2. Michael Dunne, comment in *Pump* (film), directed by Joshua Tickell and Rebecca Harrell Tickell, Digital Neural Axis, 2014.

3. Since 2007, China has almost doubled the amount of oil it draws from the global market every day. Most of it originates from the Middle East, where it is loaded onto bulk tankers and shipped through the Strait of Malacca. On China's import channels, see Lucian Pugliaresi, "The Price Collapse Winners and Losers (China & Russia)," Energy Policy Research Foundation, March 16, 2015. On China's consumption, see U.S. Energy Information Administration, "Total Consumption of Petroleum Products," 2012; on China's production, see U.S. Energy Information Administration, "Overview Data for China," May 30, 2013.

4. U.S. Energy Information Administration, "Shale in the Unites States," Independent Statistics and Analysis, May 14, 2015.

5. U.S. Energy Information Administration, "Power Plant Emissions of Sulfur Dioxide and Nitrogen Oxides Continue to Decline in 2012," February 27, 2013; Mike Orcutt, "A Drop in U.S. CO2 Emissions," *MIT Technology Review*, August 21, 2012.

6. It works out to $11.20/MMBtu (for China) versus $3.40/MMBtu (for the United States). "China's Shale Gas Costs, Etc.," *Bloomberg*, May 29, 2014.

7. "China's Shale Gas Bust," *MIT Technology Review*, August 12, 2014; "China Cuts 2020 Shale Gas Output Target as Challenges Persist," *Platts*, September 18, 2014; "China Finds Shale Gas Challenging, Halves 2020 Output Target," *Reuters*, August 7, 2014. Spain burns around 30 BCM/y, roughly equal to China's target for shale gas production in 2020. U.S. Energy Information Administration, "Dry Natural Gas Consumption," 2013.

8. David Sandalow et al., "Meeting China's Shale Gas Goals," Columbia/SIPA, Center on Global Energy Policy, September 2014.

9. Chi-Kong Chong and Vessela Tcherneva, "Europe's Vulnerability on Russian Gas," European Council on Foreign Relations, March 17, 2015.

10. J. Leijonhielm and R. L. Larsson, "Russia's Strategic Commodities: Energy and Metals as Security Levers," Swedish Defense Research Agency (FOI), User Report FOI-R—1346—SE, Stockholm, November 2004. On the use of energy as a weapon in Ukraine, see David Koranyi, "Transatlantic Energy Security and the Ukraine-Crisis: A Blessing in Disguise?" *NATO Review* (May 2014), p. 5.

11. Alex Barker, Stanley Pignal, and Gerrit Wiesmann, "Gazprom Raided in EU Antitrust Investigation," *Financial Times*, September 27, 2011.

12. European Commission, "Antitrust: Commission Sends Statement of Objections to Gazprom for Alleged Abuse of Dominance on Central and Eastern European Gas Supply Markets," April 22, 2015.

13. Today the ownership requirement is 75 percent. Merchant Marine Act of 1920 (P. L. 66-261).

Notes

14. Another example would be the Interstate Commerce Act of 1887, 24 Stat. 379, 49 U.S.C. § 1 et seq., 49 U.S.C.A. § 1 et seq.
15. Daryll E. Ray, "Relaxation of the Jones Act Could Help Midwest Maintain Hold on Southeast U.S. Grain Markets," Agricultural Policy Analysis Center, University of Tennessee, July 9, 2002.
16. In the case of the Deepwater Horizon spill, President George W. Bush eventually issued an exemption to foreign ships, but only after considerable delay. On the other absurd episodes, see Corey Kilgannon and Marc Santora, "40,000 Tons of New Jersey Salt, Stuck in Maine," *New York Times*, February 18, 2014; Malia Blom Hill, "The Sinking Ship of Cabotage," Capital Research Center, April 2013.
17. U.S. Energy Information Administration, "Shale in the United States," Independent Statistics and Analysis, May 14, 2015.
18. John Frittelli, "Shipping U.S. Crude Oil by Water: Vessel Flag Requirements and Safety Issues," Congressional Research Service, July 21, 2014.
19. Curtis Tate, "More Oil Spilled from Trains in 2013 than in Previous 4 Decades," *McClatchy*, January 20, 2014.
20. R. G. Edmonson, "Domestic Shipping Faces Choppy Waters," *Journal of Cargo*, May 2, 2011.

Bibliography

Adkins, Roy. *Nelson's Trafalgar: The Battle That Changed the World.* New York: Penguin, 2006.

Altstadt, Audrey L. *The Azerbaijani Turks: Power and Identity Under Russian Rule.* Stanford, CA: Hoover Press, 1992.

Andrews, E. B. "Petroleum in Its Geological Relations." *American Journal of Science*, ser. 2, 42 (July 1866).

Arnstein, Walter L. "The Survival of the Victorian Aristocracy." In *The Rich, the Wellborn, and the Powerful: Elites and Upper Classes in History*, edited by Frederic Cople Jaher. Urbana: University of Illinois Press, 1973.

Babushkin, Ivan, and C. Bobrovskaya. *Ivan Babushkin: A Short Biography.* New York: Workers Library Publishers, 1932.

Baedeker, Karl. *Paris and Environs: With Routes from London to Paris.* 15th ed. Leipzig: Karl Baedeker, 1907.

———. *Southern Germany and Austria, Including Hungary and Transylvania Handbook for Travellers.* 6th ed. Leipzig: Karl Baedeker, 1887.

Balfour, Edward, ed. *Cyclopædia of India and of Eastern and Southern Asia, Commercial, Industrial and Scientific: Products of the Mineral, Vegetable and Animal Kingdoms, Etc..* 2nd ed. Madras: Scottish & Adelphi Presses, 1873.

Baltzell, W. J. *A Complete History of Music, for Schools, Clubs, and Private Readings.* Philadelphia: T. Presser, 1905.

Beaton, Kendall. *Enterprise in Oil: A History of Shell in the United States.* New York: Appleton-Century-Crofts, 1957.

Bibliography

Beeby-Thompson, Arthur. *The Oil Fields of Russia and the Russian Petroleum Industry: A Practical Handbook on the Exploration, Exploitation, and Management of Russian Oil Properties.* London: C. Lockwood and Son, 1904.

Berger, David. *The Legacy of Jewish Migration: 1881 and Its Impact.* New York: Brooklyn College Press, 1983.

Bernstein, Peter W., and Annalyn Swan. *All the Money in the World: How the Forbes 400 Make—and Spend—Their Fortunes.* New York: Alfred A. Knopf, 2007.

Bird, Anthony, and Gottlieb Daimler. *Gottlieb Daimler, Inventor of the Motor Engine.* London: Weidenfeld & Nicolson, 1962.

Black, Charles Bertram. *The Riviera, Or, The Coast from Marseilles to Leghorn: Including the Interior Towns of Carrara, Lucca, Pisa, Pistoia, & Florence.* 7th ed. Edinburgh: A. & C. Black, 1890.

Bloomfield, Gerald Taylor. *The World Automotive Industry.* North Pomfret, VT: David and Charles, 1978.

Boddy, William, and Brian Laban. *The History of Motor Racing.* London: WH Smith, 1988.

Boesen, Victor, and Wendy Grad. *The Mercedes-Benz Book.* Garden City, NY: Doubleday, 1981.

Bone, John Herbert Aloysius. *Petroleum and Petroleum Wells: With a Complete Guide Book and Description of the Oil Regions of Pennsylvania, West Virginia, Kentucky, and Ohio.* Philadelphia: J. B. Lippincott, 1865.

Bouzanquet, Jean François. *Fast Ladies: Female Racing Drivers, 1888 to 1970.* Dorchester, UK: Veloce Publishing, 2009.

Brady, Kathleen. *Ida Tarbell: Portrait of a Muckraker.* Pittsburgh: University of Pittsburgh Press, 1989.

Brands, H. W. *American Colossus: The Triumph of Capitalism, 1865–1900.* New York: Doubleday, 2010.

Bujak, Edward. *England's Rural Realms: Landholding and the Agricultural Revolution,* London: I.B. Tauris, 2007.

Busch, Noel F. *The Emperor's Sword: Japan vs. Russia in the Battle of Tsushima.* New York: Funk & Wagnalls, 1969.

Cameron, Rondo, and V. I. Bovykin, eds. *International Banking, 1870–1914.* Oxford: Oxford University Press, 1992.

Bibliography

Carlisle, Rodney. "Coal Oil." In *Scientific American Inventions and Discoveries: All the Milestones in Ingenuity—From the Discovery of Fire to the Invention of the Microwave Oven*. Hoboken, NJ: John Wiley & Sons, 2005.

Cars, Jean, and Jean Caracalla. *The Orient Express: A Century of Railway Adventures*. London: Grand Express Books, 1987.

Chernow, Ron. *Titan: The Life of John D. Rockefeller, Sr.* 2nd ed. New York: Vintage, 1998.

Churchill, Randolph Spencer, and Martin Gilbert. *Winston S. Churchill: Young Statesman, 1901–1914*, vol. 2. London: Heinemann, 1969.

Churchill, Winston. *Churchill Speaks: Winston S. Churchill in Peace and War: Collected Speeches, 1897–1963*. Edited by Robert Rhodes James. New York: Chelsea House, 1980.

———. *The World Crisis, 1911–1918,* vol. 1. New York: Scribner, 1931.

Chyong, Chi-Kong, and Vessela Tcherneva, "Europe's Vulnerability on Russian Gas." European Council on Foreign Relations, March 17, 2015.

Cook, Joel. *A Holiday Tour in Europe*. Philadelphia: D. McKay, 1889.

Cook, Thomas. *Cook's Handbook to the Health Resorts of the South of France, Riviera and Pyrenees*. London: Thomas Cook, 1905.

Cornell, Svante. *Small Nations and Great Powers: A Study of Ethnopolitical Conflict in the Caucasus*. London: Routledge, 2005.

Costello, Augustine E. *Our Police Protectors: History of the New York Police from the Earliest Period to the Present Time*. New York: Costello, 1885.

Curzon, George N. *Persia and the Persian Question*. London: Longmans Green, 1892.

de Mendelssohn, Peter. *The Age of Churchill*. New York: Thames & Hudson, 1961.

de Waal, Thomas. *The Caucasus: An Introduction*. Oxford: Oxford University Press, 2010.

Dench, Geoff. *The New East End: Kinship, Race and Conflict*. London: Profile Books, 2006.

Dickens, Charles. *Dickens's Dictionary of the Thames, from Oxford to the Nore*. London: Charles Dickens, 1880.

Douglas-Scott, John Walter Edward. *A History of the First Ten Years of Automobilism*. London: Car Limited, 1906.

313

Bibliography

Edmonson, R. G. "Domestic Shipping Faces Choppy Waters." *Journal of Cargo*, May 2, 2011.

Endelman, Todd M. *The Jews of Britain, 1656 to 2000*. Berkeley: University of California Press, 2002.

Erickson, Edward J. *Gallipoli: The Ottoman Campaign*. Barnsley, UK: Pen & Sword, 2010.

Ericson, Steven J. *The Treaty of Portsmouth and Its Legacies*. Hanover, NH: University Press of New England, 2008.

Ernst, Joseph W., and John Davison Rockefeller. *Dear Father, Dear Son: Correspondence of John D. Rockefeller and John D. Rockefeller, Jr.* Edited by Joseph W. Ernst. New York: Fordham University Press, 1994.

European Commission. "Antitrust: Commission Sends Statement of Objections to Gazprom for Alleged Abuse of Dominance on Central and Eastern European Gas Supply Markets," April 22, 2015.

Fisher, John Arbuthnot. *Fear God and Dread Nought: Correspondence of Admiral of the Fleet Lord Fisher of Kilverstone*. 3 vols. Edited by Arthur Marder. London: Jonathan Cape, 1953–59.

———. *Memories and Records*. New York: George H. Doran Co., 1920.

Fitzpatrick, Sheila. *The Russian Revolution*. Oxford: Oxford University Press, 2008.

Flynn, John T. *God's Gold*. Rahway, NJ: Quinn & Bodden, 1932.

Forbes, Robert James, and Denis R. O'Beirne. *The Technical Development of the Royal Dutch/Shell: 1890–1940*. Leiden: Brill, 1957.

Fosdick, Raymond B. *The Story of the Rockefeller Foundation*. New York: Harper & Brothers, 1952.

Foxwell, E., and Thomas Cecil Farrer. *Express Trains, English and Foreign, Being a Statistical Account of All the Express Trains of the World*. London: Smith Elder, 1889.

Frankel, Jonathan. *Crisis, Revolution, and Russian Jews*. Cambridge: Cambridge University Press, 2009.

Franks, Clyda R. *Tulsa: Where the Streets Were Paved With Gold*. Charleston: Arcadia, 2000.

Frehner, Brian. *Finding Oil: The Nature of Petroleum Geology, 1859–1920*. Lincoln: University of Nebraska Press, 2011.

Bibliography

Frittelli, John. "Shipping U.S. Crude Oil by Water: Vessel Flag Requirements and Safety Issues." Congressional Research Service, July 21, 2014.

Georgano, Nick. *The Beaulieu Encyclopedia of the Automobile*. Chicago: Fitzroy Dearborn, 2000.

Gerretson, Frederik Carel. *History of the Royal Dutch*. Leiden: Brill, 1953.

Goldstone, Lawrence. *Birdmen: The Wright Brothers, Glenn Curtiss, and the Battle to Control the Skies*. New York: Random House, 2014.

Graham, Chris. "Ormond's Oldest Church Celebrates Name Change." *Daytona Beach News-Journal*, October 30, 2012.

Hare, Augustus. *Walks in London*. London: Daldy, 1883.

Hartman, Gary R., Roy M. Mersky, and Cindy L. Tate. *Landmark Supreme Court Cases: The Most Influential Decisions of the Supreme Court of the United States*. New York: Infobase, 2009.

Hasluck, Paul Nooncree, ed. *The Automobile: A Practical Treatise on the Construction of Modern Motor Cars, Steam, Petrol, Electric and Petrol-electric, Based on Lavergne's "L'Automobile Sur Route."* London: Cassell, 1903.

Heckford, Nathaniel. *Practical Sailing Directions and Coasting Guide from the Sand Heads to Rangoon, Etc.* 6th ed. London: H. Hughes, 1871.

Hendrix, Henry J. "At What Cost a Carrier?" Center for a New American Security, March 2013.

Henriques, Robert David Quixano. *Bearsted: A Biography of Marcus Samuel, First Viscount Bearsted, and Founder of "Shell" Transport and Trading Company*. New York: Viking Press, 1960.

Henry, James Dodds. *Baku: An Eventful History*. London: Archibald Constable & Co., 1905.

Herbertson, Fanny Dorothea. *Asia*. London: Adam and Charles Black, 1903.

Herzog, Bodo, and Gu Schomaeckrs. *Ritter der Tiefe, Graue Wölfe: Die erfolgreichsten U-Boot-Kommandanten der Welt des Ersten und Zweiten Weltkrieges*. Munich: Verlag Welsermühl, 1965.

Hewins, Ralph. *Mr. Five Per Cent: Story of Calouste Gulbenkian*. New York: Rinehart, 1958.

Hidy, R. W., and M. E. Hidy. *History of Standard Oil Company New Jersey: Pioneering in Big Business, 1882–1911*. New York: Harper, 1955.

Bibliography

Hill, Malia Blom. "The Sinking Ship of Cabotage." Capital Research Center, April 2013.

Hinton, Diana Davids, and Roger M. Olien. *Oil in Texas: The Gusher Age, 1895–1945*. Austin: University of Texas Press, 2010.

HM Stationery Office. *Return of Owners of Land, 1873,* vol. 1. London: HM Stationery Office, 1875.

Hobbs, David. *British Aircraft Carriers Design, Development and Service Histories*. Havertown: Seaforth, 2014.

Howarth, Stephen. *A Century in Oil: The "Shell" Transport and Trading Company, 1897–1997*. London: Weidenfeld & Nicolson, 1997.

Hydrographic Department of Great Britain. *The China Sea Directory, Pilot Guide*, vol. 1. London: Admiralty Hydrographic Office, 1896.

Jane, Fred. *The British Battle Fleet: Its Inception and Growth Throughout the Centuries to the Present Day*. London: City Library Press, 1915.

Jarrott, Charles. *Ten Years of Motors and Motor Racing*. New York: Dutton, 1906.

Jones, Geoffery. *The State and the Emergence of the British Oil Industry*. London: Macmillan, 1981.

Jonker, Joost, J. L. van Zanden, Stephen Howarth, and Keetie E. Sluyterman. *A History of Royal Dutch Shell: From Challenger to Joint Industry Leader, 1890–1939*. Oxford: Oxford University Press, 2007.

Keegan, John. *The First World War*. New York: Knopf Doubleday, 2012.

Kennan, George. *Siberia and the Exile System*. Boston: J. R. Osgood, 1891.

Kinzer, Stephen. *All the Shah's Men: An American Coup and the Roots of Middle East Terror*. Hoboken, NJ: John Wiley & Sons, 2004.

Kobe Chronicle Office. "Events of the War, 1904–1905." In *A Diary of the Russo-Japanese War*. Kobe, Japan: Kobe Chronicle Office, 1904.

Koranyi, David. "Transatlantic Energy Security and the Ukraine-Crisis: A Blessing in Disguise?" *NATO Review*, May 2014.

Landau, Sarah Bradford, and Carl W. Condit. *Rise of the New York Skyscraper: 1865–1913*. New Haven, CT: Yale University Press, 1999.

Larson, Erik. *Dead Wake: The Last Crossing of the Lusitania*. New York: Crown/Archetype, 2015.

Leijonhielm, J., and R. L. Larsson. "Russia's Strategic Commodities: Energy and Metals as Security Levers." Swedish Defense Research Agency (FOI), User Report FOI-R—1346—SE, Stockholm, November 2004.

Bibliography

Leslie, Anita. *The Marlborough House Set*. New York: Doubleday, 1973.

LeVine, Steve. *The Oil and the Glory: The Pursuit of Empire and Fortune on the Caspian Sea*. New York: Random House, 2007.

Linsley, Judith Walker, Ellen Walker Rienstra, and Jo Ann Stiles. *Giant Under the Hill: History of the Spindletop Oil Discovery at Beaumont, Texas, in 1901*. Austin: Texas State Historical Association, 2002.

Lodwick, John, and Calouste Sarkis Gulbenkian. *Gulbenkian: An Interpretation of Calouste Sarkis Gulbenkian*. Heinemann: London, 1958.

Lucier, Paul. *Scientists and Swindlers: Consulting on Coal and Oil in America, 1820–1890*. Baltimore: Johns Hopkins University Press, 2010.

MacMillan, Margaret. *The War That Ended Peace: The Road to 1914*. New York: Random House, 2013.

Madureira, Nuno Luís. *Key Concepts in Energy*. Berlin: Springer, 2014.

Man, John. *Attila: The Barbarian King Who Challenged Rome*. London: Macmillan, 2009.

Manchester, William, and Paul Reid. *The Last Lion, Winston Spencer Churchill*. Boston: Little, Brown, 1983.

Marvin, Charles. *The Region of the Eternal Fire: An Account of a Journey to the Petroleum Region of the Caspian in 1883*. London: W. H. Allen & Co., 1884.

Massie, Robert K. *Dreadnought*. New York: Random House, 2012.

———. *Nicholas and Alexandra: The Fall of the Romanov Dynasty*. New York: Random House, 2000.

McCully, Emily Arnold. *Ida M. Tarbell: The Woman Who Challenged Big Business—and Won*. Boston: Houghton Mifflin Harcourt, 2014.

Mellon, William Larimer, and Boyden Sparkes. *Judge Mellon's Sons*. Privately printed, 1948.

Morton, Frederic. *A Nervous Splendor: Vienna, 1888–1889*. London: Weidenfeld & Nicolson, 1980.

Nauges, Céline, and Caroline van den Berg. *How "Natural" Are Natural Monopolies in the Water Supply and Sewerage Sector? Case Studies from Developing and Transition Economies*, Policy Research Working Paper no. WPS 4137. Washington, DC: World Bank Publications, 2007.

Nevins, Allan. *John D. Rockefeller: The Heroic Age of American Enterprise*. New York: Scribner's Sons, 1940.

Bibliography

Olien, Roger M., and Diana Davids Hinton. *Oil and Ideology: The Cultural Creation of the American Petroleum Industry*. Chapel Hill: University of North Carolina Press, 2000.

Orcutt, Mike, "A Drop in U.S. CO2 Emissions." *MIT Technology Review,* August 21, 2012.

———. "China's Shale Gas Bust." *MIT Technology Review*, August 12, 2014.

Peritz, Rudolph J. R. *Competition Policy in America: History, Rhetoric, Law*. Oxford: Oxford University Press, 2001.

Peters, Timothy J., and D. Wilkinson. "King George III and Porphyria: A Clinical Re-examination of the Historical Evidence." *History of Psychiatry* 21, no. 1 (March 2010).

Poley, J. P. *Eroïca: The Quest for Oil in Indonesia (1850–1898)*. Berlin: Springer, 2000.

Priest, Tyler. "The 'Americanization' of Shell." In *Foreign Multinationals in the United States*, edited by Lina Gálvez-Muñoz and Geoffrey G. Jones. London: Routledge, 2005.

Pugliaresi, Lucian. "The Price Collapse Winners and Losers (China & Russia)." Energy Policy Research Foundation, March 16, 2015.

Rappaport, Helen. *Four Sisters: The Lost Lives of the Romanov Grand Duchesses*. London: Macmillan, 2014.

———. *Joseph Stalin: A Biographical Companion*. Santa Barbara, CA: ABC-CLIO, 1999.

———. *Queen Victoria: A Biographical Companion*. Santa Barbara, CA: ABC-CLIO, 2003.

Rasor, Eugene L. *Winston S. Churchill, 1874–1965: A Comprehensive Historiography and Annotated Bibliography*. Santa Barbara, CA: Greenwood, 2000.

Ray, Daryll E. "Relaxation of the Jones Act Could Help Midwest Maintain Hold on Southeast U.S. Grain Markets." Agricultural Policy Analysis Center, University of Tennessee, July 9, 2002.

Rockefeller, John D. *Random Reminiscences of Men and Events*. New York: Doubleday, 1909.

Rogers III, C. Paul, Stephen Calkins, Mark R. Patterson, and William R. Andersen. "Antitrust in the Formative Era." In *Antitrust Law: Policy and Practice*. Dayton: LexisNexis, 2008.

Rosenbaum, David Ira, ed. *Market Dominance: How Firms Gain, Hold, Or Lose It and the Impact on Economic Performance*. Santa Barbara: Greenwood, 1998.

Bibliography

Rothschild, Nathaniel Mayer, and Victor Rothschild. *"You Have It, Madam": The Purchase, in 1875, of Suez Canal Shares by Disraeli and Baron Lionel de Rothschild.* London: Nathaniel Mayer Rothschild, 1980.

Sandalow, David, Jingchao Wu, Qing Yang, Anders Hove, and Junda Lin, "Meeting China's Shale Gas Goals." Columbia/SIPA, Center on Global Energy Policy, September 2014.

Seward, William Henry. *William H. Seward's Travels Around the World.* Edited by Olive Risley Seward. New York: D. Appleton and Co., 1873.

Shulman, Seth. "The Flight That Tamed the Skies." *MIT Technology Review,* September 1, 2002.

Smil, Vaclav. *Creating the Twentieth Century: Technical Innovations of 1867–1914 and Their Lasting Impact.* Oxford: Oxford University Press, 2005.

Spyrou, Andrew G. *From T-2 to Supertanker: Development of the Oil Tanker, 1940–2000.* Bloomington: iUniverse, 2000.

Standiford, Les. *Last Train to Paradise: Henry Flagler and the Spectacular Rise and Fall of the Railroad that Crossed an Ocean.* New York: Crown/Archetype, 2003.

Studer, A. J. "The War in Acheen and Its Effects on Commerce." In *Reports from the Consuls of the United States on the Commerce, Manufactures, Etc., of Their Consular Districts*, no. 35. Washington, DC: Government Printing Office, 1883.

Suez Canal Authority. *Suez Canal Traffic Statistics, Monthly Number & Net Ton by Ship Type, Direction and Ship Status.* 2014.

Sweetser, Moses Foster, and Simeon Ford. *How to Know New York City: A Serviceable and Trustworthy Guide, Having its Starting Point at Grand Union Hotel, Etc.* New York: Rand Avery Co., 1887.

Tarbell, Ida Minerva. *All in the Day's Work: An Autobiography.* Champaign: University of Illinois Press, 1939.

———. "John D. Rockefeller." *McClure's Magazine,* July 1905.

———. *The History of the Standard Oil Company.* New York: McClure, Phillips & Co., 1904.

Tate, Curtis. "More Oil Spilled from Trains in 2013 than in Previous 4 Decades, Federal Data Show." *McClatchy,* January 20, 2014.

Temple, Richard. *Men and Events of My Time in India.* London: John Murray, 1882.

Bibliography

Tibbals, Geoff. *Motor Racing's Strangest Races: Extraordinary But True Stories from Over a Century of Motor Racing*. London: Anova Books, 2013.

Tobin, James. *To Conquer the Air: The Wright Brothers and the Great Race for Flight*. New York: Simon & Schuster, 2004.

Tolf, Robert W. *The Russian Rockefellers: The Saga of the Nobel Family and the Russian Oil Industry*. Stanford: Hoover Institution Press, 1976.

Trollope, Anthony. *The Way We Live Now*. Leipzig: Tauchnitz, 1875.

Tuchman, Barbara W. *The Guns of August: The Outbreak of World War I*. 1962. Reprint, New York: Random House, 2009.

———. *The Proud Tower: A Portrait of the World Before the War*. 1966. Reprint, New York: Random House, 2011.

Twain, Mark. *Autobiography of Mark Twain: The Complete and Authoritative Edition*. Edited by Harriet Elinor Smith. Berkeley: University of California Press, 2010.

U.K. *Census of England, Wales, and Scotland, 1851*. Aldgate, London, HO 107/1546.

U.K. HMS *Ark Royal* Logbook. December 1914 to December 1916.

U.K. "H.M.S. Hannibal—Oil Fuel Trials." *The Parliamentary Debates*. London: Wayman and Sons, March 11, 1903.

Ulam, Adam Bruno. *Stalin: The Man and His Era*. London: Tauris Parke, 2007.

U.S. Bureau of Foreign Commerce. *Bureau of Statistics Monthly Consular and Trade Reports* 41, nos. 148–151 (1893).

U.S. Congress. Act of July 2, 1890, Enrolled Acts and Resolutions of Congress, 1789-1992. General Records of the United States Government, Record Group 11, National Archives.

U.S. Department of Agriculture. "U.S. Rice Exports by Type, Rice Yearbook 2015." March 31, 2015.

U.S. Energy Information Administration. "Dry Natural Gas Consumption," 2013.

———. "International Energy Statistics—Total Petroleum Consumption." 2015.

———. "Overview Data for China." May 30, 2013.

———. "Power Plant Emissions of Sulfur Dioxide and Nitrogen Oxides Continue to Decline in 2012." February 27, 2013.

Bibliography

———. "Shale in the United States." Independent Statistics and Analysis. May 14, 2015.

———. "Total Consumption of Petroleum Products." 2012.

———. "U.S. Crude Oil First Purchase Price." May 1, 2015.

———. "U.S. Field Production of Crude Oil." June 30, 2015.

———. "U.S. Natural Gas Imports & Exports 2014." Independent Statistics and Analysis. May 14, 2015.

U.S. Federal Trade Commission. "Exxon/Mobil Agree to Largest FTC Divestiture Ever in Order to Settle FTC Antitrust Charges; Settlement Requires Extensive Restructuring and Prevents Merger of Significant Competing U.S. Assets." November 30, 1999.

van der Leeuw, Charles. *Storm over the Caucasus: In the Wake of Independence.* Richmond, UK: Curzon Press/Caucasus World, 1997.

van der Vat, Dan. *The Dardanelles Disaster: Winston Churchill's Greatest Failure.* London: Duckworth Overlook, 2009.

Vassiliou, M. S. *The A to Z of the Petroleum Industry.* Lanham, MD: Scarecrow Press, 2009.

Vego, Milan N. *Joint Operational Warfare: Theory and Practice.* Washington, DC: Government Printing Office, 2009.

Villari, Luigi. *Fire and Sword in the Caucasus.* London: T.F. Unwin, 1906.

Vincent, Frank. *The Land of the White Elephant: Sights and Scenes in South-Eastern Asia.* London: Sampson Low, Marston, Low, & Searle, 1873.

Walkowitz, Judith R. *Prostitution and Victorian Society: Women, Class, and the State.* Cambridge: Cambridge University Press, 1982.

Wasson, Ellis Archer. *Born to Rule: British Political Elites.* Stroud: Sutton, 2000.

Waugh, Alexander. *The House of Wittgenstein: A Family at War.* New York: Doubleday, 2008.

Weinberg, Steve. *Taking on the Trust: How Ida Tarbell Brought Down John D. Rockefeller and Standard Oil.* New York: W. W. Norton, 2009.

West Publishing. "Moss et al. v. Manhattan Ry. Co. et al." In *The New York Supplement Containing the Decisions of the Intermediate and Lower Courts of Record of New York State, March 26–May 14.* St. Paul, MN: West Publishing, 1891.

Bibliography

Wilkins, Mira. *The History of Foreign Investment in the United States to 1914*. Cambridge, MA: Harvard University Press, 1989.

Williams, Beryl. "1905: The View from the Provinces." In *The Russian Revolution of 1905: Centenary Perspectives*, edited by Jon Smele and Anthony Heywood. Abingdon, UK: Taylor & Francis, 2005.

Williams, Harold. *Tales of Foreign Settlements in Japan*. Rutland, VT: Tuttle, 2012.

Winchester, Clarence, and Cecil John Allen. *Railway Wonders of the World*. London: Amalgamated Press, 1935.

Wing-Huen, Ip, ed. *Advances in Geosciences: Solid Earth (SE) Ocean Science (OS) and Atmospheric Science (AS)*, vol. 9. Hackensack: World Scientific, 2007.

Winkler, John K. *John D. Rockefeller: A Portrait in Oils*. New York: Vanguard Press, 1929.

Winton, John. *Jellicoe*. London: Michael Joseph, 1981.

Wolfe, Bertram D. *Three Who Made a Revolution: A Biographical History of Lenin, Trotsky, and Stalin*. New York: Cooper Square Press, 2001.

Wright, William. *The Oil Regions of Pennsylvania: Showing Where Petroleum Is Found Etc*. New York: Harper & Bros., 1865.

Yergin, Daniel. *The Prize: The Epic Quest for Oil, Money and Power*. New York: Simon & Schuster, 1991.

Zelikson-Bobrovskaia, Tsetsiliia Samoĭlovna. *Twenty Years in Underground Russia: Memoirs of a Rank-and-File Bolshevik*. New York: International Publishers, 1934.

Index

Index

Index

Index

Index

Index

Index

Index

Index

Index

Index

Index

334

Index

Index

Index